THE LINCOLN
MEMORIAL
& AMERICAN
LIFE

THE
LINCOLN
MEMORIAL
&
AMERICAN
LIFE

Christopher A. Thomas

PRINCETON UNIVERSITY PRESS
PRINCETON AND OXFORD

Published by Princeton University Press, 41 William Street, Princeton, New Jersey 08540

In the United Kingdom: Princeton University Press, 3 Market Place, Woodstock, Oxfordshire OX20 1SY

LIBRARY OF CONGRESS CATALOGING-IN-PUBLICATION DATA

Thomas, Christopher A., 1949–
    The Lincoln Memorial and American life /
    Christopher A. Thomas.
        p.   cm.
    Includes bibliographical references (p.   ) and index.
    ISBN 0-691-01194-X (cloth : alk. paper)
    1. Lincoln Memorial (Washington, D.C.)—
History.   2. Lincoln, Abraham, 1809–1865—
Monuments—Washington (D.C.)   3. Washington
(D.C.)—Buildings, structures, etc.   4. Memorials
—Social aspects—United States.   5. Memorials—
Political aspects—United States.   6. National
characteristics, American.   7. Lincoln, Abraham,
1809–1865—Influence.   I. Title.

                    F203.4.L73 T48 2002
975.3—dc21   200127836

British Library Cataloging-in-Publication Data
is available

This book has been composed in Aldus text and
Castellar display

Printed on acid-free paper. ∞

www.pup.princeton.edu

Printed in the United States of America

10 9 8 7 6 5 4 3 2 1

For Leslie N. Boney Jr., FAIA,
my patron and friend,
and
Elizabeth A. Swaim (d. 2000),
my good angel

CONTENTS

ILLUSTRATIONS

INTRODUCTION

THE LINCOLN MEMORIAL is an American icon.[1] Millions visit it each year, and its image pervades American life. Daily, the memorial is seen on the humble penny and the five-dollar bill.[2] On the televised evening news, if it is not the U.S. Capitol, it is the Lincoln Memorial that peeks over the shoulder of the anchor or Washington correspondent. When some person or interest, particularly on the Right, wants to summon an image of the archetypally American, the Lincoln Memorial often provides it. Like Abraham Lincoln himself, represented in the gigantic seated marble statue inside (Fig. I), the memorial is a metaphorical stand-in for values deemed to be American. To people around the world, it is one of a handful of structures, such as the Eiffel Tower, the Taj Mahal, the clock tower of Parliament in London, and the walls of the Kremlin, that are mentally inseparable from their respective nations.

The Lincoln Memorial projects an air of inevitability and timelessness. This owes in part to its spectacular, heraldic location. Regal at the west end of the Mall, like a huge white lion in repose, it is a guardian at the city's gate. More than a destination for traffic

whirling across Memorial Bridge, it is a symbolic junction between Washington and the old Confederacy, of which Virginia was the crown jewel. Partly, the Lincoln Memorial is hard to escape because it is so many things at once—a war memorial, a monument to a national hero, a temple to American ideals, and a national stage or theater on which events in American history and pageantry are performed, such as the March on Washington for Jobs and Freedom of August 1963. It is a place of both reflective private visitation and public ritual, official and unofficial. Although no longer the most visited monument in Washington, the memorial in effect plays host to the one that is—the Vietnam Veterans Memorial, dedicated in 1982. As a container for the statue of Lincoln, itself embodying a subtle sculptural balance of humanity and gravity, and for great lapidary inscriptions of two texts in which Lincoln reimagined the Union (Fig. II), his memorial is both personal and ideal, this-worldly and celestial. Many prefer it to any other memorial in Washington, especially at night.

A key to the Lincoln Memorial's effectiveness is the way it evades questions. After all, who could imagine Washington without it? We seldom think to ask, When was it built, who built it, or why? Answers to such questions seem unimportant, not just because in Washington everything—like the camel in the

Fig. I. Two African-American children gazing up at the statue in the Lincoln Memorial, ca. 1940. Photograph by Theodore Horydczak. (Library of Congress, Division of Prints and Photos. LC-H814-T-L05-085-B)

joke—is built by committee but because, like the Parthenon (a prototype for its design), the memorial is simply eternal. This illusion is owed in part to the fact that its architect, Henry Bacon, built it in the most refined Graeco-Roman classicism, which for Western culture since the Enlightenment has represented timeless perfection. A minority of visitors can name the sculptor of the statue—Daniel Chester French, "dean of American sculptors" at the turn of the twentieth century; but the building's architect, Bacon, is much less known, partly because many suppose that the Lincoln Memorial *is* the statue, and the building a mere box for it. A box, perhaps, but one exquisitely designed, and large enough to be visible from the west terrace of the Capitol, two miles away, and to have been the second most costly monumental building project in Washington's history to that point, 1911–22.[3] The memorial's apparent sacredness also discourages questioning. The dedicatory inscription high on the wall behind Lincoln's head calls it a "temple":

IN THIS TEMPLE
AS IN THE HEARTS OF THE PEOPLE
FOR WHOM HE SAVED THE UNION
THE MEMORY OF ABRAHAM LINCOLN
IS ENSHRINED FOREVER.

The memorial's Platonic scale and location, formal perfection, and apparent timelessness

Fig. II. *Tablet of Lincoln's Gettysburg Address, with mural by Jules Guérin,* Emancipation of a Race, *in south recess of Lincoln Memorial. (Photograph courtesy of the Photographic Archives, National Gallery of Art, Washington, D.C.: Dunlap Society Collection. Taken for the Dunlap Society by Richard Cheek)*

achieve another effect unusual in Washington: they place it above politics. Here is a monument, we suppose, not to partisan or sectional values but to values all Americans share.[4] The generality was intentional, for, as a monument to the Union restored after the bloody Civil War in 1865, Lincoln's memorial was built to celebrate and foster consensus and reconciliation. It *should* be appropriated by all and for whatever worthy cause, provided that cause be consistent with "American values." Though Lincoln represented the Republicans shortly after the party was distilled from Whig and abolitionist forces, this is not seen as a partisan monument, and the fact that it is sometimes used that way—for the "American Reunion" concert that marked Bill Clinton's inauguration in 1993, for example—is believed to derive, precisely, from the universal ideals the memorial is said to honor. Our cause is right, such use claims, because Lincoln's was right and was rooted in the nation's founding ideals. The Lincoln Memorial, it is believed, is a universal site honoring an indissoluble Union founded on indisputable ideals—values that political parties may occasionally approximate but never abrogate. Such is the suavity with which American civil religion transfers sacred ideals and symbols to the state.

A key argument of this book is that that illusion is, precisely, an illusion. It may seem a shocking act of sacrilege to root the planning and use of the Lincoln Memorial in material historical circumstances, but this treatment will make it apparent that, like any other site or object, the Lincoln Memorial is utterly of this world, with all its ambiguities. It was, as much as anything else in Washington, a product of politics, created by groups and interests. The Lincoln Memorial, regardless of how it has subsequently been used, was an emblem of the Republican Party of Teddy Roosevelt's and William Howard Taft's era, of the Grand Old Party at just that moment when Gilded Age plutocracy and laissez-faire were giving way to Progressive system and regulation. The memorial indeed presents, as I titled a talk, "Lincoln as Theodore Roosevelt."[5] I am not the first to notice this. In 1924, mordant leftist critic Lewis Mumford inquired, "Who lives in that shrine, I wonder–Lincoln, . . . or the generation that took pleasure in the mean triumph of the Spanish-American exploit?"[6] But iconoclasm goes even further here, to claim that the man the memorial in Washington so strikingly commemorates barely resembles the Abraham Lincoln of history; "he," rather, was a confection of a cultural and political elite bent on stripping Lincoln of his earthly imperfection and his war of its bloodiness, to make it and him into prototypes of the progressive and (for some) imperial nation that Republicans of 1901–12 hoped to shape. Sitting in effigy inside the regal memorial is the ideal American president, not Abraham Lincoln.

Any attempt to reconstruct actual historical circumstances is valuable and ultimately useful, no matter how painful it seems. It helps, perhaps, that I am an outsider—a Canadian—for Canadians, though not exactly foreign, are not quite family, either; skepticism of American intentions, whether in the Persian Gulf or over "free" trade, is a Canadian reflex. The ironic distance we keep from American

patriotic claims gives us something in common with disenfranchised groups within the United States itself, such as African-Americans—groups that since the 1930s have made the Lincoln Memorial a shrine of opposition to dominant values.

Plumbing the myths behind a place, even a hallowed patriotic icon, does not, however, mean dismissing those myths as primitive, naive falsehoods. As the stories we live by, myths are inescapable metaphors, and the most we can do is to choose which ones to honor, not to live without them in some Alpine air of cold, clear "reality." Recognizing this is not to denigrate the historian's task but to acknowledge its limits. The mediated, represented character of all "reality," including phenomena that seem to determine the course of history, such as nationalism, patriotism, ritual, and ethnic and racial identities, is a theme historians have been hammering away at for several decades. In any case, as myths go, those about Abraham Lincoln are better than most. After fifteen years of reading about him and his war, I can say that, taking into account the work of the demythologizers and "debunkers," Lincoln remains an appealing and engaging character who happened along in American history at a time of crisis and, on the whole, managed his part in that history well. Of limited formal education, he grew to express himself clearly and brilliantly, especially in writing. And, though not at all the twenty-first-century liberal I wish he had been, Lincoln acted with remarkable balance and humanity in bloody and difficult times, in the midst of an ambiguous culture. Balance accounts for the flexibility of his mythological persona, his susceptibility to appropriation for any number of causes.[7] Conservatives and liberals routinely claim him as their own; African-Americans and other racial and cultural minorities may not invariably approve his choices but find in him a useful emblem of their aspirations. This gives his memorial a resonance today it would not otherwise have and which other monuments in Washington do not possess. But it would not have that resonance had it not been so skillfully and evocatively designed. Chapter 5 shows that, starting life as a site of official, consensus ritual (public and private), the Lincoln Memorial has become a place of individual and collective reflection on wounds undressed and wrongs yet to be righted. I think that is a site worth celebrating. The Lincoln Memorial is an instance of the American genius for shaping national symbols that raise "patriotic" feelings even in a skeptical foreigner.

A more reverent book would no doubt have been written about the Lincoln Memorial twenty years ago, but I like to think it would have been duller. The thoroughly documented work of positivist scholarship on the memorial and its architect that I produced as a Ph.D. dissertation at Yale University in 1990 is perhaps duller, but it was a platform on which I and more adventurous scholars than I have built since. Material first presented there has been reworked in light of recent directions in scholarship, directions taken under the interdisciplinary umbrella of cultural studies, which includes American Studies. These new directions are worthy of comment here, as background to the text that follows.

Thanks to the spread of semiotic approaches in the humanities, scholars since the 1960s have been transfixed with studying human cultures as interconnected systems of signs rather than objective, independently existing phenomena. "[M]an is an animal suspended in webs of significance he himself has spun," writes anthropologist Clifford Geertz. "I take culture to be those webs, and the analysis of it to be therefore . . . an interpretive [science] in search of meaning."[8] Researchers in all fields have dislodged the illusion of naturalness that readily grows up around cultural—including political—practices, an illusion that proves to be the result of ingrained mental habits, not the way things are. What we regard as natural realities are actually screens of representations or signs pointing toward other realities. Deconstruction, a movement in philosophy and criticism, adds the insight that this process of representation by signs cannot be arbitrarily brought to an end but, in fact, continues in an endless cycle or "play" of signs pointing to other signs. From this idea arises the oft-heard charge leveled against deconstructionism that it is cynical and nihilistic.

Contemporary emphasis on signs, and the academic preoccupation with theory, generally, has the effect of throwing into question and destabilizing cherished, time-honored verities. The apparent relativism has political implications that, not surprisingly, alarm cultural conservatives. "Americanness" and other national essences, "freedom," "liberty," and other transcendent virtues said to underpin the authority of the state, and notions of divine Providence guiding the affairs of nations come to be seen not as self-evident realities but as ideological constructs motivated by material interests. Conservatives, of course, fear that in the absence of transcendent essences anarchic and decentering forces will divide and eventually devour their national societies. Americans, in particular, resist seeing their body of shared national beliefs as "ideology" or their government as a "regime," words usually reserved for foreign dictatorships and the backward societies they rule.[9] But recognizing the artificiality and constructedness of hallowed social institutions need not cause alarm. It can instead open spaces of choice and initiative that naturalizing of long-held customs does not allow. Sympathetically understood, the new approaches can be liberating and socially healing.

In particular, the apparent naturalness and inevitability of the modern nation-state have come under question from historians and social scientists. (Interdisciplinarity, or, as Terry Eagleton calls it, "disciplinary indeterminacy,"[10] has become the rule rather than the exception.) Benedict Anderson, a professor of international relations, stresses the way the nation, a community of persons many times too large for face-to-face contact, which nevertheless considers its members to share a common essence, must necessarily be a product first of the imagination and only later of political or military events.[11] We—at least, a political elite among us—must first imagine ourselves as Britons, or Australians, or Canadians before we take the constitutional steps to formalize that. Eric Hobsbawm and Terence Ranger point to the way that allegedly ancient traditions and practices are revived or invented to support the process of creating an organic people, purporting to prove that "we" have always, or since time out of mind, been one. Witness the proliferation of ritual and custom that sprang up around the British monarchy during Queen Victoria's reign.[12] Studies of postmodernity and "postcoloniality" (a phenomenon of the 1990s) have only intensified our awareness of how arbitrary customs truly are. To Eagleton, "The decentering and deconstruction of categories and identities assume fresh urgency in a context of racism, ethnic conflict, [and] neo-colonial domination."[13] Construction of historical memory is central to the process of shaping felt national identity. The memory of a fourteenth-century battle in which a Serbian king was "martyred" is summoned to justify the seizure and ethnic cleansing of Kosovo at the end of the twentieth.[14] The past is never truly past; for the present it becomes a "usable past"[15]—a collection of memories so assembled and arranged as to justify this or that course of action in the here and now. The past is thus not a dead letter but a living, dynamic presence.

Since the late 1970s, when debates about a condition of contemporary society labeled "postmodernity" were at their most vigorous, a large body of literature has appeared that examines collective memory, national identity, and the worldwide "heritage" phenomenon.[16] Memory operates on several scales—individual, familial, group, religious, ethnic, national, and pan-national. Where a nation's historic memory is concerned, the outlines of the narrative are usually shaped by an energetic, moneyed political and cultural elite. Often produced in times of crisis when the nation is believed to be at risk of disintegration, official memory usually promotes consensus among divergent, conflicting groups, which typically nurture their own "vernacular" versions of the past.[17] These groups are able to spread their versions of the past among their own members, but typically only the official representations of national memory are taught in public schools. America between the Civil War and the First World War was, in numbers anyway, perhaps the most racially and ethnically diverse society in Western history; consequently, cultural leaders saw an urgent need to shape and circulate collective memories of historical events, to bring these diverse elements into unity. The perceived need produced in American society, until then proudly not given to retrospection, a period of what Michael Kammen calls "ancestor worship."[18] Evoking that mood is crucial to this study. As chapter 1 explains, the portrait of Abraham Lincoln precipitated out of late-nineteenth-century biographies—hagiographies, really—was of a classically balanced figure marked by humanity and heroism in approximately equal parts, more concerned to reunite America than to free the slaves or break the will of white Southerners. This is Lincoln as Daniel Chester French represents him in the statue in the memorial in Washington. This portrayal served the goal of national reconciliation, a preoccupation of the governing American, especially Republican, elite of the period after Reconstruction. That mind-set also produced in American culture, especially its architecture, a revival of Colo-

nial forms and values somewhat spuriously associated with the period of the nation's founding.[19] It also produced a movement to apply orderly, academic classical architectural forms to the large, new building types required by the newly expanded scale of American cities.

The mood of retrospection tangible by the 1880s also produced a spate of commemorative monuments. Whereas before the Civil War few American towns could boast of public statues or monuments, suddenly these lay thick on the ground, with the enlarged industrial cities graced, sometimes incongruously, with plazas, boulevards, concourses, and circles focused on commemorative monuments. The lion's share of these represented events and figures of the Civil War, which, with its Napoleonic pitched battles and fratricidal carnage, produced countless occasions for commemoration. But present goals were active in this work, too. Detailed study of campaigns to build public monuments in New York City at the end of the nineteenth century and the opening of the twentieth led Michele Bogart to argue that in that period, especially between 1893 (the World's Columbian Exposition) and the First World War, idealizing civic monuments were built in substantial numbers to endow the turmoil of American events and the furious growth of the cities with higher purpose than mere material gain.[20] Usually designed in formal vocabularies of Renaissance and baroque derivation, by artists trained in Europe such as Daniel Chester French, Augustus Saint-Gaudens, and Karl Bitter, commemorative monuments publicly paid for and sited in conspicuous public locations served to indoctrinate youth and "Americanize" workers and the foreign-born by preaching high ideals of civic and national harmony. Often working with commemorative materials provided by the Civil War, this activity at root addressed anxieties about contemporary conditions in the society, economy, and culture.

The extraordinary amount and richness of commemorative activity following the Civil War caused Kirk Savage to observe that Lincoln's "new birth of freedom" also "ushered in a new era of the public monument." The war, he said, molded "a landscape of collective memory."[21] Central to that enterprise was defining new relations between the races, for in the wake of the Union victory and emancipation, Americans had literally to reimagine race and racial difference. When studied intently, Savage observed, public monuments to Civil War events and heroes, Northern and Southern, are seen to inscribe the racial hierarchies established by compromise when Reconstruction ended and cemented in place after 1900, hierarchies not seriously disrupted until the 1950s.

These and other recent studies of commemoration, especially as materialized in monuments, not only do not shy away from treating politics but actually emphasize it. At times, indeed, they risk reducing aesthetics entirely to politics.[22] Emphasis in the late 1970s and 1980s on politics of memory is hardly surprising given the ideological gap that opened in America between Left and Right from the Vietnam War to the Reagan-Bush years. The period witnessed a series of "culture wars," some of which concerned pub-

lic monuments, including the Vietnam Veterans Memorial in Washington. The conflicts demonstrated that commemoration is more often an ideological battleground than the neutral, high-minded enterprise imagined in retrospect.[23] By focusing on the ideology behind and within public art of the past, a generation of young, politically engaged scholars has gone beyond the aestheticism that marked much older art history. Initiative and models for this work have often come from anthropology and the social sciences, for by their nature the new studies straddle the disciplines.

In this way, valuable insight has been gained into the ways the politics of memory has worked in cherished national monuments, previously more or less taken for granted. Vivien Green Fryd sees the murals and sculpture with which the U.S. Capitol was embellished between its rebuilding after the War of 1812 and the Civil War as embodying an almost seamless ideology of imperial expansion.[24] The decorations of the Capitol, not surprisingly, overlooked the national embarrassment of African-American slavery and, by idealizing Indians, celebrated the vanishing—or banishing—of Native Americans. Dennis Montagna connects the energetic martialism of the reliefs and sculpture groups of the Ulysses S. Grant Memorial, designed in 1901–3, on the Mall below Capitol Hill, to turn-of-the-century athletic strenuosity and the drive for military preparedness. The Grant Memorial embodied the Civil War as some in the generation of the Spanish-American War remembered and exploited it.[25] Studies like these "historicize" commemorative sculpture by rooting it in the material, especially political, conditions of the period that produced it.

One of the three linchpins of the national Mall—the others are the Washington Monument[26] and the Capitol itself—the Lincoln Memorial could expect to be subjected to similar study. Scott Sandage, concentrating on the ritual uses to which the memorial was put rather than on its planning and construction (where I had focused my energies in the dissertation), studied the way in which, between 1939 and 1963, advocates of civil rights for racial minorities wrested the memorial away from its official dedication to Lincoln as Savior of the Union and in effect rededicated it to Lincoln as Emancipator.[27] They practiced a "politics of memory," which turned the political discourse of the civil religion of the white majority inside out to make it speak for their own cause. That strategy created Marian Anderson's memorable concert at the memorial on Easter 1939 and the huge March on Washington of August 1963. Albert Boime echoed this argument about the reversal of the Lincoln Memorial's signification in a lengthy article that appears in a collection of studies decoding the authoritarian political content of a number of American national "icons."[28] Boime portrayed the memorial commissioners and their artists as seamless political reactionaries who sought to bend the chance to build a national memorial to the iconic Lincoln to their politico-cultural program of controlling the populace by sedative, pacifying mythology. Though I find Boime's argument shrill and insufficiently attentive to detail, in the final analysis I agree with it

and admire his and Sandage's boldness in confronting the memorial's racial politics.

In the present politicized climate of scholarship, aesthetic considerations in any form tend to get short shrift, risking being tarred as elitist and formalizing. Yet who can deny that the Lincoln Memorial is a beautiful, evocative, and cherished site, whose political utility largely derives from that beauty? A large share of my text is therefore devoted to questions of design and appearance. To that degree, my study arises from another current in recent design and scholarship— renewed appreciation for architecture in the classical tradition. "Classicism," as a general term, designates architecture derived from that of Greece and Rome, but Graeco-Roman architecture had vast range, from marble temples in the five "orders"—Doric, Ionic, Corinthian, Tuscan, and Composite— to austere, styleless palaces and fortifications, to vast market and bath complexes built by the Romans with concrete core walls faced with brick and stone.[29] Not only is "classical" architecture not a unified phenomenon; it comes to us today filtered through a series of European movements of the fourteenth to nineteenth centuries known as the Renaissance, the baroque, neoclassicism, and academic classicism. Admittedly, though, Henry Bacon derived a good deal of his ornament for the Lincoln Memorial, if not its underlying form, unusually directly from ancient Greek sources as archaeologically reconstructed. In the case of Washington today, it is probably more accurate to speak of neoclassicism or even neo-neoclassicism; but let us agree to use

xxv

"classicism" as shorthand for architecture based on antique precedent.

So understood, classicism is deeply identified with American ideals and American memory—what is valuable and worth preserving, along with what is defective. Classicism is protean, polyvalent. In the hands of David in France and Jefferson, Mills, and Latrobe in America, it was a vehicle of revolutionary, not conforming, attitudes. For Americans it became a national family of styles: banks and courthouses, as we know, are often columned and porticoed, occasionally bizarrely. Accordingly, the revived appreciation of classical traditions that arose approximately at the mid-1970s is a particularly American manifestation of a larger architectural movement commonly called "postmodernism."[30] Often—for example, in much of the work of Michael Graves and that of Robert Venturi, Denise Scott Brown, and their associates—postmodernists have revived classical elements in fragmentary, eccentric, and ironic ways. Others, however, have quoted from antique, Renaissance/baroque, and neoclassical models more literally and consistently: Allan Greenberg, cited in chapter 5, is an instance. In architectural education, too, it has become possible in the past decade, for the first time since the 1930s, to receive training in classical design.[31] Often these schools are identified with conservative social values, but the politics is normally not that simple. Appreciation for classicism, and for eighteenth- and nineteenth-century vernacular traditions in building and laying out towns at pedestrian scale, also underpins the so-called new urbanism of the 1990s.[32] That

classicism is a vital and relevant tradition, with progressive, even radical potential, becomes evident from the fact that it continues to generate articulate contemporary design. Much is classical, for example, in Maya Ying Lin's powerful Vietnam Veterans Memorial in Washington (see chapter 5), widely regarded as the first and most moving example of a new type of commemorative monument—perhaps the first new type since Sir Edwin Lutyens pioneered the cenotaph in London after the First World War.[33] Like the past and memory, classicism is anything but a dead letter, and the attention given to formal matters here signals that.

Political and cultural themes predominate in this book. Chapter 1 asks, Why a grandiose memorial to Lincoln? It carries the prehistory of the present monument as far as the making of the McMillan Plan for Washington in 1901–2. A major work of imagination, the McMillan Plan included as a key feature the first important proposal for a memorial to Lincoln in the capital since an abortive campaign for one in the late 1860s. Immediately after the Civil War and his assassination, Lincoln had been too exclusively associated with the Union cause and the Republican Party to be conspicuously memorialized in the capital. But after Reconstruction collapsed in 1877 and the nation entered its late-century industrial and imperial growth, Lincoln's stock rose. While still a party hero, he became more acceptable to white Southerners and Democrats as his mythical persona became more divorced from his historic person. The decisive electoral win of the GOP in 1896 was good for Lincoln's cult. The trouncing of Spain in the "splendid little war" two years later and the return of economic prosperity under the Republicans created a mood of national triumphalism. One manifestation was the making of the McMillan Plan by a strongly Republican team of artists and architects. The plan can be read as a visual representation of the progressive but genteel Republican program to expand the federal government's authority under a powerful presidency. The Lincoln Memorial that ended the Mall axis in the plan recalled the war president and party patron, but it also presented the image of the ideal president, strong but compassionate. That ideal was approximated to a remarkable degree and at almost the same moment in the administration of Theodore Roosevelt.

Chapter 2 takes the narrative of building the memorial up to 1911, when the project was authorized. Through most of the decade after 1901, the McMillan Plan languished, obstructed by the House of Representatives under Speaker Joseph G. Cannon, who detested the plan. In 1908–9, when the centennial of Lincoln's birth was marked, it temporarily seemed possible that a plan could be agreed on to memorialize Lincoln, for both Republican stalwarts (like Cannon) and progressives of both parties claimed him as a patron. At that time competing memorial schemes were presented, but their backers could not unite behind any of them. The stalemate was broken in 1910 with the creation of the Commission of Fine Arts, which steadfastly supported the McMillan Commission's vision of a memorial in Washington.

The Lincoln Memorial Commission, chaired by President Taft, was created, and two promising American classical architects were chosen to propose designs for a memorial.

Chapter 3 traces the evolution of the memorial's design, from a skewed quasi competition in 1911–12 that pitted architect Henry Bacon against John Russell Pope in creating designs tailored to a confusing collection of sites in the capital, through a fairer intermediate stage in which they competed to design a memorial in Potomac Park (as in the McMillan Plan), to the final selection of Bacon as the memorial's architect. The competitive process attracted extraordinary attention to Washington and to the American architectural profession. Since 1912 was a watershed year in American politics, the designs for the Lincoln Memorial became a lightning rod for the tension between and within the parties. Although there were loud objections to the architects' classical designs, and cries that something more "American" should be built to honor Lincoln, in January 1913 Congress authorized the building of Bacon's design for a Graeco-Roman temple.

Chapter 4 traces the construction of the Lincoln Memorial from 1913 to 1922, a period that included an eighteen-month lapse in wartime. Bacon's choice of snow-white Colorado-Yule marble for the building's visible superstructure occasioned a battle between the predominantly Republican memorial commission and Woodrow Wilson's newly arrived, high-minded Democratic administration, which mirrored intense conflict in American life between forces representing the New and the Old. As a classical temple resting on skyscraper foundations of steel and concrete, the memorial embodied a duality of traditionalism and modernity, a recurrent theme in its history. The quarrying of the marble for the superstructure, a herculean task that required near-military organization and the day's most advanced technology, served Bacon's refined contemporary Greek design. The chapter also presents the memorial's major internal features, including Daniel Chester French's colossal marble image of Lincoln inside the sanctuary. His conception of Lincoln married idealized, eternal portrayal to the rendering of a humane and approachable modern man. The statue and other carved and painted features emphasize the memorial's dedication to Lincoln as Savior of the Union, to the all but complete neglect of his role as Emancipator.

Chapter 5 considers the private and public uses to which the memorial has been put since its completion, starting with the dedication in 1922. Among public uses, those in official ritual can be distinguished from what John Bodnar calls "vernacular" uses. Private visits usually represent a cross between secular tourism and "civil religion," in which practices originating in sacred contexts are transferred to patriotic icons. The appropriation of the memorial by civil rights demonstraters, which weakened its official, Republican dedication to Lincoln as Savior of the Union in favor of a more libertarian image of the Emancipator, most colors our perceptions of the memorial today. Hints of this shift were already heard in the memorial's official dedication in 1922, but it was really Marian Anderson's concert on the steps on Easter Sunday in 1939 that began to reshape the symbolism of the Lincoln Memorial in the public mind. The March on Washington for Jobs and Freedom, of August 1963, climaxed a series of highly ritualized civil rights demonstrations held at the memorial from 1940 onward. In turn, the new dedication of the memorial has set a trajectory for its subsequent uses, official and unofficial. The monument's identification with oppositional values helps explain the location of the Vietnam Veterans Memorial, dedicated in 1982, under its fatherly wing.

In a research project spread over fifteen years, leading first to a dissertation and then to a book, I have incurred too many debts to discharge easily or, in some cases, at all. The list that follows is as complete as I can now make it. My first and greatest debt is to Vincent Scully, who suggested the topic and, as my Ph.D. supervisor, helped bring it to first birth. He is a consummate teacher who has treated me with honesty, generosity, and tact and has led countless students and architects to appreciate the excellence of American classical architecture. A number of ideas here, especially in chapter 5, started with things he said, in class and out. Thanks are also due to Jules Prown, George Hersey, Alan Trachtenberg, and Jerome Pollitt, all of Yale, who read early versions of the text and contributed to it from their specialized knowledge.

From the start, I received encouragement and practical help from specialists in Washington, starting with Tony P. Wrenn, former archivist of the American Institute of Architects (AIA) and long an admirer of Henry

Bacon's work. He stood behind this book from the beginning. Others who showed interest early on and have continued to help in ways professional and sometimes personal are Antoinette J. Lee of the National Park Service, Cynthia Field of the Smithsonian's Office of Architectural History, Sue Kohler and Charles Atherton of the Commission of Fine Arts, C. Ford Peatross of the Library of Congress, Barbara Wolanin, curator of the office of the Architect of the U.S. Capitol, and independent scholar and historian Pamela Scott. Bill and Becky Bushong hosted me in the city several times and shared their knowledge of its history and, in Bill's case, of Glenn Brown and the AIA. The late Paul Goeldner of the National Park Service's regional office shared with me the contents of an interview with a builder of the memorial and, shortly before he died, gave me a memorable tour of the roof and undercroft of the Lincoln Memorial. Audrey Tepper, also of the Park Service, helped with technical matters that came to light when the memorial was restored in the early 1990s. Michael Richman and Steven Bedford generously opened their files on Daniel Chester French and John Russsell Pope, respectively. Richard Guy Wilson, of the University of Virginia, and Richard Longstreth, of George Washington University, supported the project all along and contributed points of information. Others in the Washington area I wish to thank include John Dwyer and the staff of the National Archives, Cartographic Branch; Renée M. Jaussaud and Donald Jacanicz, National Archives, Scientific, Economic, and Natural Resources Branch; James Goode, then of the Smithsonian Institution; Dr. Martin K. Gordon, U.S. Army Corps of Engineers; Howard Gillette Jr., George Washington University; and Donald Jackson, of the National Capital Planning Commission.

A person always deeply committed to this research project, which in effect he started, is Leslie N. Boney Jr., FAIA, of Wilmington, North Carolina. Something of a spiritual son to Henry Bacon, the memorial's architect, Leslie has over the years been to me host, collaborator, benefactor, visitor, critic, gadfly, correspondent, well-wisher, and friend. This work is largely a tribute to him. Through him, I came to know the architect's nephew, Henry Bacon McKoy (now deceased), and Henry's daughter and son-in-law, Anne and Dewey Parks Jr., of Greenville, South Carolina. I value their support. Another long-standing debt is to Elizabeth Swaim and her assistant, Diana Perron, in Archives and Special Collections of Wesleyan University's Olin Memorial Library, at Middletown, Connecticut. The accounts here of Henry Bacon's career and the memorial's design and construction are based in large part on documents in the Bacon collection there, to which Elizabeth gave me access for six months in 1986. Sadly, she died in May 2000, too early to read this book. I dedicate it, in part, to her.

Several other people made contributions to the biography of the little-known Bacon. These include Sherry Birk (American Architectural Foundation), Kathy Marquis and Hope Brand (MIT Libraries), Wendy Shadwell (New-York Historical Society), Abigail Booth Gerdts (National Academy of Design), John H. Dryfhout (Saint-Gaudens National Historic Site), Paul Ivory and Wanda M.

Styka (Chesterwood), and Janet Parks and Lisa Rosenthal (Avery Architectural Library, Columbia University).

Research for the book required many visits to and a period of residence in Washington. During 1988–90, I was a Kress predoctoral fellow at the National Gallery of Art's Center for Advanced Study in the Visual Arts (CASVA). Dean Henry Millon, Assistant Deans Shreve Simpson and Therese O'Malley, and the Center's staff, especially Deborah Gomez and Helen Tangires, were warm hosts during that time. The Center's other scholars and fellows also made agreeable and stimulating company. I think particularly of Mark Antliff, Milton Brown, Tracy Cooper, Kristian Jeppesen (who suggested the parallel to the Temple of Concord in chapter 3), Lothar Ledderose, Patricia Leighten, John Tagg, Bernice Thomas, and my friend and office-mate, Jeffrey Weiss. The project that became the book benefited from a year as a Kress curatorial postdoctoral fellow at the National Gallery in 1990–91. Maygene Daniels and the staff of Gallery Archives, including Ann Ritchie, Kurt Helfrich, and the kindly late Richard Saito, were welcoming hosts. Others at the National Gallery I wish to thank are Ted Dalziel, Lamia Doumato, Andrea Gibbs, the late Jerry Mallick, Tom McGill, and Ruth Philbrick. It was my good fortune to arrive in Washington a decade after the Dunlap Society had conducted an exhaustive campaign to document the historical buildings and monuments of the capital for the national Bicentennial. The Society *was* Bates and Isabel Lowry, who generously permitted me to use illustrations from their series in this study.

In and around Washington, I would also name Joseph and Mary Katherine Theis and the Reverend Joseph Komonchak, of Catholic University, who assisted in major personal ways. Joe Theis became involved in the scholarly work, too: an investigator, he patiently ferreted out several obscure points of information and tracked down photographs, working especially hard on the photo of the Clinton inaugural concert (Fig 5.7).

The faculty and staff of the two art history departments in Canada where I taught during the preparation of the book, the University of Western Ontario and the University of Victoria, also contributed. At Victoria, I owe particular scholarly insights to Catherine Harding and Kathlyn Liscomb. Don Pierce and Chris Marshall printed innumerable photos, and Karen McDonald supplied images (including one of her own of the Parthenon). Karen Shearer, Berdine Jonker, Lenore Hietkamp, Eva Campbell, and Debi Saul served as research assistants; Lenore played a particular role, dredging up obscure bibliographic details and solving challenging computer problems.

Colleagues in other academic departments in Canada and the United States have read and commented on sections of this book. These include Robert Bruegmann (University of Illinois at Chicago), Leland Roth (University of Oregon), David Brownlee (University of Pennsylvania), Scott Sandage (Rutgers University), Todd Stephenson (Brown University), and, again, Richard Guy Wilson and Richard Longstreth. Independent scholar Marcelle Robinson, of Braintree, Massachusetts, assisted me in the areas of Bacon family history and classical archaeology and, in the process, became a warm friend. Architect Allan Greenberg, quoted in chapter 5, both commented on portions of my manuscript and shared one of his own with me. Mark E. Neely Jr. (Louis A. Warren Library and Museum) and Gabor S. Boritt (Gettysburg College) helped on recent viewpoints on Lincoln. Vivien Green Fryd, of Vanderbilt University, and Kirk Savage, of the University of Pittsburgh, read and conscientiously commented on the penultimate and final versions of the text, respectively, for Princeton University Press. Their critical knowledge of American political and cultural history enriched the study enormously. And, though we never met, Robert Bannister of Swarthmore College set me straight on many aspects of the Progressive Era by posting the syllabus of his History 44 on the World Wide Web. In a category of her own is Carol Herselle Krinsky, of New York University, who read and reread, sensible and meticulous editing pencil in hand, multiple chapters and drafts of the manuscript for the past several years. Her generosity and sage, sometimes sharp, advice gave me heart to continue. My sympathetic editors at Princeton University Press— Elizabeth Powers, Deborah Malmud, Thomas LeBien, Ellen Foos, and Maura Roessner— helped form a vision of the finished manuscript and work toward it.

An embarrassingly long series of grants and fellowships made research and writing possible. A short-term grant from Frederick R. Mayer and the American Arts office of the Yale University Art Gallery allowed me to set out in 1985. Predoctoral fellowships from the Social Sciences and Humanities Research Council of Canada (SSHRCC), the Henry Luce Foundation and the Yale Art Department of Art History, and CASVA in association with the Kress Foundation and a writing grant from the Architectural History Foundation in honor of Vincent Scully let me complete the dissertation. Part-time writing under a postdoctoral fellowship from the SSHRCC produced a first draft for a book, but involvement with Princeton University Press, beginning in 1995, changed the project's shape. Since then, several internal research grants from the University of Victoria and a welcome outside grant made it possible to finish the book. The outside help came from the Graham Foundation for Advanced Studies in the Fine Arts. Offered at a time, early 1997, when for several reasons the book manuscript was in some jeopardy, the grant provided support for research travel, publication photographs, teaching release, and research assistance that allowed the book to be finished.

Other persons and agencies whose help, of various kinds, I gratefully acknowledge are Robert Adams (Olin Library, Wesleyan University); Mardges Bacon (Northeastern University); Michele H. Bogart (State University of New York–Stony Brook); David Brodherson (New York City); Harry R. Bumba (American Automobile Association); Richard Chafee (Providence, Rhode Island); Isabelle Gournay (University of Maryland and Society of Architectural Historians, Latrobe chapter); Arnold Goldstein and Jeff Gaumer (Department of the Interior, National Capital Parks–Central); Maria Goodwin (U.S. Mint); the late Frederick Gutheim (Columbia, Maryland); John Haynes and Marvin Kranz (Library of Congress);

Richard Joncas (Stanford University); Neil Levine (Harvard University); Cynthia Pease Miller (Office of the Clerk, U.S. House of Representatives); Dennis Montagna (Philadelphia); Victoria Newhouse and Karen Banks (Architectural History Foundation); Jeffrey Karl Ochsner (University of Washington); David Potts (Gettysburg College); Paul Spreiregen (Washington, D.C.); Robert A. M. Stern, Architect (New York City); Florian Thayn (curator's office, Architect of the U.S. Capitol); Sarah Turner (American Institute of Architects); David Van Zanten (Northwestern University); Thomas Walton (Catholic University of America); Sally Webster, Mary Woods (Cornell University); and Mary K. Woolever (Art Institute of Chicago).

An author's personal debts are always the greatest but the least definable. Regrettably, my father, Alex J. Thomas, who proofread an earlier version, did not live to see the book appear. Maureen Jones Thomas made contributions that cannot be measured, in moves made and hours, money, and presence sacrificed, as did our two children, Joseph and Christopher.

THE LINCOLN
MEMORIAL
& AMERICAN
LIFE

CHAPTER 1

"Greatest American": A Memorial to Lincoln?

He knew to bide his time,
And can his fame abide . . .[1]

THE ASSASSINATION OF President Abraham Lincoln in his own capital on Good Friday, 1865, just days after Lee had surrendered to Grant at Appomattox, came on Americans, especially of the North, as a dreadful shock. Washington, said Edmund Clarence Stedman, was "converted into a vast mausoleum by the national calamity . . . like an immense black and white flower."[2] Amid the anger and revulsion that the assassination caused in the North, Lincoln was raised to the empyrean as a national god, especially in the mouths of preachers, many of them abolitionists and radical Republicans, on that following "Black Easter" morning. Some did not shrink from comparing Lincoln to Christ and rhetorically asserting that he, too, was being resurrected to a stirring afterlife as the nation's patron in its work of rebuilding:

And now the martyr is moving in triumphal march, mightier than when alive. The nation rises up at every stage of his coming. Cities and States are his pallbearers and the cannon speak the hours with solemn procession. Dead! Dead! Dead! Is Washington dead? Is David dead?

Disenthralled of flesh, risen to the unobstructed sphere where passion never comes, he begins his illimitable work. His life is now grafted upon the infinite and will be fruitful as no earthly life can be.[3]

The godlike Lincoln constructed by the preachers after his death differed greatly from versions of him that had been current during his lifetime.[4] When Lincoln arrived, furtively, in Washington in March 1861 to assume the presidency of a nation on the verge of breakup and war, neither he nor the capital city to which he came stood in high repute with Americans. His election, representing the triumph of the Republican Party, a coalition of opponents to slavery formed in 1854, had been enough to cause some slaveholding states of the South immediately to announce their secession from the Union. The situation only worsened after he was inaugurated later that month. Lincoln's decision in April to defend Fort Sumter precipitated the war that had so long been feared, and, though it started slowly, that war dragged on for four terrible years. At the beginning of his term, public opinion of Lincoln was not high. White Southerners saw him as a provocation; to many in the North, he was a temporizing, ineffectual bumpkin. Nathaniel Hawthorne, after meeting Lincoln in 1862, called him "about the homeliest man I ever saw";[5] and Lincoln's distinctive physiognomy and carriage gave cartoonists a field day. But as the war continued, qualities of leadership emerged in him, and he rose in the esteem of most Northerners. "Copperheads," or Northerners—mostly Democrats—who opposed the war, never took to him, however, nor did radical Republicans, who thought him too tender by half toward the white South and not nearly determined enough to emancipate the slaves. But support for Lincoln was strong enough that he handily won reelection in 1864 at the head of the Union Party, formed from moderate Republicans and "War" Democrats to meet the national emergency.

Just as Lincoln's qualities were not immediately apparent, so, in 1860, Washington, D.C., did not seem to have fulfilled its promise as the first "new" capital of the modern era.[6] Chosen by Congress in 1790 in a compromise between Northern and Southern states, the diamond-shaped site straddling the Potomac, ten miles to a side, had been laid out as a city by the French officer of engineers Pierre Charles L'Enfant. He imagined his abstract, geometric neoclassical scheme as an allegory or microcosm of the novel institutions of the American government and the vast natural riches of its "inland empire."[7] The city's official and social core would be an L-shaped "grand avenue" —today's Mall—linking the federal Capitol and the President's House (what we call the White House), with, at its fulcrum on a hillock overlooking the Potomac, a great equestrian statue of George Washington, Revolutionary general and first president. These and other "principal points"

of the federal city would be linked by broad radial avenues and an intersecting grid pattern of secondary streets, with formal squares and circles at the major junctions. The capital got a good start with the building of the Capitol and the President's House in time for the government to occupy them when it arrived in 1800, but the British damaged these buildings so badly in the War of 1812 that the government nearly abandoned Washington. In the Jacksonian era of the 1830s, three major new government buildings, designed (or substantially redesigned) by Robert Mills in the fashionable and symbolic Greek Revival style, were begun on the high ground north of the Mall—the U.S. Treasury and the Patent Office (both 1836) and the General Post Office (1839–42)—but by 1842 the visiting English writer Charles Dickens could mock Washington as "the City of Magnificent Intentions" with "[s]pacious avenues, that begin in nothing, and lead nowhere . . . and ornaments of great thoroughfares, which only lack great thoroughfares to ornament."[8] Washington was small, unkempt, and culturally isolated, for the federal government was weak and Congress met there during only a few months of the year. Moreover, being in the upper South, the city bore what was for many Americans the additional stigma of being a center of slaveholding and, until 1850, slave trading. Partly to offset the contempt in which the federal government and its capital were held, in the late forties and early fifties some members of the American cultural and congressional elite tried to improve the patchwork of public grounds and gardens that L'Enfant's "grand avenue" had become, as a unified and picturesquely landscaped public garden with an uplifting moral and educational mission.[9] Shortly before that, James Renwick's red sandstone "castle" for the Smithsonian Institution (1846–51) was built on the Mall, and about the same time a start was finally made on building a towering obelisk memorial in honor of George Washington. Its construction was interrupted in 1855, however, and the improvements to the city that were actually carried out were so slight that the genteel writer Henry Adams could say of Washington, "As in 1800 and 1850, so in 1860, the same rude colony was camped in the same forest, with the same unfinished Greek temples for workrooms, and sloughs for roads."[10]

The coming of the Civil War did not improve the city's appearance—beef cattle were kept in pens on the monument grounds to feed the federal armies, and many public buildings were turned over for use as hospitals—but did much to enhance its prestige and strategic importance to the Union.[11] A border city, Washington stood near the epicenter of the campaigns in the East and was convulsed by the war. In the early period in particular, the Union's hold on the city was sometimes tenuous. Yet Lincoln would not abandon Washington to the Confederacy and for symbolic reasons would not consent, despite the emergency conditions, to halting construction of the enormous cast-iron dome being added to the Capitol to balance its wings, which had recently been enlarged. "When the people see the dome rising," he said, "it will be a sign that we intend the union to go on."[12] The city also benefited from the greatly widened authority the war gave the federal government in a vast range of matters, from the cut and color of Union army uniforms, to the reorganization of the country's banking system, to the decision to subsidize the building of the first railroads to the Pacific. Under Lincoln and the Republican Party in Congress, a modern nation was being made of what had been a voluntary compact of states. In a sense, the war reinvented Washington and the federal government, and, as a result, Lincoln cast a long shadow over the city even after he was gone. So, the memorial to him erected after 1911 at the end of the Mall axis can be viewed as a long-delayed tribute to his critical role in building the federal city.

LINCOLN, REPUBLICANS, AND RECONSTRUCTION

However they had felt toward Lincoln in life, radical Republicans made of him in death a martyr to promote their firm program of reconstructing the South. The apotheosis of Lincoln was, in a measure, modeled on that of Americans' other semidivine president, George Washington.[13] Washington, early on, had assumed godlike stature as Father of the Nation, and he had flourished in this role throughout the National Period, reemerging with particular force in the 1850s, while his monument was being built in Washington. So, when Lincoln appeared as a candidate for canonization in 1865, he was, almost from the moment of his death, compared with and associated with Washington. Popular prints of him rushed out after the assassination, such

A. LINCOLN,
Died
April 15th 1865.

as that in Figure 1.1, which was patterned on an older image of the apotheosis of Washington that still hung in many American homes, show Lincoln being received into heaven as a second Washington. Images like this suggested to Northern Unionists—for the South also laid claim to Washington's memory—that in his selfless devotion to the Union Lincoln was Washington's true successor, or even Washington reincarnate. Imagery of Lincoln drawn from Protestant Christianity and classical myth—both very widespread in America in that day—tended to intertwine. A further complication was the tendency to portray him in a contradictory way, as, on one hand, a frontier folk hero and Man of the People and, on the other, a transcendent American Christ. These images continued to coexist somewhat uneasily and, as we will see, accounted in part for the controversy that arose in the early twentieth century over what form Lincoln's national memorial should take.

Nineteenth-century Americans took party politics very seriously, and partisan symbols were jealously guarded. In this climate Lincoln, though a moral hero to much of the nation, became, specifically, Republicans' symbolic property, and it was they, almost exclusively, who encouraged his cult.[14] By and large Republicans, whatever their internal divisions, had been the firmest supporters of Lincoln's policy of total war to restore the

Union and of his eventual decision to emancipate the slaves. During and after the war, they were the party of central authority, favoring the vigorous exercise of federal leadership to organize and modernize the U.S. economy on industrial lines as that of a true nation-state rather than a decentralized agrarian republic. As the Union's commander in chief and a president unafraid to wield unprecedented federal and executive power during the wartime emergency, ruling at times as though Congress barely existed, Lincoln was a useful symbol of central authority for postwar Republicans. On the other hand, Lincoln was middle-of-the-road on some matters connected with Reconstruction, including race, and it is not clear that had he lived he would have fully supported the policies of his party's radical right wing, in the ascendant after the war, to reconstruct the devastated South as an interracial society in which whites and African-Americans would coexist on equal terms.[15] Nevertheless, he had prosecuted the war to its conclusion and issued the Emancipation Proclamation, allowing the Radicals to appropriate him as a martyr for their cause.

In early 1867, as soon as the Radicals had sufficient strength in Congress to wrest control of Reconstruction from President Andrew Johnson, they continued the "ghoulish tugging at Lincoln's shroud" by moving to memorialize him in the capital.[16] The very month it passed the Reconstruction Act, the Radical-dominated Fortieth Congress enacted a bill to create a private Lincoln Monument Association, like the one originally formed to build the Washington Monument. The plan arose from a nexus of other schemes

Fig. 1.1. D. T. Wiest. In Memory of Abraham Lincoln. *Engraving, 1865, after one by John J. Barralet, 1802. (Collection of Library of Congress. Courtesy of The Lincoln Museum, Fort Wayne, Indiana, no. 3282)*

elsewhere in the country to honor Lincoln, emancipation, the African-American "race," and the ideal of a truly interracial nation.[17] The stated intention was to erect a monument "commemorative of the great charter of emancipation and universal liberty in America." The association, one of whose trustees was Representative Shelby M. Cullom, a Springfield lawyer who had been a student and protégé of Lincoln's and would be part of every attempt to honor him in Washington for the next half century,[18] commissioned a design for a monument from local sculptor and bronze founder Clark Mills. The association mounted a nationwide fund-raising campaign as gigantic as the monument—of bronze, naturally—that Mills planned (Fig. 1.2), which was described as "the grandest work of its kind . . . ever erected." It was to include thirty-six statues, of Union generals, "figures emblematic of the war and its results," members of Lincoln's cabinet, prominent abolitionists, allegorical figures of "Liberty, Justice, and Time," and, at the summit, a seated figure of Lincoln himself shown in the act of signing the Emancipation Proclamation. Emancipation was also celebrated in a series of statues and relief tablets at midheight, which presented the "Negro" in an allegorical three-stage cycle progressing from slavery to freedom. The wording of the law, the character of Mills's scheme, and the placement of Lincoln at the summit of a tower of representatives of the war movement make it clear that honoring the man himself was secondary to celebrating his Emancipation Proclamation and the goal of the interracial nation-state that was at the heart of the Radical program.

Even the location of the monument—the northeast corner of the Capitol grounds—symbolized the power of Congress, especially that of the House of Representatives, which had seized the reins of government from the executive and sought to impeach Johnson. The proposed monument would have represented a slap in the face to Lincoln's successor.

For a variety of ideological, practical, and representational reasons, the project collapsed. Before the mid-1870s, Radical Reconstruction was in trouble, frustrated by white Southerners and deserted by the Northern interests that had promoted it. Well before the formal end of Reconstruction in the debacle that followed the presidential election of 1876, former Unionists showed they wanted to put the war behind them and, in the midst of the "age of confidence," concentrate on national affairs, especially the settling of the West and the pressing financial and social problems that attended industrialization. In the sectional "reconciliation" that followed, the welfare, even the physical safety, of African-Americans in the South was sacrificed and forgotten.[19] So there was no support in Congress, with Southern white interests again represented there, for the association's project, which in any event had been muddied and watered down to a "representational hodgepodge."[20] In the end, the only monuments to Lincoln on the theme of emancipation erected in the capital were Thomas Ball's Freedmen's Memorial, in Lincoln Park, east of the U.S. Capitol (and replicated in Boston), dedicated in 1876, in which the African-American kneels submissively before his emancipator; and a statue of the standing Lincoln (holding

Fig. 1.2. Clark Mills. Model of proposed monument to Lincoln on grounds of U.S. Capitol, commissioned 1867. (Photograph courtesy of the Photographic Archives, Washington, D.C., Dunlap Society Collection. Take for the Dunlap Society by Richard Cheek)

the proclamation), unveiled in the rotunda of the U.S. Capitol in 1871, modeled by Vinnie Ream Hoxie.[21] Probably, even under better circumstances, Mills's design would have been too ambitious and iconographically complex to be realized in America in 1880, especially by an artist who lacked academic training. By 1880 the monument association claimed to have collected $100,000 from private subscriptions, but this was likely a great exaggeration. By the time Mills died three years later, he had cast only one of the freestanding figures, that of Chief Justice Salmon P. Chase. Even in France, whose government-sponsored system of academic training and artistic patronage was the seedbed of such sculptural programs encoding political meanings in allegory, a monument on this scale would have been remarkable; in America it was impossible. Only Frédéric-Auguste Bartholdi's colossus of Liberty for New York Harbor, dedicated in 1886—a French monument, in fact—and some schemes volunteered to the government in 1879 to complete the Washington Monument, but not adopted, matched Mills's in scale and ambition.[22]

The aim of building a large, federally sponsored memorial to Lincoln languished throughout the late nineteenth century, for, sadly, as much as most Northerners revered Lincoln and enjoyed reading endless hagiography about him, the last thing they and their federal legislators wanted was to rub salt in old wounds. Fragile national confidence and the fact that for fifteen years after 1877 Republicans and Democrats held an approximately equal balance of strength in Congress, and so could not afford to antagonize one another over symbolic matters, explain the near-total absence of talk in Congress of building a memorial to Lincoln in the capital until after the election of 1896, which the Republicans won decisively.[23] By contrast, finishing the Washington Monument was seen as the government's prime symbolic obligation to its founder in the city named after him. What better emblem could there be of his children's reunion? In the centennial year of 1876, Congress assumed responsibility for the project, and the capstone of the 555-foot obelisk was set in December 1884. Yet Lincoln went officially unhonored and seldom even named, except in fulsome speeches by Republicans on his birthday each February 12, which became the party's annual love feast.[24] During the eighties, then, Lincoln receded from politics into the domain of culture, bat-

tening there in preparation for his political resurrection in the late nineties.

Washington, D.C., meanwhile, flourished in the Gilded Age thanks to the federal government's heightened role in national life during and after the Civil War. In the nineties alone, the city's population effectively tripled in size, from 100,000 to 279,000. In the eighties and nineties, as will be detailed elsewhere, even the presidency rose in prestige, and Washington began to attract an aristocracy of wealth and talent possessed of enterprise and ideas and to look the part of a national city. The State, War, and Navy Department building, of 1871–88 (now the Old Executive Office Building), beside the White House, was among the grandest buildings in the Second Empire style anywhere; and the Library of Congress, built facing the enlarged U.S. Capitol in 1871–97, brought the cosmopolitan, French Beaux Arts aesthetic to Washington.[25] But in some respects the city was less inspiring. The grandeur of official Washington contrasted vividly with the squalor of its slums, especially its black slums, a problem that still bedevils the city. And the Mall, antebellum idealists' hopeful symbol of national renewal, had fallen into fragmentary condition since the war.[26] Surely its least agreeable feature was the Baltimore & Potomac's station, train sheds, and track bed at Sixth Street, but otherwise the grounds, though scrappy and discontinuous, had a generally pleasant quality, with government buildings, museums, and the like built around their edges, each nested in semiprivate grounds. The City Canal, originally an improvement but long a nuisance, which for decades had paralleled the Mall to the north and crossed it below Capitol Hill, was filled in to create B Street, now Constitution Avenue. And in 1882, as the Washington monument was being finished, the Army Corps of Engineers embarked on a vast, eighteen-year project of dredging the marshy tidal bay west of the Monument grounds and creating eight hundred acres of parkland where sedge and mud had been. Here would eventually rise the Lincoln Memorial.

REINVENTING LINCOLN AND THE WAR

In the same troubled years between the end of Reconstruction and the midnineties, the mythical, remembered Lincoln was reshaped in a way that proved crucial to the eventual decision to build his memorial. The reshaping of Lincoln took place in the discourse of culture rather than of partisan politics, for, in keeping with the general desire to stress what all Americans had in common, he was remembered less as a figure of controversy between parties and sections than as a sad, wise philosopher-statesman of universal significance. Even if Democrats felt the less said of him the better, and if no Southern town would have raised a statue of him on the courthouse lawn, Lincoln gradually became a less threatening symbol and an instrument in the growing sense of a powerful, united American nation.

This "Lincoln" was mainly the product of the genteel, generally Anglo-Saxon and Republican, cultural elite of the Northeast and upper Midwest, which viewed with alarm the effects on the country of rapid industrialization, immigration, and urbanization.[27] Where was the white, relatively egalitarian republic of farms, towns, and small cities they had known in their youth? Imbued with Matthew Arnold's notion of culture as "sweetness and light," a substitute religion or healing balm for a materialistic society composed of "an ignorant proletariat and a half-taught plutocracy" the divisions between whom threatened "barbarism,"[28] this group portrayed Lincoln as a cultivated and spiritual if still vigorous representative of the leadership democracy could produce at its best. For such intellectuals, often associated with literary magazines and the new universities, Lincoln had the dual virtue of his humble origins and his rise to prodigious power, learning, and morality, a combination that made him a useful model of ideal Americanism to an elite that was wedded to the rhetoric but not the substance of democracy.[29] Already Lincoln's best speeches were considered modern classics of American civil religion. What an example he was to place before western silver miners and ranch hands or eastern factory workers newly arrived from Italy or Slovenia! So, idealized, universalized portrayals of him, which would have seemed laughable a quarter century earlier to an audience that had known Lincoln in his lifetime, became the stuff of biographies in the late nineteenth and early twentieth centuries, which portrayed him as a mix of Christian saint, Hellenistic philosopher, and New England scholar. Ida M. Tarbell, later famous as a journalistic muckraker, called Lincoln, in a hugely popular serialized life of him that began to appear in 1895, "the simple, steady,

Fig. 1.3. *Augustus Saint-Gaudens (sculptor) and Stanford White (architect).* Lincoln the Man *("The Standing Lincoln"), Lincoln Park, Chicago, 1884–87. (Photo: U.S. Department of the Interior, St-Gaudens National Historic Site. Used with permission)*

resolute, unselfish man whose supreme ambition was to find out the truth of the questions which confronted him in life, and . . [to follow] the truth he discovered."[30] The sculptor Augustus Saint-Gaudens, a member of the mainly Republican cultural elite of New York, portrayed him in the celebrated statue *Lincoln the Man* (or simply "The Standing Lincoln"), unveiled in Lincoln Park in Chicago in 1887, as a contemporary human being who embod-

ied a universal intellectual ideal (Fig. 1.3). Lincoln is shown inwardly weighing his words before addressing the American people, presumably at Gettysburg.[31] Remarkable, however, is the omission, here and in most portrayals of him in the period, of the least reference to his role as emancipator of the slaves. Yet even so apparently politically harmless a statue, which until French's statue of him in Washington was dedicated in 1922 was Americans' favorite sculpted image of Lincoln, would not have been tolerated in Washington until after 1900.

Especially in the 1880s, the picture of Lincoln began to grow haloed and diffuse as memories of the Civil War were increasingly wrapped in gauzy haze. As war veterans aged and were replaced by a new generation, the war tended to be viewed either with academic sangfroid, as the inevitable result of a sectional conflict that was economic, not moral, in origin, or with overheated romanticism as "the war of the modern Roses in the Western World" and "an American epic."[32] In that epic, the heroes of the two sides became as interchangeable as the bronze monuments that were raised to commemorate them; meanwhile, the principles for which they had fought were overlooked. How real, then, was the reconciliation effected between the sections? In their effort to forget the bitter sectionalism and party conflict of the 1850s to the 1870s and to concentrate on the new issues of national change, white Americans of the eighties and nineties tended to downplay the bitter memories of wartime and to shade distinctions between the sections, focusing instead on what united them as "American all."[33] The impulse is understandable, but it made Northerners and even Republicans ignore unpleasant contemporary realities such as the treatment of immigrants in Northern cities and of African-Americans in the South, who were rapidly being restored to terror and peonage. The plight of blacks would grow even worse after 1900.

Throughout America, nevertheless, patriotism flowered. In that period was born the modern cult of the flag—putting it on prominent display in schools, churches, and business places, reciting the Pledge of Allegiance before it, singing, "The Star-Spangled Banner" as a national anthem, and so on.[34] The Republican Party, in its repeated attempts to win control of Congress, took with special avidity to patriotic rhetoric and symbolism, but most responsible for the new piety, which entangled patriotism and religion, were veterans' and hereditary groups, especially the Grand Army of the Republic (GAR), a huge, highly influential patriotic society of Union veterans, and the Daughters of the American Revolution (DAR),comprising women who could trace their lineage to Colonial times. The GAR made it one of its special missions to spread the celebration of Memorial Day each year in May. Besides the Civil War, the Revolution was also evoked as a seminal, conscience-bearing period in national life. After 1876 a Colonial Revival in design and ethical values was trumpeted throughout American culture.[35] Patriotism and national self-congratulation reached fever pitch over the heady Spanish-American War of 1898 but had been building since the end of Reconstruction.

Patriotism and nationalism naturally had their own distinctive flavor in the South. About 1880 a "New South" movement emerged in large commercial centers such as Atlanta, Nashville, and Birmingham, calling on the South to let the past be past and to integrate its economy and society with national, Northern-dominated patterns. "New South" meant both admitting military defeat and acknowledging the failure of the Old South and the need for a new order.[36] One leading New Southerner was Woodrow Wilson, raised in Virginia, South Carolina, and Georgia but come to prominence in the North, where he presided over Princeton University before being elected governor of New Jersey and, in 1912, president. While nostalgic for the Old South of tradition and gentility, Wilson was a nationalist who saw it as the white South's new task to take its place in national life, furnishing a class of leaders as it had in the Antebellum who combined the best of old and new.[37] His vision of the future, however, required that the past be reinterpreted, and in *Division and Reunion* (1893) and the magisterial *History of the American People* (1901–2), Wilson had just the answer. These widely read works spread the new clinical interpretation of the war as a clash of economies drained of moral content, for Wilson, though as president the archpriest of Progressivism, was by temperament and breeding deeply conservative. He viewed the aftermath of the Civil War as nothing less than the "overthrow of civilization,"[38] a view of Radical Reconstruction that long dominated historiography. On the popular level the rescue of Southern pride was accomplished by the "Confederate tradition" or "celebration," which glorified the heroic virtue of white Southern warriors by means of reunions, rituals such as those of Confederate Memorial Day, and monument-building. Promoted particularly by the United Confederate Veterans (UCV), a Southern analogue to the GAR, the movement to exalt the Lost Cause issued in the deployment of countless Confederate memorials across the South, especially between 1900 and 1912, and larger ones, too, including monuments to Robert E. Lee and Jefferson Davis, unveiled in 1890 and 1907, respectively, along Monument Avenue in Richmond.[39]

Paradoxically, the mythological Abraham Lincoln benefited in two ways from these new, amoral, and by turns sanitary and romantic versions of the war. Even to some white Southerners like Wilson, he came to seem a noble, tragic figure, the sad oracle of the clement Second Inaugural who, had he but lived to carry out his humane postwar policy, might have protected his white Southern children from the excesses of Reconstruction.[40] In addition, amid the glorifying and memorializing of war heroes at the turn of the century, it came more and more to appear unseemly that he *not* be honored prominently, however reluctant some in the federal capital were. How could Republicans and ex-abolitionists and Unionists do nothing for Lincoln's memory while Lee, Jackson, and Davis were glorified?

TURN-OF-THE-CENTURY TRIUMPHALISM AND THE McMILLAN PLAN

The election of 1896 proved epochal and altered the fate of Lincoln's memory in official Washington. For the first time in twenty years the Republicans, under the new, affectionate label of the "Grand Old Party," won control of not just the presidency, in the reassuring person of William McKinley, but also both houses of Congress, ushering in a dozen glorious years of unbroken electoral victories for the party. During the recession of the early and midnineties, chaos and anarchy had seemed to be at the door, so the firm rebuff given the Democrats and Populists, or People's Party, both of which had nominated the electrifying reformer William Jennings

Bryan for president, seemed to most Americans to herald a return to stability and confidence.[41] Support for McKinley ran the gamut from organized labor to big business, and even the economy began to recover as he took office in March 1897. Ever popular, McKinley then channeled the war fever that had been abroad in the yellow press for several years into the brief, heady Spanish-American War in the spring of 1898. While the "splendid little war" by no means received unanimous support, it made American confidence rebound to great heights. Domestic prosperity reached levels never before seen, and eventual success in Cuba and the Philippines, the annexation of Hawaii, and leadership overseas, especially in opening China to free trade, convinced Americans they had become a world power and force for good. The sense of national unity and triumph was so enormous that McKinley could boast in 1901, "I can no longer be called the President of a party; I am now the President of the whole people."[42] Republicans skimmed the cream of the bounteous optimism, and in a celebrated address given in 1904 to mark the party's fiftieth anniversary, arch-Republican Secretary of State John Hay crowed, "History affords no parallel to the vast and increasing prosperity which this country has enjoyed under Republican rule."[43]

In this climate, the reputation of Lincoln, the party's patron, soared again. Long useful as a partisan symbol and now cleansed to a degree of damaging sectionalism, Lincoln was freed to be a contemporary exemplar who incidentally helped his party. In the late nineties a stream of Lincoln legislation flowed through Congress: the Peterson house in Washington, to which he had been carried before his death, was purchased as a museum, and bills called on the government to build national monuments to him at Gettysburg and Washington.[44] Though none succeeded, perhaps a national monument in the capital did not have long to wait. In the atmosphere of hyperpatriotism, what David Herbert Donald called "getting right with Lincoln" and asking, as a Republican reflex, what Lincoln would do about this or that issue became staples of political discourse.[45] Theodore Roosevelt, who succeeded McKinley as president in 1901, kept a portrait of Lincoln over his office mantel in the White House, saying, "When I am confronted with a great problem, I look up to that picture, and I do as I believe Lincoln would have done. I have always felt that if I could do as he would have done were he in my place, I would not be far from right."[46]

In that confident, jingoistic period, one proposal to honor Lincoln in the capital stands out above all others—the one contained in the plan developed in 1901 by the Senate Park Commission, or McMillan Commission, to terminate a lengthened Mall axis with a great memorial to him in line with the dome of the U.S. Capitol and the shaft of the Washington Monument (Fig. 1.4). The most concrete and compelling vision for a Lincoln Memorial since that of 1867, the commission's proposal was a feature of a daring plan to reshape the core of federal Washington for the new century. It channeled Republicans' long-held

Fig. 1.4. McMillan Commission. Perspective of proposed Lincoln Memorial, concourse, and reflecting basin, 1901–2. Rendering by Robert Blum. (Charles Moore, Improvement of the Park System)

desire to discharge their spiritual debt to Lincoln and gave that desire fresh, visionary form.[47]

The McMillan Plan was made on the pretext of the centennial, in 1900, of the removal of the seat of government to Washington. Two years earlier, during the Spanish-American War, local citizens had asked the president to help them build some "permanent structure which would commemorate not only the [centennial] but also the exceptionally happy condition of our people at this time, when to so marked a degree there is noticed the absence of all sectional feeling."[48] Recovery from the Civil War, the sense of a nation reborn, economic prosperity, and celebration of victory in the Spanish-American War were all themes of the centennial. The

McMillan Plan also sprang from the movement for urban reform that had originated in the 1880s and reached its peak about 1905, the heyday of muckraking journalism.[49] Architects and urban reformers, many trained in the new universities, were seeing cities as quasi-biological organisms that could be put under a microscope and reconfigured using the startling new principles of social science, for "science" and "expert" were mantras of such Progressives. They cited as a model the World's Columbian Exposition held on the Chicago lakefront in 1893 (Fig. 1.5), which was widely viewed as a modern miracle of social engineering and aesthetic harmony despite—in part, because of—the apparent traditionalism of its architecture.[50] Architects, partly to boost their profession, sought to achieve the same order, rationality, and visual dignity in actual cities, citing as their ideal the "City Beautiful," of which the McMillan Plan for Washington would be the first large example. There, of all places, the nation would see the architects' craft at work.

Fig. 1.5. East end of Court of Honor and Peristyle, designed by Charles B. Atwood, World's Columbian Exposition, Chicago, 1893. (Avery Architectural and Fine Arts Library, Columbia University in the City of New York: C. D. Arnold Collection)

The plan was the result of an alliance between two genteel reformers—Glenn Brown, national secretary of the American Institute of Architects (AIA), and James McMillan, who chaired the Senate Committee on the District of Columbia. Brown was a Southerner who had studied architecture in the North and had come to revere the neoclassical architecture and urbanism of early Washington. He was a dedicated spokesman and lobbyist for the architectural profession who recognized how crucial the federal government had become to the nation and labored for it to work to architects' advantage.[51] He persuaded the AIA to move its headquarters from New York to Washington, where it took over the Octagon, a house of 1799 designed by James Thornton, first architect of the Capitol. Brown saw Washington's drab condition in 1900 as an opportunity for architects to show what they could do to improve *all* American cities if given the chance and the centennial as the moment to strike. He arranged for the AIA to hold its annual convention in Washington in 1900 and orchestrated the program to have experts in the emerging field of city planning present

15

heavily illustrated proposals to show federal officials, especially McMillan, how a commission of specialists could beautify and aggrandize the capital.[52]

As the first "active American aesthetic presence" in Congress in some decades,[53] McMillan shared this vision of fusing strong government to beauty in architecture and landscape. Genial, soft-spoken, and a generous host, he was unusually dedicated to art and culture as sources of respite, style, and legitimacy. A multimillionaire who had made his fortune building railroad rolling stock in Detroit, he was among the most powerful Republicans in Washington, a member of the Allison-Aldrich circle that dictated policy to the Senate. The District committee was his hobby. A nonentity until his arrival in Washington in 1889, it became, with his interests and Washington's rapid growth, his ideal theater of action. During the nineties McMillan worked to improve the capital's health and safety, building a new sewer system of which Brown, a specialist in sanitary design, thought highly. Along with McMillan's Harvard-educated secretary Charles Moore, who became Brown's fast friend, they gravitated toward each other immediately.

In March 1901, bypassing the House of Representatives altogether and so earning emnity for the plan from Joseph G. ("Uncle Joe") Cannon, the powerful, irascible chairman of its Committee on Appropriations and soon to be Speaker,[54] McMillan got the commission of experts appointed that Brown and the AIA wanted. The excuse was offered that the group would confine itself to studying the District's parks system for McMillan's com-

mittee, hence the title Senate Park Commission. But plainly more was at stake than that.

The commission was Republican through and through. It would report to McMillan and his Republican-dominated committee and through it to the Republican-controlled Senate. Every influential party member in the chamber would certainly have been lobbied by McMillan and his commissioners. The project also appealed to President Theodore Roosevelt, who entered the White House in the fall of 1901 after McKinley was assassinated. The commissioners' own politics are harder to determine, for then, even more than now, it was thought bad form in genteel circles to speak openly of politics. Nevertheless, all four commissioners were very likely Republican in sympathies. Architects Daniel H. Burnham and Charles F. McKim, landscape architect Frederick Law Olmsted Jr., and sculptor Augustus Saint-Gaudens were all former Unionists and, in some cases, abolitionists.[55] All were of the idealistic cultural elite of the northeastern cities or, in Burnham's case, Chicago—the stratum to which postwar Republicanism most appealed, if not in its most bellicose and imperial forms. All—though this is less true of the bohemian Saint-Gaudens, who in fact took less of a hand in the Washington work than the others—were businessmen-artists who mixed easily in the upper-class, cosmopolitan social circles from which the business-driven Republican leadership of the day was drawn. And all were strong patriots associated with the attempt after the Civil War to forge a truly American art. McKim, the one mainly responsible for the design of the "new" Mall, including the addition of the Lincoln Memorial, was the son of a Quaker abolitionist from Pennsylvania associated with William Lloyd Garrison and John Brown. As boys McKim and a friend had tramped the battlefield of Gettysburg soon after the battle, and later, as an architect, he played a key role in the Colonial Revival.[56] Saint-Gaudens, "the example par excellence of the Civil War sculptor, the sculptor of history,"[57] collaborated with McKim and his partner Stanford White in producing the most eminent memorials to war heroes in the country, including those to Farragut (1877–80) and Sherman (1892–1903) in New York City and to Colonel Robert Gould Shaw in Boston (1884–97).[58] The four were the same group, virtually, as had orchestrated the design and layout of the World's Columbian Exposition, with all its patriotic and aesthetic associations.[59] Burnham, who chaired the McMillan Commission, had been the fair's director of works. So, the four were a logical choice for McMillan. On the other hand, the fact that the Republican Cannon, despite his intense reverence for Lincoln (he and Cullom were viewed as the gatekeepers in Congress to the great man's memory), detested the commission and its plan suggests that the project was directed not to the party's populist traditional wing with its strength in the West and Midwest—the "common man" whom Cannon purported to represent—but to the new Republican Party shaped in the eighties and nineties from plutocrats, the urban middle class, and moderate reformers.

In January 1902, when the McMillan Commission presented its plan, models and lav-ishly rendered drawings evoked a vision of the capital of the future (Fig. 1.6), in the greatest contrast imaginable to the jumbled, empirical Washington of that day. While they obeyed their mandate to devise for the federal district an integrated park system like Boston's, what clearly most interested the commissioners was the capital's ceremonial core—the Mall and its appendages, including the barren tract west of the Washington Monument reclaimed from the river and hopefully called Potomac Park. Not surprisingly, the treatment they proposed for the Mall evoked the axial Court of Honor at the exposition of 1893, except that for the water basin there they substituted an arrow-straight greensward four hundred feet wide, lined by trees, walks, and drives, and uniform ranks of pale neoclassical buildings of medium height. This sort of treatment, emphasizing polite leisure, would appeal to the plutocracy from which most senators and their wives were drawn. Moreover, it would finally realize L'Enfant's dream of a "grand avenue" at the capital's heart. The broad lawn axis, amply furnished with fountains, would join the slope of Capitol Hill at the east, landscaped by Olmsted's father some decades before, to the grounds of the Washington Monument, which would be formalized by masonry terraces (which proved too heavy to build) and carry on westward with a canal or reflecting basin down the center for another mile to the new riverbank. Here would be raised the Lincoln Memorial at the center of a *rond-point*, or circular road (see Fig. 1.4). For it, the commissioners—that is, McKim—imagined "a great portico of Doric columns rising from an

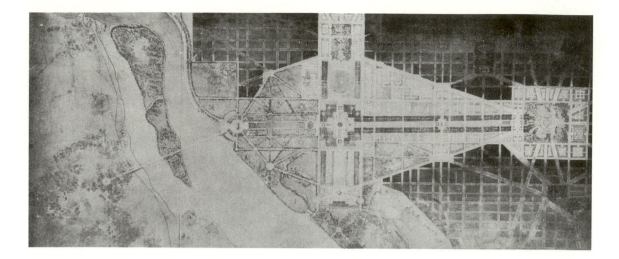

unbroken stylobate" or viewing platform
overlooking the river, supporting a monumental tablet engraved with one of Lincoln's
addresses and having a statue of him in front,
facing back toward the Monument and the
Capitol.

The dedication and placement of the Lincoln Memorial were among the commissioners' boldest strokes. They had considered
locating the memorial at the south end of the
cross-axis of the White House, to which, in
the end, they assigned a circular, pantheon-
like memorial of indeterminate dedication
(where the Jefferson Memorial is today).
They had eventually decided, however, that
since in their view Lincoln was "the one man
in our history as a nation who is worthy to be
named with George Washington," his memorial should be aligned with the founder's
monument and the dome of the Capitol, the

symbol of the government both presidents
had served. They dedicated the memorial not
to the man Lincoln but to Lincoln as Savior of
the Union, and indeed to the Union itself.
This explains why McKim wanted the memorial's form to "possess the quality of universality." In fact, imagery of the Union and the
Northern cause abounded in the plan. At the
far east end of the Mall, at the foot of Capitol
Hill, where a memorial to General Grant had
already (in 1901) been authorized,[60] the commissioners envisioned a grander Union
Square, with equestrian statues of a trio of
Northern generals (including Grant and Sherman), turning their backs to the Capitol in a
row as though protecting it from attack. In
addition, off the circle of the Lincoln Memorial, at an oblique angle, would run a memorial
bridge to Virginia, ending at the foot of the
hill on which stands Arlington House, the
mansion Robert E. Lee forsook to take command of the Confederate army, in what had
become the nation's premier military cemetery, holding the remains of the heroized
Union dead.[61] The arrangement made the Lin-

coln Memorial a point of symbolic reunion for the nation. So, besides making use of the reclaimed land and creating a western terminus for the lengthened Mall and a gateway to a new riverfront parks system, McKim's Lincoln Memorial was crucial to the commission's Unionist imagery for the Mall. Such bias would have been unthinkable a decade earlier, before the Spanish-American War, which was widely considered the joint enterprise of the reunited North and South. On the other hand, the Union the memorial design credited Lincoln with saving was presented no longer simply as the Northern states of 1861–65 but as the Union of *all* Americans Lincoln had left behind. Thus the commissioners sidestepped charges of sectionalism and triumphalism.

The plan they made was received enthusiastically by those in power in Washington. Through Secretary of War Elihu Root, a behind-the-scenes supporter, they received a sympathetic hearing from President Roosevelt, who opened the exhibition of the plan in the Corcoran Gallery and was given a private showing by Senator McMillan.[62] Secretary of State John Hay, who as a young man had been Lincoln's private secretary, responded most touchingly to the plan:

> When [Hay] realized the meaning of the conception—that Lincoln, standing with Washington in the history of this country, should also stand with him in memorial symbolism in the nation's capital—the Secretary said that the reasoning was sound in both logic and sentiment. Then and there he accepted the location and the design of the Lincoln Memorial on the axis of the Capitol and the Washington Monument, saying that he regarded it as inevitable. The design of the memorial, simple, dignified, of great beauty in its proportions and classical in its form, strongly appealed to him; for he felt that underneath the rough and often uncouth exterior of Lincoln there was a serene beauty of character which found expression in language comparable to the Psalms in majestic grandeur and depth of human feeling; while in the Gettysburg Address President Lincoln had spoken words of sublimity parallel to the classic oration of Pericles over the dead of Thermopylae.[63]

More than likely, Roosevelt's explicit permission had been sought to include a Lincoln memorial.[64] The plan continued to have support in high places: even after McMillan inconveniently died a few months after the plan was published, Root and Senator Francis G. Newlands of Nevada, an early conservationist and, intriguingly, a Democrat, became its staunchest supporters in the government.[65]

In its clarity, daring, and magnificent presentation, the plan realized the hope of Brown, Burnham, and other advocates of civic art that it would dramatize the City Beautiful for the nation and spread it elsewhere. The plan's beauty is often praised, and more recently the political and professional context in which it was made has been analyzed; but less studied is what the plan signified or represented. What exactly, in concrete political and cultural terms, did the plan, especially the proposal for the Lincoln Memorial, mean?

First, it sought to take up L'Enfant's theme

of the "grand avenue" but to render it on the grand, imperial scale befitting the great power America was fast becoming. The plan imagined a Washington influenced by and competing with European imperial capitals as they had been aggrandized in the late nineteenth century, especially Paris of the Second Empire and Third Republic.[66] The plan, however, had distinctly American content. Its idealism represented an effort to confer on the central government, which had been the despair of reformers in the late nineteenth century, a new dignity and sense of mission. Since the end of the Civil War, most reformers and Republicans had been calling for a stronger, more orderly and professional federal government, seen as less vulnerable than state and city authorities to corruption, and the economic and social challenges facing Americans in the late century were increasingly national in scope. In the mideighties Woodrow Wilson had written, "There are voices in the air which cannot be misunderstood. The times seem to favor a centralization of governmental functions such as could not have suggested itself as a possibility to the framers of the Consitution."[67] In fact, "nationalism," besides designating centralization, patriotism, and sectional reunion, became a code word for reform.[68] So, the austere grandeur and dignity of official Washington in the McMillan Plan was a characteristically centralizing, Republican call for an organized, efficient, reformist order, to which the primacy accorded the arch-nationalist Lincoln added emphasis. Henry James, on his visit in 1904, saw this clearly:

The "artistic" Federal city already announced spreads itself then before us . . . a city of palaces and monuments and gardens, symmetries and circles and far radiations. . . . This imagery has, above all, the value, for the considering mind, that it presents itself as under the wide-spread wings of the general Government, which fairly makes it figure to the rapt vision as the object caught up in eagle claws and lifted into fields of air that even the high brows of the municipal boss fail to sweep. The wide-spread wings affect us, in the prospect, as great fans that, by their mere tremor, will blow the work, at all steps and stages, clean and clear, disinfect it quite ideally of any germ of the job, and prepare thereby for the American voter, on the spot and in the pride of possession, quite a new kind of civic consciousness.[69]

One reason the plan appealed so insistently to Unionist memories of the Civil War was that it represented the Republican program to cleanse and strengthen the federal government.[70] Harking back to the war and the leadership the party had given it had become Republicans' perennial campaign strategy. Whatever the issue of the day—the tariff, the gold standard, restrictions on immigration, the labor question, imperialism—Republican speakers could be depended on to weave references into speeches urging their positions on those issues to the party's founding mission to end slavery and fight the war. On Lincoln's Birthday, on Memorial Day, and in election campaign speeches, voters were tirelessly reminded—as they occasionally still are—

that Republicans were "the party of Lincoln," who by following him into battle had saved the Union and brought prosperity and renewed nationhood. "The Republican Party had a noble origin," boasted Hay in his anniversary speech of 1904. "It sprang directly from an aroused and indignant national conscience. . . . If there is one thing more than another in which we Republicans are entitled to a legitimate pride, it is that Lincoln was our first President. . . . [W]e who have always tried to walk in the road he pointed out can not be deprived of the tender pride of calling ourselves his disciples, and of doing in his name the work allotted to us by Providence."[71] Veterans of the GAR, grizzled enough by 1900, were regularly trotted out to give speeches calling for loyalty to the Union and the Grand Old Party, a strategy that had reached fever pitch in the shrill, desperate campaign of 1896.[72] The Civil War revival of that year, which captured the martialism of the midnineties and was reinforced two years later by jingoism and national pride arising from the war with Spain, largely explains the McMillan Commission's emphasis on the war.

For McMillan and his fellow sponsors of the plan, of course, referring to the war was a risk, for it might antagonize Southerners and Democrats, along with Republican traditionalists and "stalwarts" (conservative nonreformers), such as Cannon in the House, who did not want the expensive plan made at all; but, as with everything McMillan did, the risk was calculated. The decision to honor Lincoln, arch-embodiment of the Union and federal authority, by a great terminal memorial was the greatest danger of all. The risk was reduced by knowing that by that time, even to many Southerners, the Union had become what Lincoln had conceived it to be: a spiritual bond among Americans of all states and sections, from which white Southerners had briefly wandered but to which they had been welcome—indeed, compelled by historical forces—to return.[73] Accordingly, Lincoln himself had become more palatable to all. Furthermore, McKim and the other commissioners had taken pains to ensure that the structure and location of his memorial should cause it to give as little offense as possible. It would be a transparent screen of columns at the end of the bridge from Arlington, a metaphorical city gate welcoming Southerners, neither barring sight of nor blocking access to the Mall from Virginia. At the same time, on the Washington shore it would create a raised platform affording beautiful views of the sun setting over the river. In type it was a park structure, as the Lincoln Memorial eventually built would not be, and so relatively harmless. Apart from inscriptions on it quoting heroic speeches, the memorial McKim imagined was virtually drained of ideological content. What had started as a partisan political exercise was reborn as "expert," bureaucratic, formal expression.

Another reason Lincoln belonged at the fulcrum of the progressive Republican plan for the capital was that he symbolized a strong presidency. However he might have behaved in more normal times, as wartime president Lincoln had markedly expanded the scope of the office at the expense of that of Congress. The congressional Radicals sought to correct the imbalance when his successor, Andrew Johnson, provoked them by enacting what they considered too lenient a program of Reconstruction in 1865–66. Under Johnson and Grant, then, Congress functioned almost independently of the executive, much to the detriment of that office, which in the early Republic had been a strong one, more or less parallel to that of a British prime minister.[74] Under Grant, said George F. Hoar, "The most eminent Senators . . . would have received as a personal affront a private message from the White House expressing a desire that they should adopt any course . . . they did not approve. If they visited the White House, it was to give, not to receive advice."[75] Although presidents after Hayes (1877–81) acted with more independence than Grant, the approximate balance of power between the parties until the midnineties led to a tug-of-war between Congress and the Executive Mansion, as the presidential residence was officially called until Theodore Roosevelt renamed it "White House" after 1901. So, until the end of Grover Cleveland's second administration, in 1897, the presidency remained a relatively weak office, chiefly of executing or vetoing legislation devised by Congress. "That high office has fallen from its first estate of dignity," wrote Woodrow Wilson in 1885, "because its power has waned; and its power has waned because the power of Congress has become predominant."[76] Today a president is expected to set policy and priorities, prepare legislation, work with Congress to secure its passage, and carry it out through the various departments of the executive branch, but such an activist presidency was foreign to the late nineteenth century. Then, presidents generally held office because they were party stalwarts who were both socially acceptable and compromise figures. By the 1880s, however, a weakened executive was not satisfactory to reformers, for whom the pressing economic and social issues of the day required strong national government with a vigorous executive at the helm, nor to genteel scholars and critics like Henry Adams and Woodrow Wilson, who viewed party politics in all its corruption as dirty, degrading, and beneath the country's "natural" leaders. As an undergraduate at Princeton in 1879, Wilson had lamented that the president was "merely the executor of the sovereign legislative will,"[77] and he began to construct a theory of government, which he got the chance to apply thirty years later, around the need for a strong executive.

The turmoil of the late eighties and early nineties caused many thoughtful Americans to agree with Wilson. So, during his first term (1885–89), Grover Cleveland acted more independently of Congress than his predecessors, indeed with some haughtiness. Later he wrote, perhaps with Theodore Roosevelt's example in mind, "[T]he Presidency is preeminently the people's office."[78] Cleveland's successor, McKinley, having long served in the House himself, ruled Congress by his winning personality and steel ties to the party. McKinley's leadership in the Spanish-American War and his cabinet's, especially Hay's, active interest in raising America's profile in the world further enhanced the prestige of the presidency. So, when Wilson reissued his book *Congressional Government* in 1900, he noted that, since 1885, when it had first appeared, "Much the most important change to be noticed is . . . the greatly increased power and opportunity for constructive statesmanship given the President."[79] Now, for Republicans the emblem of strong, wise leadership was Abraham Lincoln. Besides standing for morality, Americanism, and the party, he was the figure of the strong executive. So the decision to include in the McMillan Plan a memorial to him in line with the key symbol of the legislature, the dome of the Capitol, and in succession to the monument to Washington should be read in part as an appeal for strong presidential leadership in the twentieth century.[80]

Theodore Roosevelt, the hero of the Spanish-American War, though born into the aristocracy of New York City, was a savvy, pragmatic politician as well as an idealistic if snobbish reformer and mugwump. He brought into office in September 1901 a theory of an activist presidency he erroneously attributed to Jackson and Lincoln.[81] All residual powers the Constitution did not specifically reserve to Congress, he believed, were in the purview of the president, who was responsible to the American people, not the legislature. This energizing new concept and Roosevelt's leonine personality were the engine that drove the most vigorous administration the country had seen in a hundred years—more vigorous, even, than Lincoln's. Through the Speakers of the House, whom he courted, Roosevelt engineered a legislative program that, to a degree previously unseen,

regulated business, established a public interest in land, water, and forests, and asserted magisterial leadership in the world under a Pax Americana. Nothing personal or political seemed beyond Roosevelt. While in office he was awarded the Nobel Peace Prize for settling the Russo-Japanese War and found time to entertain lavishly, exercise vigorously, and even publish literary writings. The public adored him, though there were those, naturally, who mistrusted his bold new script for the presidency. But even the Democratic contender Woodrow Wilson was forced to admit, "Whatever else we may think or say of Theodore Roosevelt, we must admit that he is an aggressive leader. He led Congress—he was not driven by Congress."[82] This institutional revolution, though not permanent, was a lesson from which Roosevelt's successors took instruction, especially Wilson himself, who by 1907 was saying, "The President is at liberty, both in law and conscience, to be as big a man as he can be. His capacity will set the limit."[83] Though only a metaphor for real government and power, the Lincoln Memorial that the McMillan Commission imagined at the end of the Mall embodied the growing sentiment that not just Lincoln but whoever occupied the presidency should be a "big man."

In light of all this, the coincidence is almost too neat that Roosevelt assumed the presidency in the very weeks that the McMillan Commission was refining its plan for official Washington. It is as though, despite his absolutely antithetical appearance and temperament, he *were* the Lincoln of the plan. The point can be pushed one step further. A remarkable feature of turn-of-the-century America was the appearance, in many fields of activity, of giants, some of whom became president, while others did not. In fact, the cult of strong personality is part of what gives the period its romance and high drama. Apart from Roosevelt and Wilson, one thinks of William Jennings Bryan, Clarence Darrow, Frank Lloyd Wright, William James, J. P. Morgan, Andrew Carnegie, Jane Addams, Eugene Debs, W.E.B. Du Bois, John Reed, and so on. In American politics it was "a second golden age" equaling that of the founders, an era that set a standard of public life later periods only hoped to emulate.[84] The reappearance in national myth of Lincoln and his metamorphosis into a figure of gigantic proportions, and the plan to build a great memorial to him on the nation's town green, so to speak—full in the face of the American people—symbolized confidence in the power of the human person to shape history and change the world, an attitude very far from our own quite skep-

tical appraisal of human action, which, with reason, tends to give at least equal attention to less comforting aspects of American life.

The McMillan Plan ends the beginning of the story of the Lincoln Memorial. In its beautiful and compelling presentation, the plan made a memorial to him, indeed, a new kind of capital city, imaginable. Like a knot, the plan's Lincoln Memorial joined several themes: the history and symbolism of the Republican Party; a vision of the American city of the future; a sense of the Union as a bond between Americans of all sections and countries of origin; a picture of the United States as a great—perhaps the greatest—modern nation, having a divine mission to spread prosperity and democracy to humanity; and the idealized interpretation of Lincoln as national patron, patriotic visionary, epitome of social and cultural harmony, and spokesman for the renewal of the national government and the presidency.

CHAPTER 2

1902–1912: "What Shall the Lincoln Memorial Be?"

PRESSURE TO GET GOING on the Lincoln Memorial began to rise even before the McMillan Plan appeared. In December 1901, with plans and models still under way, old Senator Cullom introduced a bill to provide for such a monument, but when his colleagues saw the McMillan Plan, they asked Cullom to bring his bill into harmony with it, for Lincoln's memorial was the plan's western anchor. In March 1902 a meeting was held with Cullom and other representatives of Congress, the Park Commission, and Roosevelt's administration. Before that meeting, McKim, Saint-Gaudens, and Moore performed a quasi-religious rite as a gesture of faith: "[They] explored the wastes of Potomac Park until they got the Monument on a line with the dome of the Capitol, and there, on the bank of the Potomac, they drove a stake to mark the site of the Lincoln Memorial."[1] But there was a long way to go before the commissioners' vision became reality, and even by the "slow and byzantine" standards of campaigns for national monuments,[2] a long fight was ahead. Not for another ten years, until 1912, would action on the Lincoln Memorial be decisive, and even then a final fight lay ahead in Congress. The plans for the memorial had the good or perhaps ill fortune

to be caught up in the political and social tempests of the Roosevelt, Taft, and Wilson periods, when a new America was coming into being. That era was the stage for crucial battles between new and old orders and new and old models of democracy, so the form, location, and design of the Lincoln Memorial, though only pawns in the larger battles, were heavily fought over.

In early 1902 the McMillan Plan's supporters believed success was at hand. This was a measure of their naïveté. With their lavish plan a vast public success, the railroad station that had squatted on the Mall soon to be removed, major memorials to Grant and Lincoln authorized where the commissioners wanted them, and talk even being heard of a memorial bridge to Virginia, the armature of a new and richly symbolic federal center seemed to be in place.[3] Although a revised version of Cullom's bill met heavy weather in the House, which had been snubbed in the making of the plan, it did become law in June 1902. It created a Lincoln memorial commission consisting of Roosevelt's secretary of war, William Howard Taft; Secretary of State John Hay; and the chairs, both Republican, of the library committees of the

25

two houses—George Peabody Wetmore for the Senate and James P. McCleary for the House. To give the commission a nominally bipartisan and nonsectional character, two Democrats were included: an aging ex-Confederate and noted orator, Senator George Graham Vest of Missouri; and Representative James Richardson of Tennessee.[4] McKim supplied an estimate of just over $2 million to build his memorial according to the plan, an unprecedented sum for a federal monument but one that seemed not out of order given that four of the commissioners were Republican and that three of these—Taft, Hay, and Wetmore—were known backers of the McMillan Plan.[5]

Those who supported the plan, though, neglected the effectiveness of opposition to it in the House led by "Uncle Joe" Cannon. As chair of the Committee on Appropriations and, soon, House Speaker, Cannon practiced a tyrannical form of one-man rule known as "Cannonism," which earned him the nickname "the Czar"; and, with many more vital issues at stake in negotiations between the House, Senate, and White House than the design of public monuments, Cannon could readily play spoiler to any plan for a Lincoln memorial he disliked. On the one hand, his age, personal popularity, fanatical Republicanism—he was a leading party stalwart—and early ties to Lincoln made his support for the memorial crucial; on the other, he despised the McMillan Plan because the House had been passed over in its making and because it represented the new, expansive, nationalizing Rooseveltianism he dis-

liked. An old-fashioned party politician, he believed Congress should supply the minimum of federal regulation and interference necessary, at minimal cost to taxpayers. Notoriously parsimonious, he would scrutinize spending bills mercilessly for flab. To him, not only were the McMillan Commission and its castles in the air pure frippery, but, constitutionally, the commission was a "cuckoo's egg," an "unnatural child, born not in lawful legislative wedlock."[6] He could not forgive the insult McMillan had administered to him and the House in appointing it. Moreover, having lived part-time in Washington for several decades, he thought of the Potomac Flats, site of the putative "Potomac Park," as impossibly remote and dangerously malarial. "[T]he monument itself would take fever and ague, let alone a living man," he declared and swore to oppose "anything . . . that will not place that monument where all the people will and must see it."[7] Famously vulgar in speech (his other nickname was "Foul-Mouth Joe"), Cannon had warned Root, "There is a fight on about the location of the Lincoln Memorial and you keep out of it; it's none of your damned business. So long as I live I'll never let a memorial to Abraham Lincoln be erected in that God damned swamp."[8]

As chair of the Committee on Appropriations, then, Cannon was in a position to obstruct Roosevelt's novel, interventionist program of legislation; after 1903, as Speaker, he would not even let a bill for a memorial to his beloved Lincoln on the Flats be debated in the

House. The president's representatives and their allies on the Lincoln Memorial Commission could not therefore risk antagonizing him for the sake of a symbol, especially one he held dear. Wetmore, who chaired the commission, was a strong personal supporter of civic beautification and the McMillan Plan, but, knowing Cannon's opposition, he did not call a meeting until April 1904. Even then, the commission merely authorized McCleary "to proceed abroad and gather information concerning important monuments and memorials there" and to report back by December 1905.[9] This would seem to be superfluous given the thorough study of European gardens and capitals performed by the McMillan Commission in 1901. Most likely the meeting was deadlocked, with Wetmore, Hay, and Taft favoring McKim's design and McCleary, a "regular" Republican who owed his committee chairmanship to Cannon, temporizing or being obstructive, along with the two Democrats. It is even possible McCleary already had in mind the proposal, discussed later, he would make public in 1908; that is not known. The McMillan Plan's supporters, so sure of victory just two years before, were left to seethe, and, although they made some limited progress in following years in realizing their vision for the Mall, especially around 1905, when relations between Cannon and Roosevelt (then at the height of his popularity) briefly thawed, they could do nothing to secure the Mall's west end except to watch the landscaping of Potomac Park carefully so that nothing was done to preempt the building of a Lincoln Memorial there.[10]

THE LINCOLN CENTENNIAL AND PROGRESSIVISM

McCleary is not known to have reported on his European findings, nor did Wetmore call another meeting of the Lincoln Memorial Commission. But with the centennial of Lincoln's birth approaching in February 1909, pressure grew to memorialize him as a nation. The centennial was a major event, and Lincoln legislation of all sorts came before Congress in the two years prior: bills to place busts of him in public schools, to make his birthday an annual national holiday, and to subsidize a private campaign to buy the Lincoln family farm in Kentucky and build a birthplace memorial there.[11] With Republicans in the saddle in Washington, the lack of progress in building Lincoln a memorial, to the McMillan Commission's or anyone else's specifications, was becoming a partisan and national embarrassment.

Meanwhile, the imagery of Lincoln had undergone another change, making him still huger and more unreal than ever, as fewer and fewer American could remember him as a man. About 1900 a "composite American ideal" of him had emerged that fused his human and approachable qualities with semi-divinity in such a way that "demigod and hero became inextricably scrambled."[12] The Lincoln we meet in Edwin Arlington Robinson's poem "The Master" was "elemental when he died, / As he was ancient at his birth: / The saddest among kings of earth … Laconic—and Olympian."[13] Edwin Markham's "Lincoln, the Man of the People," composed in 1899, figures him as a Norse god formed from "the tried clay of the common road," yet "Dasht through" with "prophecy" and endowed with "sense of the Mystic Powers"—"A man to match the mountains and the sea." For Markham, Lincoln's death disturbed the cosmos, as when a "lordly cedar . . . [g]oes down with a great shout upon the hills, / And leaves a lonesome place against the sky."[14]

Partly because the anniversary marked Lincoln's birth and partly because of changing conditions in American life, the centennial redirected the process of reinvention by portraying Lincoln as a youthful pioneer on the frontier. Indeed, the image of Lincoln as titanic but humane Man of the People that dominated his hagiography through most of the twentieth century, especially up to 1960, was formed at this time.[15] Architect John Russell Pope, whom we will meet shortly, gave that image material form in his design of the National Birthplace Memorial at Hodgenville, Kentucky, whose idealized Doric exterior enshrined in its memorial chamber a more appropriate if historically dubious reminder of Lincoln's rude origins—the log cabin in which he was said to have been born.[16] By this time, of course, the frontier had become more distant ideal than present reality: the 1891 census had officially declared it closed. Rather, the stress on the young and promising but untried Lincoln had much to do with the growth of Progressivism in American life and politics in the first decade of the century.

The way in which Teddy Roosevelt's administration (1901–9) embodied zeal for reform has already been observed. Americans who considered themselves Progressives adulated him; indeed, in 1912 he campaigned for president on behalf of a schismatic left-wing offshoot of the Republicans called the Progressive Party. But what was Progressivism? Historians today agree that it was more a "clash of cultures" than simply a political movement.[17] A sanitized, bureaucratized version of the Populism of the eighties and nineties, Progressivism, a congeries of submovements for change, diagnosed the same ills as the Populists—overconcentrated wealth and disreputable party politics—but looked confidently to orderly governmental reform to create efficient administration and a broader distribution of power. Essentially, Progressivism made reform palatable to the growing middle class. The McMillan Plan and the cause of civic reform and beautification, generally, were typical products of turn-of-the-century Progressivism.

By 1908, however, the situation had subtly changed. As reform causes became more respectable, Progressives of more radical views became dissatisfied, and a noticeable shift to the left took place within the forces of reform, with a consequent hardening in conservatives' positions. Fears of labor violence, race riots, and social disruption reached their highest levels in over a decade, fueled by a financial panic in October 1907 and a mild recession that followed, as tension grew between reactionaries and reformists. During his second term in office (1905–9), even the sunny "TR" became increasingly upset at the intransigence of conservative judges and Republican Party "regulars" in Congress, such as Cannon, and was able to enact the reform measures for which he is remembered only thanks to a fragile de facto coalition of progressive Republicans and congressional Democrats. The Republicans were slowly losing their hegemony in Congress, losing ground to the Democrats in the elections of 1906 and 1908 and suffering a bitter rift in their own ranks that was concealed only by the thinnest veneer of party unity, a veneer to which shared symbols such as Lincoln were crucial. By 1908, when talk of a memorial to him revived, Progressivism had grown in appeal as a political philosophy. Its bible, *The Promise of American Life* by Herbert Croly, appeared the following year.[18] Croly praised the thrust of Roosevelt's reform efforts but called for even more forceful and concerted national action, guided by a class of expert administrators, to overhaul the American economy and government so that democracy, an evasive hope so far, could be realized in concrete economic terms. "Reconstructive" democracy, he argued, could become real only by delegating to government, especially the federal government, authority to restrain the aristocracy of money, which had made nonsense of true equality. "Democracy" and "the People" were keywords of Progressives.

Understandably, Lincoln as a figure for the regenerative potential of Democracy appealed widely to working-class and middle-class Americans of the time. He was a protean symbol, appealing to a wide spectrum of reformers. For Croly, Lincoln was the great Democrat not chiefly because he was a Man of the People but because he transcended that norm. His was the view of an educated, literary reformer who personified Progressivism's elitist face. To him, Lincoln represented "the permanent type of consummate personal nobility" who "shows us by the full but unconscious integrity of his example the kind of human excellence which a political and social democracy may and should fashion."[19] But spokesmen for positions well to Croly's left also enlisted Lincoln for their causes. For the first time Democrats, who by and large were, except in matters of race, more reformist than all but "insurgent" Republicans, began to claim Lincoln as their symbolic property, too. Wilson appealed to his memory in the 1912 presidential campaign.[20] In the hands of Brand Whitlock, a radical civic reformer, Lincoln became in 1909 a protosocialist or labor unionist who preached the priority of labor over capital and, by standing up courageously to slave power, opposed "the power of money, which always supports the conservative and aristocratic side."[21] That is also how Jane Addams and other collectivists and socialists saw him, paving the way for Lincoln's symbolic appropriation by Democratic New Dealers in the 1930s. Progressives of all political shades identified, like Roosevelt, with Lincoln as a model of "mastery"—strong and impartial executive leadership. "O, rulers of this mighty land! / O, selfish leaders, great and small! / Let Lincoln teach you how to rule, / He is the model for us all."[22] In compassion he had no peer. As protector of the young, troubled, and unfortunate, he even mediated between classes, as suggested by an illustration that accompanied a magazine story written in dialect by reformer Ida Tarbell about Lincoln's kindness (Fig. 2.1).[23]

Fig. 2.1. *"Don't mind me, Billy. The Lord generally knows what he's about."* (Illustration to Ida M. Tarbell, *"Father Abraham: Another 'He Knew Lincoln' Story,"* American Magazine 67, no. 4 [February 1909]: 329)

Thanks to the surge of Progressivism in the middle years of the decade, then, Lincoln became a symbol around which both reformers and Republican Party stalwarts like Cannon could cluster. The centennial of his birth in 1909 made these propitious years for his reputation; on the other hand, his breadth of appeal muddied his memory and fostered conflict among his votaries over where and how to commemorate him. By mid-1908 three possible forms of memorial were being proposed. The first was the scheme shown in the McMillan Plan, which lacked the political support it needed to pass, especially in the House, and, moreover, by that time seemed stodgy, unreal, and aesthetic to more radical reformers who cared more for a "City Functional" or "City Practical" than a "City Beautiful."[24] So the plan now faced opposition from both left and right. The second was a proposal, contained in a widely read magazine article by James McCleary that appeared in September, that the government build a "Lincoln Road" or "Lincoln Way" from Washington to Gettysburg, the symbolic centers of his cult.[25] Silent for four years, McCleary had left Congress and was now second assistant postmaster general in Washington. Had he already formed the idea of such a road in 1904, when he was authorized to go canvassing in Europe for ideas? We do not know; what is certain is that he now envisioned a modern Via Appia: in Lincoln's honor:

Down the middle of the road let there be a greensward forty or fifty feet wide . . . [with h]ere and there flower gardens and other decorative features. . . . On each side of this central line of beauty let there be a smooth roadway forty or fifty feet wide. . . . One of these roadways may be reserved for swift-moving vehicles like automobiles, and the other for slow-moving vehicles like carriages and wagons. Outside of these driveways could be double-tracked electric railways . . . separated from the driveways by hedges. . . . Bordering the "Lincoln Road" on each side there should be a row or rows of stately trees . . . [framing] fine views of mountain or valley or river.

Built with federal dollars, maintained by money from tolls and traction franchises, and ornamented by state governments and patriotic societies, McCleary's Lincoln Road would be useful—like the kindly, homespun Lincoln—and even arch-supporters of the McMillan Plan, such as Daniel Burnham and Cass Gilbert, were hard put to criticize it. Gilbert even suggested extending the road to Richmond to make it a memorial to the dead of both sides and—a deft idea—combining it with the architectural memorial of the McMillan Plan.[26] Desperation was entering McMillan ranks.

Glenn Brown later charged, "The Roadway to Gettysburg appealed to auto manufacturers and auto owners, as well as the real estate owners who wanted to speculate in land along the proposed route."[27] Though undoubtedly correct, his charge was narrow, for in fact the road scheme had a useful and idealistic element, and good roads were a major cause of political and cultural Progressives.[28] American roads of 1900 were dreadful—worse than those of seventy-five years earlier, when canals and railroads had begun to make travel by road outmoded. In the 1880s bicyclists had begun to agitate for the building of good roads, and a decade later pioneering motorists had joined them. In a country as far-flung as the United States, with travel a national obsession and the potential market for cars enormous, the lack of paved roads outside city limits, and often within, was a major obstacle to "automobility." Lobbying for improved roads was a major goal of the American Automobile Association (AAA), created in 1902. The association called for the building of a continuous paved highway from New York to San Francisco, then only a dream.[29] The relatively prosperous first decade of the century was crucial to the transformation of the auto from a luxury article to a mass-produced one. The year 1908, alone, when McCleary proposed his Lincoln Road, saw the incorporation of General Motors, the introduction of Henry Ford's "car for the masses," the Model T or "Tin Lizzie" (which he would shortly start to manufacture on assembly lines), and the first annual Good Roads Convention, drawing delegates from across the nation.[30]

Although it engaged the self-interest of automakers and their suppliers, the movement for good roads had wider backing than that. It was a constituent part of Progressivism, appealing particularly to the Farm Belt states of the West and Midwest. The motor industry was based in the Midwest, but the Good Roads movement's appeal in the region ran deeper than that. Populists had favored improved roads as a democratic alternative to the monopolistic railroads and traction companies and as a means of overcoming rural isolation. "[P]oor country roads meant poor country schools, poor churches, poor community relationships, and isolated farmers, as well as financial losses."[31] Better roads led to improved rural education and mail delivery, McCleary's two key causes. Though a party regular rather than a Progressive, McCleary was a former schoolteacher from Minnesota, whose nickname was the "schoolmaster-politician." His responsibilities as second assistant postmaster general centered on the transportation of domestic and foreign mails. (On his watch, the post office experimented with delivering mail by automobile in cities.)[32] Outside cities, a powerful stimulus to improve roads was the need to extend the rural free delivery (RFD) of mail, since the U.S. Postal Sevice would not offer RFD to areas lacking improved, graded roads.[33] Farmers and mailmen in isolated areas were clamoring for door-to-door postal delivery, and farmers' organizations, coordinated by the National Grange, became, along with the AAA, the key lobbyists for Good Roads. For these reasons, good roads were espoused by Progressives of both parties, including Bryan and Roosevelt, who urged the federal government to involve itself in building and maintaining roads. So far, apart from creating an "office of road inquiry" in the Department of Agriculture, this was an area the government had refused to move into and would continue to do so as long as Joe Cannon was Speaker. Road-building was just the sort of big, Roosveltian idea he opposed. Still, McCleary's plan was clever and grew in strength later. If the federal government could be induced on any pretext to build a road across state lines, preferably several state lines, a valuable precedent would be set, and naming it after the sainted Lincoln would emphasize the road's practical and benevolent purpose, giving it the "Lincoln atmosphere."[34]

Nevertheless, nothing came of several bills for a Lincoln memorial road introduced in Congress. Cannon blocked them, as part of a larger conflict with Roosevelt that tied Congress in knots throughout 1908–9. The plan for a memorial road perhaps made subliminal gains in the Senate when, during a debate on memorials immediately before Lincoln's Birthday, senators from the Far West and Deep South spoke in favor of building a road in his honor from Washington to Richmond, an idea that took on a life of its own, but by the end of 1908 the tide of opinion in the press and Congress had turned against the road scheme.[35]

A third way to honor Lincoln in the capital, at odds with the McMillan Plan, was also proposed in 1908. Samuel Walker McCall, who chaired the House Committee on the Library, introduced a bill in May "for the enlargement of the Capitol grounds and for the erection of a monument or monumental memorial to Abraham Lincoln."[36] The purpose was to replace a disreputable neighborhood of small, old buildings in private ownership between the Capitol and the new Union Station with a precinct of parks and government office buildings, which would impress persons arriving in the capital by train. (The scheme was later carried out.) Though not specifically recommended by the McMillan Commission, the project would tidy up Congress's backyard and fit with the plan's Rooseveltian spirit of

public grandeur. The ambitious project had come to include a Lincoln memorial, a gratuitous but, to Speaker Cannon, helpful feature. He and the superintending architect of the Capitol, Elliott Woods (who owed his position to Cannon), were two of the three commissioners who would supervise the proposed project, and despite its overall cost of over $3 million, Cannon's fingerprints were all over the plan. Not only would building the Lincoln Memorial between the Capitol and the station keep it away from Potomac Park, but the memorial would meet Cannon's demands for visibility, for no one passing between the station and the Capitol could miss it, and relative cheapness—a million dollars, as opposed to twice that in the park. Again, Glenn Brown astutely but narrowly explained that the park and slum-clearance project on Capitol Hill appealed to "three classes—those who desired to beautify and emphasize the railway station; those who desired to increase real estate values in this section, and the pride many representatives had in Capitol Hill . . . combined with the desire of many Representatives to destroy the integrity of the Park Commission plans."[37] Brown detested Woods, with whom he feuded constantly. Having written a history of the U.S. Capitol and knowing the building and its grounds better than anyone else, Brown had expected to be named superintendent in 1901; but Cannon, as chair of the Committee on Appropriations, had chosen Woods, a slight for which Brown forgave neither.[38]

Moreover, Daniel Burnham had a conflict of interest in the matter. Though chair of the McMillan Commission—some even spoke of the "Burnham Plan"—and a member of the unofficial consultative board Roosevelt had appointed to succeed the McMillan Commission, he also headed the architectural office in Chicago that had just completed Union Station and was understandably anxious to aggrandize its surroundings. These included an awkward, outsized, elliptical plaza in front, which eventually became home to the Christopher Columbus memorial fountain.[39] Briefly, in 1908–9, Burnham and his design assistant Pierce Anderson conspired with Woods to promote the inclusion of a Lincoln memorial in the proposed formal precinct between the station and the Capitol. Of Anderson's hundreds of sketches for varied memorial schemes, the one that was Burnham's favorite showed monumental Doric colonnades enclosing the ungainly plaza and meeting, across the mouth of Delaware Avenue, in a pair of huge shell-like half domes honoring Lincoln and framing a vista of the Capitol (Fig. 2.2).[40] These aedicular shrines would have held chambers in which passersby could pause and meditate on Lincoln's greatness.

Brown was so focused on city planning that he appears to have missed the point that McCall's bill would have lassoed Lincoln's memory for Congress, rather than the executive. This feature eerily evokes Clark Mills's plan of 1867. During Roosevelt's lame-duck period as president, November 1908 to March 1909, his relations with Cannon, never more than superficially cordial, deteriorated still further to become downright grim. McCall, too, was a fiscal and constitutional conservative who, though not usually Cannon's crea-

ture, took his side in this instance.[41] In that context, the McCall scheme should be seen as an assertion of the authority of Cannon and Congress over that of the free-spending, expansionist White House, which had consistently supported the McMillan Plan. Seen in this light, the scheme was more than an annoying impediment to implementing the McMillan Plan or evidence of Congress's mistrust of architects as a profession, as scholars have argued,[42] but part and parcel of Roosevelt's battle with Congress over power and national ideals. Clearly, the president himself saw the issue in that light. When the danger McCall's bill posed to the Lincoln Memorial of the McMillan Plan sunk in, Brown set to orchestrating a furious public-relations campaign to blacken the bill, which reached fever pitch in January and February 1909.[43] In January, as his presidency drew to a close, Roosevelt was informed of the danger and, enraged yet again at Cannon's obstructionism, referred the matter as he had other Progressive causes to an expert commission by executive order, bypassing Congress and infuriating his opponents there, who now included most Republican members of both houses. They saw this as yet another act of Rooseveltian high-handedness.

Roosevelt's national Council of Fine Arts included Brown and other artistic luminaries.[44] On February 11, at its first and only meeting, the council duly pronounced that the Lincoln Memorial should be built as and where the McMillan Plan specified. But the verdict had no legal force, and the council was one of several executive commissions the House refused to fund that spring in Can-

Fig. 2.2. Pierce Anderson (for D. H. Burnham & Co.). Perspective, 1908–9, looking south on Delaware Avenue from plaza of Union Station toward U.S. Capitol, Lincoln Memorial in foreground. (Collection of curator's office, Architect of U.S. Capitol)

non's last standoff with Roosevelt. Nevertheless, the furious lobbying of the AIA and the artistic, patriotic, and veterans' groups in Brown's alliance had its effect, and McCall did not in the end call his bill up for debate. Instead, he moved a joint resolution (of both houses) on February 9, Lincoln's centennial day, to strike yet another commission to study the thorny question of how to memorialize him. Even that measure, though it passed, led only to pious rhetoric.[45] Would Congress never act?

By centennial day, then, the plan for a memorial road was in eclipse, and that for an architectural memorial on Capitol Hill was blocked. The McMillan Commission's vision of a portico memorial in Potomac Park was also moribund, and nothing except a little landscaping and roadwork suggested it would ever be built. Such a memorial was just another option, stirring but in no way mandatory. The battle for a Lincoln memorial might have continued for another decade.

BREAKING THE GORDIAN KNOT

In March 1909, William Howard Taft, poles apart from Roosevelt in temperament, succeeded him as president. Though not Roosevelt's first choice for his successor, Taft was a man of solid accomplishments.[46] His celebrated girth and joviality concealed the rigorous mind of a jurist, and as civilian governor of the Philippines after the Spanish-American War and then as Roosevelt's secretary of war, he had shown genuine administrative ability.

He was also a Republican Party loyalist. As a lawyer—he went on from the White House to be chief justice—Taft had reservations about the constitutionality of some of TR's reform measures, which caused him to take a more cautious line and seem less committed to reform than his predecessor. This was hardly fair: he was not the master showman TR was, but his administration demonstrated as much actual zeal for reform as Roosevelt's had, and did so in harder political times. Tensions in the country ran even higher than they had during Roosevelt's second term, and relations between regular and "insurgent" Republicans were still more abraded. But Taft got little credit for his accomplishments and was called by some "Taft the Blunderer." With his tendency to compromise and conciliate, he had an unfortunate way of making even good decisions appear weak, and in the end he served only one term, caught in 1912 between Roosevelt's Progressive, or "Bull Moose," Party and the Democrats under Wilson.

Though always a staunch supporter of the McMillan Plan, Taft immediately rescinded Roosevelt's executive order creating the Council of Fine Arts. He had doubted its legality from the start and wanted to chart his own, amicable if possible, course with Congress. It was, however, this sort of rigorously honest and well-intentioned act that caused reformers to suspect his commitment to their cause and, eventually, to dismiss him as a fat-cat party regular. But Taft had something else in mind. He made it known that he would sign legislation, if others initiated it, to create a permanent council or bureau of fine arts, something Glenn Brown had been agitating

for since the early nineties. In early 1910, Root, a conservative Republican, introduced legislation he and Senator Francis Newlands, a Democrat, had drafted to establish a national commission of fine arts. At just that moment, in mid-March 1910, with the bill before the joint Committee on the Library, Cannon was stripped of much of his power by a revolution in House rules engineered by Democrats and Republican insurgents. This allowed the bill to pass, creating the U.S. Commission of Fine Arts, which still exists.[47] The commission's mandate was limited at first to "advising upon" questions relating to "statues, fountains, and monuments" on public sites in the District of Columbia, but a series of executive orders issued under Taft and Wilson gradually widened its authority. The creation of the Commission of Fine Arts, with an implicit commitment to realizing the McMillan Plan, was a precondition to executing its scheme for a Lincoln memorial. Underlining the commission's lineage from the McMillan Commission, Taft appointed to it only acolytes of the plan. Burnham himself was assigned the chair, despite his temporary defection from orthodoxy; others appointed were Frederick Law Olmsted Jr., Moore, architects Thomas Hastings and Cass Gilbert, Frank Millet (a longtime associate of Burnham's), and sculptor Daniel Chester French.[48] The measure smacked of the cool detachment and professional expertise Progressives loved. Presenting the proposed commission to Democrats in his home state of Nevada, Senator Newlands called it an instrument of constructive democracy, an ideal by which "the people in their collective capacity can do things for the general good hitherto entrusted only to private interests. . . . These works were for many years conducted under the spoils system. . . . They were the subjects of trades, intrigues, and compromises."[49] On the other hand, Taft's commission had the high social and artistic tone with which more conservative Republicans were comfortable. The progressiveness of the McMillan Plan, we have seen, could no longer be taken for granted. This might make it harder to sell the plan's Lincoln Memorial to the new, more populist species of Progressive.

With the Commission of Fine Arts in place, Brown set immediately to agitating for the appointment of a new congressional Lincoln Memorial Commission. Though a body composed of politicians could be undependable, this time the art commission, however weak, would be there to nudge it into line. The need to create a Lincoln commission became still more urgent in November 1910, when the badly divided Republicans lost ground in the midterm elections to Congress. The party's long reign, ushered in in 1896, seemed to be nearing an end. It would lose control of the House in March 1911 and, quite possibly, the White House in the presidential election the year after. Members of Congress, like Cullom and Cannon, old enough to remember Lincoln would certainly be gone from Washington by 1913. Since a Democratic Congress could not be expected to promote memorial-building to Lincoln, Brown and his allies in government decided to act before March 1911. Given the divided state of the party, the congressional commission had to be set up with care. To promote it, Brown shaped a

wider, more business-centered alliance than before, focused on the Washington Chamber of Commerce and, under its aegis, the Committee of One-Hundred on the city's future.[50] In December 1910, Brown urged Cullom to introduce legislation in the Senate for a prestigious commission "to procure and determine upon a location, plan, and design for a monument or memorial" in Lincoln's memory in Washington.[51] Cullom's bill became law on February 9, 1911. The act created a bipartisan commission of seven, whose names were specified in the act (Fig. 2.3). Choosing the seven was a deft balancing act. Naming the president to the commission gave it stature and placed a loyal friend of the McMillan Plan in the chair. There were the two old inevitables, Cullom and Cannon, and the Democrat who was now the most powerful man in the House, minority leader and incoming Speaker, Champ Clark. Cannon might prove fractious but could hardly be overlooked, and his appointment was a consolation prize for the loss of the Speaker's chair. The other Democrat named, to give the group a national flavor, was the aging ex-Confederate Senator Hernando Money of Mississippi (who died in 1912). Wetmore and McCall, both Republicans, represented the joint Library Committee. Tilted toward supporters of the McMillan Plan, the commission enjoyed wide support in Congress and was proof against whatever happened in the election of 1912. It was a very senior, distinguished, and by and large conservative group, including no insurgent Republicans and only one possible Progressive, Champ Clark. Despite political differences, all the members

A $2,000,000 MEMORIAL TO LINCOLN APPROVED

This commission approved the design of Henry Bacon for the magnificent memorial to the first martyred President, which is to stand in Potomac Park, Washington. Work on the memorial will begin next fall. Left to right, sitting, Ex-President Taft, Speaker Champ Clark, Former Senator Wetmore, of Rhode Island, Senator Martin, of Virginia, and "Uncle" Joe Cannon. In front, seated, Ex-Senator Cullom, of Illinois. In background, Col. Cosby, Superintendent Washington Parks, Henry Bacon, and H. Vale, Secretary to the Commission.

Fig. 2.3. The Lincoln Memorial commissioners. Senator Hernando Money (Miss.) has been replaced by Senator Thomas Martin (Va.) as Southern representative. (Library of Congress, Prints and Photos Division. LC-USZ62-107171)

had mastered the art of compromise and could feign congeniality—useful at a time when personal relations among some of them were strained. Taft, though he respected Cannon as a politician and had avoided appearing to support the rules revolution that gelded the Speaker's power, was clearly pleased by it and personally offended by Uncle Joe's "vulgarity and blackguardism."[52] Cannon, for his part, blamed the president for secretly backing the insurgent cabal and, in April 1911, snubbed

Taft in public, a favor that was shortly returned.[53] Clark, on the other hand, did not think Taft nearly an avid enough supporter of the insurgents;[54] and outside the House, where they were of course enemies, he and Cannon were personal friends, united perhaps by their dislike of Taft. Personal animosities perhaps account for the little progress the memorial commission made in its first year. Certainly, Brown had his misgivings: "[S]peaker Cannon Senator Wetmore and rep. McCall were the principal advocates of the Lincoln Memorial on the Railway Station site. Cannon is actively . . . working for the station site, McCall and Wetmore are now supposed to favor the Park Commission site. We feel doubtful of McCall as he was such an earnest advocate of the station site only a year ago. Money and Champ Clark are unknown quantities. The President is undoubtedly for the Park Commission site."[55] Taft, however, had packed the Commission of Fine Arts with supporters of the McMillan Plan, and the act enabling the Lincoln Memorial authorized the memorial commissioners to confer with the art commission. In any event, Congress had the final say over what would be built, and it controlled the purse strings: a mere $50,0000 of the total anticipated budget of $2 million was made available immediately for such expenses as "procuring plans or designs." All the rest required specific appropriation. Its experience with Roosevelt freshly in mind, Congress was wary of writing blank checks for ad hoc commissions.

When the Lincoln Memorial Commission met in the White House on March 4, Taft was named to the chair and engineered a resolution to seek the advice of the Commission of Fine Arts on how to proceed, a predictable gambit.[56] Several possible sites were identified in the request, on which the art commission was asked to comment. For the moment, all initiative in the project of the Lincoln Memorial passed to that commission from the politicians. To the dismay of some of the memorial commissioners, however, the Commission of Fine Arts took until July 17 to reply officially. The fine arts commissioners were anxious to make a good impression with their maiden effort, for which in effect they had been convened, and debated every aspect of the proposed Lincoln Memorial in detail.[57] In particular, Shelby Cullom, who had not long to live, grew restive at these delays.

Meanwhile, the two commissions were besieged with pleas for jobs on the construction site and places in the anticipated design competition, and a host of strange but sincere suggestions for the memorial. These included a sketch for a colossal monument with obelisks at the corners and relief panels at the base depicting events in Lincoln's life; a scheme for "a pyramid of granite, larger, higher, and of better workmanship than that of Cheops"; and a plea from a temperance advocate that Lincoln's monument pay tribute to his alleged aversion to "the liquor traffic." The submissions dramatized the ambivalence that marked public debate in the period between, on the one hand, ideal and, on the other, functional, or "living," memorials.[58] The Commission of Fine Arts, however, concerned itself solely with the questions of where, in what exact form, and by whom the memorial scheme shown in the McMillan Plan could best be implemented. Never was the meaning or appropriateness of a Lincoln memorial subjected to penetrating scrutiny, nor were questions permitted about its purpose and audience. The *Washington Post*, however, asked "for whom and for what purpose such a memorial is to be erected," since the presidential commissions "seem to be possessed with the idea that Congress has appropriated $2,000,000 simply to erect some great work of art."[59] For instance, a highway project was dismissed from the start on the grounds that the legislation specified a memorial "in the city of Washington."[60] That that idea would rear its head again later owed much to the hermetic process of decision making, which raised the hackles of those outside the art community, for this was a period uncommonly sensitive to appearances of cronyism.

Although it inherently preferred the site for the memorial shown in the McMillan Plan, the Commission of Fine Arts weighed others, as well, which enjoyed various kinds of support. These were identified in an editorial in the *Washington Evening Star* possibly ghostwritten by someone, perhaps Glenn Brown, close to the art commissioners.[61] The question of a memorial on Capitol Hill had still not been dismissed, but, though "conspicuous and commanding" there, it would not be the equal of a memorial in Potomac Park at the Washington end of the proposed memorial bridge to Virginia. "The bridge itself," said the writer, "should be viewed as an integral part of the memorial." If "the great avenue or boulevard" linking Potomac Park to Arlington and, eventually, George Washington's Mount Vernon were built, Lincoln's memorial would not, as Cannon feared, be "unworthily exiled and buried in a swamp." The *Star* also commended a third site, but less glowingly: Meridian Hill, on Sixteenth Street a mile and a half north of the White House, a place the writer thought "ideal for a grand arch, the beginning of a Lincoln avenue to Gettysburg." The comment suggests both the neighborhood's prestige and the continued strength of the highway lobby. Thanks to the campaigning of Mary Foote Henderson, wife of a wartime Republican senator from Missouri, whose turreted sandstone home, Henderson, or Boundary, Castle, stood there, Meridian Hill was poised to become the capital's premier residential and diplomatic district.[62] Mrs. Henderson pictured

that part of Sixteenth Street as an American "Avenue of the Presidents." She had tried and failed to have a presidential "palace" built on the hill to replace the White House, which in 1900 was still small and dowdy.[63] With the collapse of that project she had tried, with some success, to turn the hill into a diplomatic enclave. At her urging, in 1910 the government had bought a sliver lot running up the rise along the east side of the street, where the threat of an African-American slum forming was the greatest. The future of this lot, later Meridian Hill Park, had not been settled by 1911, and it dawned on Mrs. Henderson to ally herself with the supporters of a Lincoln memorial highway to Gettysburg, for which the narrow strip of rising ground with a spectacular view over the city would be ideal for a terminal memorial.[64] Because of her influence, Meridian Hill was one of the sites the Commission of Fine Arts felt compelled to address in its report, as we will see.

Two other hilltops north of central Washington were touted as potential sites for the memorial, too, though the *Star* did not mention them. One was the grounds of the Soldiers' Home, at the head of North Capitol Street, the axis running due north from the U.S. Capitol.[65] Because, like Meridian Hill, the site commanded a splendid view of the city, the McMillan Plan had envisioned on it "a very grand formal entrance, . . . a triumphal arch commemorative of a great soldier and statesman."[66] The association would be particularly apt in that the Soldiers' Home housed veterans of the Civil War and that, during the war, Lincoln had lived on its grounds in summertime to escape the miasmic night air around the White House. Some, like Cannon, who had lived through the war were inclined to favor this site, and that is why the commissioners debated it.[67] The drawback was that the neighborhood was too working-class to appeal to Washington's beau monde. The other possible hilltop was that of Fort Stevens, one of the ring of forts thrown up to protect the city during the war, where Lincoln had briefly stood under fire in July 1864 against the army of Confederate general Jubal Early. The suggestion to build his memorial there, though, seems to have been a gimmick to "boom" real estate in the area, a ruse that was immediately recognized, and the Commission of Fine Arts all but ignored the site.[68]

As expected, the commission's report of July 17, 1911, was a ringing defense of a memorial in Potomac Park, as "concise, straightforward, and orderly" as a legal brief.[69] Alternatives were addressed briefly, most of them in an appendix, for it was clear where the commission stood on this issue most vital to the McMillan Plan's integrity. Most attention, given the support they still enjoyed in Congress, was given to sites near the U.S. Capitol. A memorial anywhere in the Capitol's vicinity must, however, inevitably form part of its background, the commission observed; the politics of such locations received no comment. True, a site near Union Station would be accessible to the public, but "[a]n axiom of exposition practice . . . is that the least desirable place for an exhibit is near a busy entrance." Meridian Hill was called too busy and constricted to accommodate a memorial of suitable grandeur, and Fort

Stevens and one other site on Seventh Street were dismissed as unrelated to the monumental city plan. Finally, while a bridge memorial to Lincoln could "supplement" an ideal memorial, it lacked the "abstraction" to be the Thing in Itself. By contrast, a memorial in Potomac Park, built free of "embarrassing obstacles," would have "complete and undisputed domination over a large area. . . . A monumental structure standing in a broad plain surrounded by an amphitheater of hills is as widely seen and is as impressive as one upon a hilltop." Yet, far from isolated, Potomac Park was "destined to be the chief center of outdoor reunion in Washington." The familiar words of John Hay on first seeing the models of the McMillan Plan, by now vested with the status of Scripture, were quoted: "As I understand it, the place of honor is on the main axis of the plan. Lincoln, of all Americans next to Washington, deserves this place of honor. He was of the immortals. You must not approach too close to the immortals. His monument should stand alone . . . isolated, distinguished, and serene."

After reaching a unanimous recommendation to build in Potomac Park, the commissioners turned to questions of form and choice of designer. Not wanting to infringe on the artstic freedom of the person selected, the commissioners observed merely, echoing the McMillan Plan: "To avoid competition with the Capitol or the Washington Monument, the Lincoln Memorial should not include a dome and should not be characterized by great height, but by strong horizontal lines." As to choice of designer, the commission's recommendation was a compromise after a two-day debate: to invite a single architect to "submit designs of various types and afterwards develop that one which your Commission may approve," or, if a design competition were thought necessary, to conduct it according to the highest professional standards. This was a controversial and awkward position to take, since the American Institute of Architects, from whose ranks several of the commissioners were drawn, had been trying for decades to open government commissions to competition among architects in private practice. In 1893 the institute had won passage of the Tarsney Act, which broke the monopoly of the Supervising Architect of the Treasury on federal building-design commissions and opened some, at least, to fair competition.[70] Now, with a design commission as prominent as that of the Lincoln Memorial at stake, one might have expected the Commission of Fine Arts to show consistency by recommending a competition. But such a competition, if freely and properly run, might produce unpredictable results, not wholly in keeping with McKim's ideas in the McMillan Plan. It could, after all, be argued that the memorial had in a sense been designed already and that what was needed was a reliable executor. Minutes and other documents show that the commissioners were intensely divided on how to proceed. Frank Millet, the vice-chair and the man most involved in drafting the report, wanted a board or jury composed jointly of government officials and artistic experts collectively to study the memorial and determine a design for it. Effectively an end run around the Lincoln Memorial Commission, his suggestion shows how deeply Millet mistrusted the politicians serving on it. Others, including the idealistic Burnham, seem to have favored a competition. The compromise recommendation provided for a design competition if one could not be avoided without losing face, yet keeping it under tight rein by requiring that leading architects be retained to draw up the program and manage the competition. It would be a two-stage contest, with a first phase open to all comers, followed by a closed one between the winners of the first and others "chosen solely for their eminent record of successful executed work." The scheme represents the bifurcated, elitist character of the aesthetic Progressivism that underpinned the Commission of Fine Arts, a character that was already generating democratic and populist reaction.

Millet was right: some of the politicians on the Lincoln Memorial Commission, especially Clark and Cannon, were unreliable. When that commission met a week later to study the report, Cannon, still determined to avoid building in Potomac Park, threw up yet another alternative site—Arlington National Cemetery. His change would have required a minor amendment to the enabling act, since Arlington is in Virginia, not the District of Columbia, but in proposing it he "counted on the support of the Southern members of the Commission," Clark and Money.[71] Millet countered Cannon's stratagem by having an influential ally in Congress approach Clark to point out that "[i]t would never do for this Republic to adopt the custom of the ancient Romans, by erecting the monument of the conqueror on the lands of the conquered." At the meeting the next day, when Cannon's proposal was revisited, Clark was heard to parrot Millet, whereupon Taft joshed Cannon, "Well, Uncle Joe, it seems that you and I will have to give up Arlington."[72] Cannon might never have relinquished his reservations about building in Potomac Park had McCall, resigned to not building on Capitol Hill, not framed a diplomatic resolution to return to the Commission of Fine Arts for advice on choosing a designer "to enable the Lincoln Memorial Commission to determine whether it will finally approve the site recommended." A noncommittal enough step aimed at disarming Cannon, this would meet the widespread impatience for action on the long-delayed memorial and strengthen the case for building in Potomac Park.

The fine art commissioners arrived at a designer's name with relative ease. It must be someone closely associated with McKim, who had died since the work on the McMillan Plan, and someone who could be depended on to present a design for the memorial in sympathy with the older architect's, economical to disarm criticism in Congress while also striking enough to overcome Cannon's doubts. "Messrs. Henry Bacon and Wm M. Kendall" were proposed, the minutes say. William Kendall, McKim's former design assistant and the successor to his section of the McKim, Mead & White practice, was the senior and better known of the two but was considered cold and something of a snob, a man who could be difficult with draftsmen, office staff, and other architects.[73] He would not function well in a project requiring the tact and collaborative gifts demanded by politically sensitive work in Washington. Someone his equal in

design but more socially adept was called for. On the second ballot, Henry ("Harry") Bacon was chosen. Though little known outside artistic circles, Bacon had a sterling reputation within them. Burnham, who had known him for two decades, considered that "the mantle of McKim had fallen" on him.[74] Burnham viewed as an advantage the fact that Bacon "had then done no great building": as "a man not of actual achievement but of supreme promise," he "would put his very life into [this] task."[75]

"AN EMBODIED CONSCIENCE"

Henry Bacon Jr., aged forty-four (Fig. 2.4), was an "architect's architect," known to other artists but so discreet that his office door, at 160 Fifth Avenue, New York, did not identify his profession.[76] Frank Millet, Bacon's friend and mentor of nearly twenty years, had to supply the Lincoln Memorial commissioners with a thumbnail biography of him:

Henry Bacon . . . brought up in the office of McKim, Mead and White, engaged as designer in the World's Fair at Chicago, Burnham and I having sent for him specially on account of his taste and sound knowledge.

Since then has been mostly on his own. Never advertises and has done little commercial work (office building, &c.) and on that account is not known to the public. A bank in Union Square, New York City, is one of his well-known works and is very fine. He has designed a number of tombs and memorials, that of Mark Hanna, among others, and is especially useful to sculptors in designing

Fig. 2.4. Photo of Henry Bacon, ca. 1900. (Century 83 [1911–12]: 369. Photo: author)

pedestals and other monumental features. He is generally recognized by the profession as one of the best equipped men in the profession and one of the very best designers. He is not accustomed to go into competitions but his design for the great Pennsylvania Museum of Fine Arts, which, however, was never built, was thought by the jury to be a masterpiece. This shows that he is capable of designing large structures. He is modest and sympathetic in temperament, and excellent to work with, as I know myself. He has no partner and is therefore free-footed and having no large jobs, commercial or other, he can devote all his attention to the work now before him.[77]

Bacon was born in Watseka, Illinois, in 1866, the son of a distinguished civil engineer of old Massachusetts stock whose work in railroad and harbor design took him to the upper Midwest and, after the Civil War, to the South. The future architect was raised mainly in southern coastal North Carolina and considered Wilmington his home. From his father and older brother, Frank, Harry acquired his interest in building; from both parents, he acquired a respect for education, a love of music, art, and culture, and conservatism in ethics and aesthetics. His heritage, like the character of the Lincoln Memorial, blended Congregationalist New England with Lincoln's Illinois and the postwar South.

In 1884 Harry enrolled at the Illinois Industrial University at Urbana, now the University of Illinois, to study architecture, but he stayed only a year. He then moved to Boston, where he had family roots and could study informally under Frank (Francis H.), a noted architect, draftsman, archaeologist, and interior designer.[78] He also wanted to position himself to win the Rotch Travelling Scholarship administered by the Boston Society of Architects, which would pay for European study travel. Through Frank he became involved in the burgeoning revival of Colonial design and found work in a local architectural office that specialized in it. Harry, too, became a fine draftsman and perspectivist in pen-and-ink, whose work often appeared in architectural journals. He also came to the attention of McKim, Mead & White, the New York practice whose modern classical work was turning the American profession on its ear. His brother's example also impelled him toward contemporary adaptations of classicism. In the early eighties, Frank had organized a major archaeological expedition to Asia Minor. He later published its findings in reports illustrated with his own drawings, of legendary beauty and precision, which reinforced the turn to classicism in American public architecture and design during the 1890s, around and after the Columbian Exposition.[79] The expedition brought Frank and, through him, Harry into contact with the strange and culturally resonant attempts in the late nineteenth century to locate the site of Homer's Troy. The brothers married a pair of expatriate English sisters, of the family that owned the mound at Hissarlik believed to contain the remains of the legendary city. A family friend quipped, "Small wonder [Harry] Bacon had a flair for the Greek Classic when his wife's family owned Ancient Troy"![80]

In 1889, Harry realized his goal of winning the Rotch Scholarship, allowing him two years of scholarly travel in Europe and Asia Minor. Predictably, what captured his attention most was antique Greek and Roman remains. The travels had long-term results. The skill he developed in adapting classical designs, especially for ornament, to modern building programs made him extremely useful to McKim, Mead & White, to whose office he returned in 1891, staying six years. It was a good moment to be there, for in the nineties the practice appealed greatly, in social tone and the exquisite quality and understatedness of its work, to the cultivated gentry of the Northeast and upper Midwest, the stratum in which Republicanism ran highest.[81] Harry served as assistant to Charles McKim, the

most sternly classical of the three partners, but sometimes helped the mercurial Stanford White, too. In 1892–93 he represented the firm in Chicago on the site of the World's Columbian Exposition being hurried to completion; there he came to the attention of Burnham and Millet. Bacon's contribution to the design and supervision of some of the firm's leading projects of the nineties, such as the Rhode Island State House, the Brooklyn Museum, and the Robert Gould Shaw Memorial in Boston, was such that he probably deserves partial credit for them.[82] From the partners he imbibed a taste for straightforward floor plans and elegant, well-scaled ornament based on classical and Renaissance models in preference to the complex and rather showy effects in space and surface favored by Beaux Arts architects of the "Modern French" persuasion.[83]

Successful though he was with McKim, Mead & White, Bacon loathed the atmosphere of the "plan factory," feeling it turned skilled draftsmen and assistants into cogs in wheels, and in 1897 he and James Brite, another veteran of McKim's office, formed a partnership of their own. Already known for their winning design for a Philadelphia museum of fine arts (which was not built), Brite & Bacon built a practice at the turn of the century in small institutional buildings, especially banks and public libraries, in and around New York, and elite town and country residences. Brite & Bacon's entry in the prestigious design competition for the New York Public Library at Fifth Avenue and Forty-second Street, though it did not win, was considered best submitted by a young firm. In institutional projects Bacon

Fig. 2.5. Henry Bacon. Eclectic Society House, Wesleyan University, Middletown, Connecticut, 1904–7. Main portico. (Photo: author)

generally took the lead, and the firm's work was marked by fastidious design and execution. After 1903, when the partnership dissolved, Bacon worked alone. Directing a small, trusted staff and maintaining tight personal control over each project, he made many drawings for them himself, even workaday contract drawings, and viewed architecture as a form of handcraft, an attitude increasingly rare in a harried, businesslike profession.

Critic Royal Cortissoz called him "an embodied conscience."[84]

Bacon's buildings are few—one bridge, one hospital, one department store, one school, one observatory, one little railroad station— each building select and painstakingly wrought. Of brick or stone, foursquare and small to medium-sized, they are simple, even puritanical, in plan and treatment. An austere redbrick fraternity house at Wesleyan Univer-

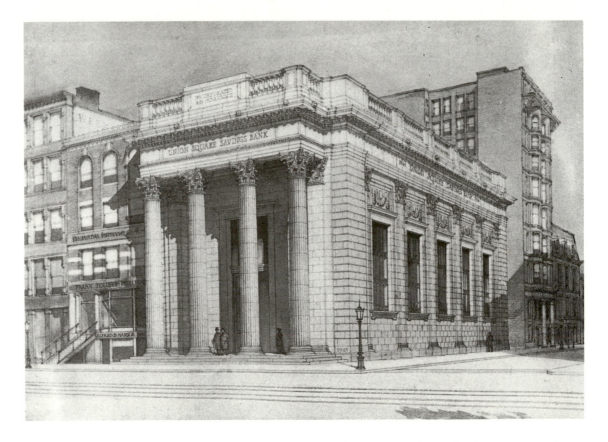

Fig. 2.6. Henry Bacon. *Perspective of Union Square Bank, Union Square East, New York City.* (Architecture 12 [December 1905], 186)

sity in Middletown, Connecticut, evokes the puritanism of the Federal and Greek Revival periods in New England. Its wooden portico of four giant Doric columns, with a frieze of triumphal wreaths replacing the canonical triglyphs, startlingly adumbrates design themes he developed fully in the colonnade of the Lincoln Memorial (Fig. 2.5). A savings bank in Manhattan has a grander, more Roman aspect, but its carved ornament, especially the rich swags over the windows of the side wall, has its sources in American neoclassical architecture (Fig. 2.6). Bacon's buildings

are like reprises of moral values associated with early America, values lost and lamented in the wealth and turbulence of the early twentieth century. Yet, despite their historicism, they were up-to-date in structure and services, as the Lincoln Memorial would be.

Disposed to small projects of great refinement, Bacon especially gravitated to the design of monuments and memorials. He usually undertook these in collaboration with sculptors, especially Daniel Chester French, who became his virtual partner.[85] The architect's role was to design the architectural setting for the monument–the pedestal for a statue, or the frame for a relief panel, and the landscaped terrace on which it stood. Idealized in tone, monuments, even major ones, were

Fig. 2.7. Daniel Chester French (sculptor) and Henry
Bacon (architect). Memorial to the Melvin brothers,
Sleepy Hollow Cemetery, Concord, Massachusetts,
1897–1907 (mainly 1906–7). (Henry Bacon Collection, Wesleyan University Library, Special Collections & Archives)

relatively small and simple objects, whose
effect depended on decorative refinement and
emotional poignancy—Bacon's great
strengths. He was, besides, a skilled and sympathetic collaborator. A memorial he and
French designed for a cemetery plot in Concord, Massachusetts, for three brothers who
had died in the Civil War epitomizes the two
artists' humane, elevated style, the elegiac air
capturing the dignified sadness with which
Northerners, especially New Englanders,

remembered the war (Fig. 2.7). Perhaps
Bacon's most typical monument of the decade
before the Lincoln Memorial is one on which
he worked alone, the mausoleum of Marcus
A. Hanna in Cleveland (Fig. 2.8). Hanna was
the great organizer of the Republican Party—
the architect of McKinley's stunning victory
in 1896 and a ramrod party regular in whom
party and person were one; so here Bacon
confronted an absolutely partisan program.[86]
Inwardly opulent but outwardly austere, his
diminutive white-granite Doric temple, with
freestanding columned porticoes sheltering
elaborate bronze doors, recalls a classical
Greek treasury, but one modified to contain
and commemorate an American public figure.
The columnar order of the porches and the
frieze of svelte American pine boughs and

Fig. 2.8. Henry Bacon. Mausoleum of Marcus A. Hanna, Lake View Cemetery, Cleveland, Ohio, 1904–6. Photo of east end, October 1906. (Henry Bacon Collection, Wesleyan University Library, Special Collections & Archives)

cones—again, replacing the standard triglyphs and metopes of the Greek Doric—anticipate features of the Lincoln Memorial's exterior, designed seven years later. As in the memorial, simple, snow-white classicism evoked the party's claims to moral and economic leadership of the nation, the tone McKim had set for the new Washington in the McMillan Plan. In strengthening the metaphorical link between pristine classicism and the moral authority and fiscal sobriety of Republicanism, Bacon had indeed inherited the "mantle of McKim." The older architect, in fact, had wanted him to supervise the making of drawings and models for the plan, although by then Bacon had left his office, and only the fact that Brite & Bacon was then competing for a federal design job in Washington prevented Bacon from accepting the prestigious opportunity. So, by 1911 Bacon was no neophyte in Washington and even had a tangential link to the McMillan Plan.[87] All this lies behind the decision of the Commission of Fine Arts to put his name forward. To an uncanny degree, Bacon was suited to the task the commission set for him—in geographic origins, ties to McKim, interest in early American and Greek classical design, specialty in designing monuments, and skill in commemorating Republican and Civil War heroes.

THE COMPETITION AND THE ROAD

Clearly, though, Joe Cannon remained hostile to the Commission of Fine Arts and the plan it was sworn to defend. Still trying to thwart the building of the memorial in Potomac Park and eliminate Bacon as sole consultant, Cannon offered a countermotion to create a consultative committee to study other sites, but it was defeated.[88] He then took advantage of the sentiment among some architects that a competition should be staged to have a resolution passed that appointed a second young architect, John Russell Pope, to prepare alternate designs for memorials at the Soldiers' Home and on Meridian Hill. (He, too, had abandoned hope of building on Capitol Hill.) The resolution gave Cannon a chance to reward Elliott Woods, his loyal subordinate, who was behind the efforts to bring Pope into the project of the Lincoln Memorial.[89] The resolution seemed to be harmless enough, and Taft let it pass, though he did not support it. It would create the appearance, though not the reality, of a competition, since the architects were employed for different sites on different terms; it would, it was hoped, demonstrate the superiority as a site of Potomac Park; and it would please Clark, who was now known to favor a memorial

highway (which could end at Meridian Hill Park).[90] The resolution represented thoroughly Taft-like compromise and would, at the very least, draw national attention to the campaign for a Lincoln Memorial and strengthen Bacon's design for Potomac Park by setting up Pope as a trial horse.

Pope made an ideal spoiler for the art commission's neat strategy. Slightly younger than Bacon, he had better academic credentials and was a designer of greater speed and versatility.[91] After studying architecture at Columbia University in the early 1890s, Pope had won two fellowships, one endowed by McKim, to travel and study in Europe. Study at the new American School of Architecture, later called the American Academy, in Rome had familiarized him with ancient and Renaissance remains. This was followed by three highly successful years at the École des Beaux-Arts in Paris. Pope's European experience gave him particular sympathy for Roman architecture, a powerful thread in American public architecture, and the fluency of a top-notch Beaux Arts designer in a range of historic styles. Born into cultivated circumstances, Pope moreover had a social tone that wealthy, refined clients appreciated. Up to 1911 he had mainly designed houses, but he yearned for commissions for monumental buildings, the summit of the Beaux Arts architectural hierarchy. His bold, eclectic classical design for the Temple of the Scottish Rite in Washington, on which he was then at work, showed imagination and suggested what he might do with Lincoln's memorial (Fig. 2.9), and his Lincoln credentials were excellent, thanks to his design for the National Birthplace Memorial

Fig. 2.9. John Russell Pope. Perspective of Temple of the Scottish Rite, Sixteenth and S Streets, NW, Washington, D.C. (Architectural Record 29 [June 1911]: frontispiece. Photo: author)

in Kentucky. Taft himself sat on its directing board. Pope had become friends with Woods, supervising architect of the U.S. Capitol, through the temple project and had approached him in January 1911, asking him to put his name forward when the Lincoln Memorial was revived. A design for Meridian Hill was a natural challenge to Pope: with the temple below the hill to his credit, and the Henry White house—and soon another, that of Irwin Laughlin—on its crest, he was establishing himself as the architect of Mrs. Henderson's grand avenue. Though he felt some compunction in competing to design the Lincoln Memorial because he was Bacon's friend, Bacon encouraged him to seize the opportunity Cannon's resolution presented.[92]

Meanwhile, in the background lay the movement for a memorial road, which was reborn in summer 1911. Speaker Clark's declaration in early August that he favored a road to Gettysburg was not made in a vacuum but, as with Mary Henderson's plan for an arch on Meridian Hill, in the context of Midwestern Progressive politics and its zest for "automobility." On July 28, on the heels of the report by the Commission of Fine Arts, Clark's Democratic colleague from Missouri, Representative William P. Borland, had introduced a bill to amend the act creating the Lincoln Memorial Commission by removing the requirement that the memorial be built in Washington and adding a stipulation that the memorial commission adopt a plan for a national "Abraham Lincoln Memorial Highway" from Washington to Gettysburg. In his speech in Congress, which became a rallying cry for the highway campaign, Borland waxed Lincolnian: "A $2,000,000 pile of stones can neither increase his fame nor exemplify his character. . . . Shall we make [a memorial] that is as dead as his own mortal clay, or as vital as his immortal spirit?"[93] Aesthetic features would be incorporated in the form of "entrance arches at the terminals [and] ornamental bridges." Borland framed his appeal in Progressive terms, claiming to speak for the People, and asked the memorial commission to postpone a final decision long enough to let "the people of the entire country . . . express preferences."[94] How the popular will could be gauged was not specified: the language was that of referendum, a mechanism Progressives favored, but what took place in fact was a public-relations campaign. Taft responded, as he often did, with scrupulous fairness, but in a way that looked like dithering. Despite promising Cullom to act speedily, he pri-

vately received a delegation of the highway party, heard its arguments, and invited it back to meet the memorial commission. Seeming to go first one way, then the other, Taft's commission then antagonized the delegation by refusing to see it. One member, Colonel McElroy of the Grand Army of the Republic, was so infuriated he promised a "nation-wide agitation for a boulevard to Gettysburg."[95] Suddenly a question that had seemed closed was reopened, and everyone was unhappy. This was a typical response to Taft's moves, which all but guaranteed defeat for him at the polling booth in 1912. Soon the local press and the Chamber of Commerce, which by and large had sided with Brown to that point, were clamoring for a bridge and federal highways to Gettysburg and Richmond honoring Lincoln. In this situation, Cannon's dilatory tactics were especially dangerous. Sensing this, Shelby Cullom sought to separate the issues by introducing a bill in the Senate for an interstate network of highways, with a trunk road from Washington, D.C., to Seattle called the "Lincoln National Interstate Highway."[96] The motor interests would get what they wanted, and so would those who wanted a Lincoln memorial built in Washington. Though Cullom's bill did not pass, it is useful to ask why the long-dead plan for a memorial road revived, which the legislation was calculated to exclude.

The answer lies in the excited state of federal politics in 1911–12 and in Progressives' attachment to automobility. The Republicans were hopelessly divided between "standpatter" and insurgent factions, and Taft's enemies had succeeded in protraying him as an old-style, top-hat Republican. Even Roosevelt, who had placed him in the White House and was usually sensitive to party unity, decided to run against Taft in 1912 for the "Bull Moose," or Progressive, Party. For the Democrats' part, their midterm electoral successes in 1910 showed them that, for the first time in nearly a generation, they might win a major national victory in 1912. Across the country, especially in the Farm Belt, Progressive feeling was running at levels never before seen, with Democrats in control of the House and several Progressive state administrations, including Woodrow Wilson's in New Jersey. In April 1911, *The World's Work*, a middle-class "uplift" magazine, boasted: "In the direction of progressive social and political legislation, the present year has been one of extraordinary activity." Naturally, the federal Democrats emphasized populist and Progressive positions, causing Taft's, including the campaign for a Lincoln memorial, to seem more antiquated still. Clark, a populist in the mold of William Jennings Bryan, emphasized "the People's" needs, hoping to capture the Democratic presidential nomination in 1912. He almost succeeded, being beaten out by Wilson only narrowly.

Progressivism, we have seen, was an amorphous congeries of causes, united mainly by the sense that they represented change. Automobility was central to Progressives, for it represented fast, free movement and bridged culture and politics, marrying modernity to middle-class populism.[97] In an age when religion, especially Protestantism, was powerful, automobiling and good roads were spoken of evangelically as a "new awakening."[98] The

campaign for a Lincoln memorial road would not go away, then, because automobiling and the movement for good roads would not go away. A total of 356,000 passenger cars were produced in 1912 alone (besides 22,000 trucks and motor buses), nearly a fourfold increase in three years.[99] Yet Henry Ford was still on the verge of implementing the true assembly line! Unless the nation's road system was drastically improved, the production of cars had effectively saturated the market already, for they could seldom be used outside towns and cities. This was especially true in the West, where barely passable roads would fan out from each town like the spokes of a wheel and end abruptly, leaving a no-man's-land between that town and the next. When Westerners wanted to go from town to town, they still had to go by train! Now, political Progressivism was by and large strongest in the West, where democratic feeling ran high and the need for change was felt the most. By 1911–12, auto manufacturers, auto clubs, car racers, and motorists were adamant: the roads must be improved, and the federal government was the only agency with the scope and resources to meet that demand. That is where the Lincoln highway entered. Motorcar companies and the metallurgical and rubber industries were among those that lobbied the Lincoln Memorial Commission for a memorial road as an alternative to a sculptural or ideal memorial.[100] Indeed, James McCleary, a key spokesperson for a Lincoln highway, became secretary of the American Iron and Steel Institute in 1911.[101]

The resurgence of the movement for a Lincoln memorial road during 1911, then, is not surprising. Taking advantage of the latest developments in the emerging field of public relations, the movement was highly organized. The Lincoln Memorial Road Association of America was created in 1910, under McCleary as president, to promote a road as "the most appropriate form for a national tribute of affection to America's best beloved son."[102] The immediate goal was, through Borland's highway bill (H.R. 13045), to divert the $2 million appropriated for a national memorial to the building of a road to Gettysburg. Property owners in Pennsylvania and Maryland were speculating in land along the proposed route.[103] But that was only the thin edge of the wedge, and the association boasted that the Pennsylvania legislature was committed to building an east-west trunk road connecting with the Lincoln road at Gettysburg. Backers in Ohio, Indiana, Illinois, Iowa, and the western states supported the extension of the road. So, the little road in Lincoln's honor was the nucleus of a plan for a paved national highway. And McCleary's was not the only scheme for such a road connected with Lincoln's name. In 1912, Carl G. Fisher, founder of the Presto-Lite headlight company and the Indianapolis Speedway and five-hundred-mile road race and an early developer of Miami Beach, began to promote the building of the "Coast-to-Coast Rock Highway," with the backing of other Indianapolis automakers. At the urging of Henry B. Joy, president of the Packard Motor Car Company of Detroit, Fisher's and McCleary's projects were combined under Lincoln's banner. Said Joy, "Let good roads be built in the name of Lincoln."[104]

By late 1911, with Borland's bill in place, zeal for Lincoln and automobility had combined to make the project of a Lincoln memorial road so powerful that a Boston editor wondered if those backing the building of an ideal memorial in Potomac Park fully grasped their opposition's strength.[105] Later, Glenn Brown admitted they hadn't until it was almost too late.[106] In retrospect, Cannon's presentation of a second architect and his introduction of alternative sites almost played into the hands of those who hoped to divert the appropriation for the Lincoln Memorial to a road, but, given his feelings about federal involvement in road-building, that was surely not Cannon's intention. But his dilatory tactic and the quasi competition it caused gave advocates of a road in Lincoln's honor time to marshal support and add confusion to the memorial project. Because until now the history of the Lincoln Memorial has been written by partisans of the Commission of Fine Arts, the delays initiated by Clark and Cannon have been viewed dimly, as deleterious and nearly fatal to the project. Instead, they should be seen within the drama of Progressivism and the crisis that split the Republican Party in 1911–12. Again, Lincoln's memory was wielded as an axe in a battle over deeper issues in American life.

CHAPTER 3

Design: Tradition, Modernity, and Americanism

WHATEVER ONE MAKES OF the Lincoln Memorial Commission's decision to set up a skewed design competition between Pope and Bacon, there can be no question it transformed an otherwise routine commission by aesthetic bureaucrats and the coronation of a single architect into one of the most colorful design duels in the history of American architecture. That competition between two able designers and draftsmen, the developments in the background that it sidestepped, and the debates on the character of American life in the new century inspired by these events epitomized a key moment of transition from traditionalism to modernity, from the established to the mobile.

For the architects, the Lincoln Memorial posed a complex iconographic problem because it had to be a hybrid of several historical types. On one hand, it was a monument to a national hero, like a monument to the founder or unifier of a modern state, such as the Victor Emmanuel monument in Rome, of 1885–1911 (Fig. 3.1). But, in this case, national rhetoric held that the nation's savior was a modest man of no pretension. The transformation I have traced of Lincoln from backwoods democrat and first among equals to national and universal emblem—without, however, sacrificing either—complicated the memorial's symbolism, forcing it from the

start to play a double game. His memorial should, perhaps, be more like that of a parliamentarian than a liberator; yet, because of his role in the Civil War and emancipation, that could not be ignored either.

Second, Lincoln's monument was to be the primary memorial to that war in the capital. But it could have nothing triumphal about it, so as to avoid offending the white South and casting doubt on the degree and depth of postwar reunion. Instead, the memorial should set a reflective, elegiac, and compassionate tone, like the remembered Lincoln himself. But if it were too modest, it would fail adequately to celebrate the Union that had emerged from the war and the modern bureaucratic and imperial state America had in the meantime become. These were among the issues with which the architects had to wrestle, and they had a rich but limited array of Euro-American historical models.[1] Fortunately, their generation of architects knew its history well, often from firsthand examination.

Past heroes had often been commemorated by statues, and McKim's design for the memorial shown in the McMillan Plan included one (see Fig. 1.4). But a statue alone would not suffice, visually, to terminate the Mall vista nor, symbolically, to honor Lincoln as the embodiment of national ideals. The McMillan

55

Fig. 3.1. Giuseppe Sacconi. Monument to Victor Emmanuel II, Rome, 1885–1911. (Photo by Ian Britton. FreeFoto.com)

Commission had expressly ruled out vertical forms of memorial, which might compete and be confused with the Washington Monument; furthermore, a memorial column or obelisk might seem bombastic. Another obelisk, the Commission of Fine Arts noted, would show "poverty of invention" and portend the spectacle of "a Cyclopean stockade of obelisks bustling from the Capitol to the Potomac."[2] Lincoln's memorial was, instead, to be horizontally regal and reposeful. McKim had envisioned a monumental gateway or triumphal arch, like Berlin's Brandenburg Gate, without, however, seeking to evoke triumphalism, but rather collective victory and peaceful passage. Related classical forms include the colonnaded stoas (roofed passageways) of Greek town squares and the columned enclosures framing altars in classical Greek and Hellenistic sanctuaries, such as the Great Altar of Zeus at Pergamon. These, too, emphasized the horizontal line and often stood at the summit of stepped compositions. The Victor Emmanuel monument, which members of the McMillan Commission would have seen under construction in Rome in 1901, is an elaborate version of one of these, with an Altar of the Nation on an intermediate terrace, but they would have thought it too baroque as a model for an American monument (see Fig. 3.1). More in tune with puritanical American taste was the chaste but expansive "peristyle" that had terminated the Court of Honor of the World's Columbian Exposition, with its McKim-like triumphal arch and quadriga at the center (see Fig. 1.5).

Fig. 3.2. Kallikrates and Iktinos (architects) and Phidias (sculptor and overseer). Temple of Athena Parthenos (the Parthenon), as rebuilt 447–432 B.C.E. Remains, from the northwest. (Photo: Karen MacDonald)

Bacon, we will see, tried similar forms as secondary designs for the Lincoln Memorial.

The main alternative to these, and the line of inquiry the architects principally pursued, was the antique, especially Greek, temple form. A sacred building, the temple was the dwelling place of the god or goddess, but in Western civilization since the eighteenth century it has tended to connote moral perfection. The Parthenon of Athens, rebuilt by Pericles as a thank offering for Greek victory over the Persians in the early fifth century B.C., was long viewed as the most perfect building of antiquity, perhaps of all time (Fig. 3.2). In its prime, the Parthenon's exterior of white Pentelic marble, enclosed in a Doric colonnade, was lavishly adorned with polychrome figural carving, and its rich, dusky interior enshrined a costly and over-powering cult image of Athena made of gold and ivory. An inaccurate image of the Greek temple as pure white and austere, however, has haunted the European and especially American imagination.[3] From the War of 1812 until the Civil War, Americans associated it with democracy, of which ancient Greece was said to be the birthplace, building countless homes, stores, churches, and public and federal buildings in temple form. Thus, the ancient, especially Greek, temple resonated deeply for patriotic American architects working in Washington a few decades later. Less resonant, but not insignificant, was the circular temple. In Greece, where it originated, the round temple seems to have connoted heroic death. Roman builders, skilled in molding structures and spaces and in creating visual spectacle, took avidly to the circular

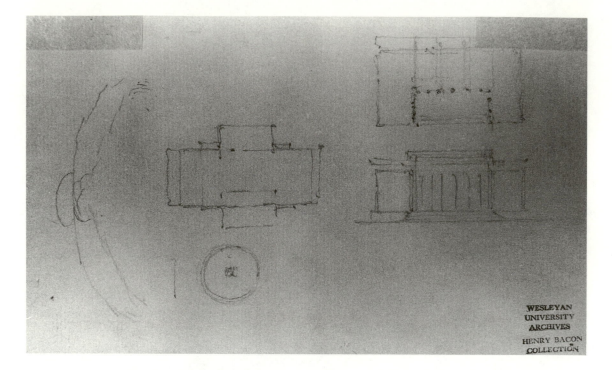

*Fig. 3.3. Henry Bacon. Rough sketches for Lincoln
Memorial, early August 1911. Pencil on paper.
(Henry Bacon Collection, Wesleyan University
Library, Special Collections & Archives)*

form, as the Pantheon, erected under Hadrian
in Rome in the second century C.E., illus-
trates. Nevertheless, though both architects
considered memorializing Lincoln in circular
forms, the designs had unsuitable cosmic
overtones and could not adequately terminate
the arrow-straight vista, two miles long, of
the Washington Mall.

BACON'S FIRST DESIGN

Even before the Lincoln Memorial Commission appointed him as its consulting architect
in August 1911, Bacon had set other work
aside and begun to concentrate on developing
a design for the memorial.[4] Likely, his supporters on the Commission of Fine Arts had
notified him of the impending appointment.
This was one of the greatest opportunities for
an American architect of his generation, and
the intensity with which he worked can be
judged from the fact that he made twenty-five
trips to Washington in five months.[5] The
drawings in his collection at Wesleyan University document his subtlety in refining the
design, especially its proportions.

From the beginning, Bacon believed the
memorial should be "to a degree a Greek temple,"[6] a closed building rather than the open
platform and peristyle, or colonnade, that
McKim had shown. He held to this belief
throughout most of the design process and
modified it only with some reluctance near
the end. He favored a closed building for two
reasons: first, that Washington's climate,

Fig. 3.4. Henry Bacon. Sketch for elevation of proposed Lincoln Memorial, with notes and detail of "Sculptured Frieze," August 6, 1911. Pencil on paper. (Henry Bacon Collection, Wesleyan University Library, Special Collections & Archives)

especially in winter, was not such as to encourage contemplation of ideals in the open; second, that the sacred awe votaries would have experienced within the cella (sanctuary chamber) of an ancient temple was impossible to attain in an unroofed (hypaethral) building. "The power of impression by an object of reverence and honor," he was quoted as saying, "is greatest when it is secluded and isolated. . . . This principle of seclusion is an old one. At the height of achievement in Greece is found the Athena, in the Parthenon, and one of the seven wonders of the world was placed within the Tem-

ple of Zeus at Olympia."[7] Accordingly, the earliest known sketches for his design show him studying a U-shaped, columned building framing what appears to be an open courtyard at the top of a flight of steps (Fig. 3.3).

By August 6, 1911, Bacon had developed a plan and form for the memorial close to those he would present to the memorial commissioners four months later. He already envisioned an oblong marble memorial hall surrounded by Greek Doric columns, modeled on those of the Parthenon and supporting a heavy entablature with a frieze of wreaths and states' names, rising above the colonnade into a Roman attic, or upper story (Fig. 3.4). Inside, the memorial hall would consist of three chambers, the central one containing a statue of Lincoln; the other two, address tablets on the side (or end) walls (Figs. 3.5 and 3.6). The interior is rather busy, typical of a

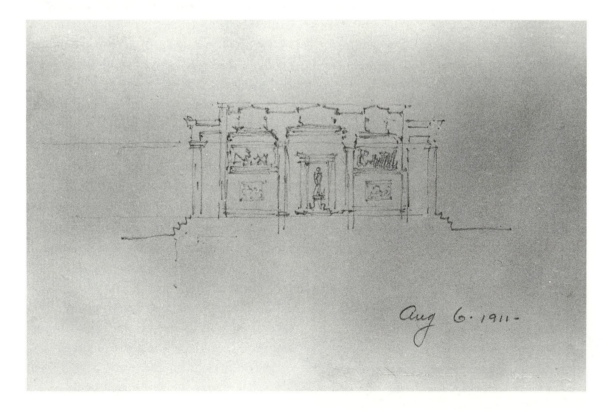

At the time of Lincoln's death (according to the World Almanac) there were 36 States that had been admitted to the Union Counting the 13 original thirteen States. It is a curious coincidence that I happened to draw 36 cols around the building without counting them though I had an idea after making the drawing of having them represent the States — At that time I didn't know the number of States at the close of the war H. Bacon

Aug 6. 1911

Aug 6. 1911-

Fig. 3.5. Henry Bacon. Sketch of plan of proposed Lincoln Memorial, August 6, 1911, and handwritten notes. Pencil on paper. (Henry Bacon Collection, Wesleyan University Library, Special Collections & Archives)

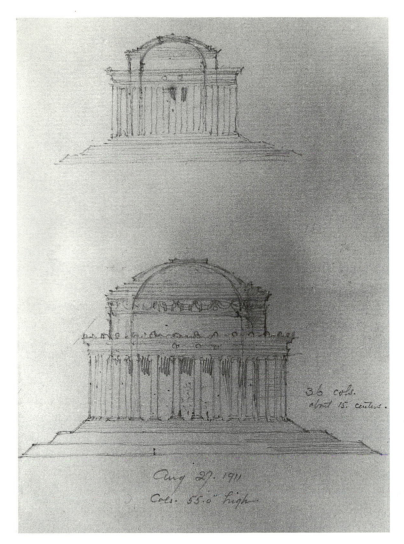

Fig. 3.7. Henry Bacon. Sketches for a circular Lincoln Memorial, combining sections with elevation and notes, August 27, 1911. Pencil on paper. (Henry Bacon Collection, Wesleyan University Library, Special Collections & Archives)

first scheme and natural enough, in that fusing all the arts in a single work was a cherished ideal of the American Renaissance.[8] Features he would shortly eliminate include a sculpted frieze high on the outer walls, inspired by the outer Panathenaic frieze of

Fig. 3.6. Henry Bacon. Sketch for transverse section through proposed Lincoln Memorial, August 6, 1911. Pencil on paper. (Henry Bacon Collection, Wesleyan University Library, Special Collections & Archives)

the Parthenon, and carved or painted tablets inside. Only the address tablets in the side chambers would be retained.

He briefly considered a circular form for the memorial in late August, transferring to a Pantheon-like building with a shallow dome the decorative system of his rectangular design (Fig. 3.7). The scheme is reminiscent of that for a rotunda at the foot of the Washington Monument that its architect, Robert Mills, had originally planned (Fig. 3.8).[9] Again, Bacon

61

SKETCH OF

WASHINGTON

NAT: MONUM:

BY

ROB: MILLS,

ARC:.

Fig. 3.8. Robert Mills. Sketch for Washington National Monument, Washington, D.C., 1845. (RG 42, Washington Monument Association Papers, National Archives and Records Administration)

showed thirty-six Greek columns, in this case apparently Ionic, the stepped-in Roman attic, and heraldic friezes at both levels. The interior was likewise similar to that of his rectangular design. Apparently unhappy, he developed the circular design no further.

Whereas McKim had proposed to celebrate the Union by means of an open peristyle and Lincoln by an outdoor statue before it, Bacon proposed to honor both in a single building. He told his friend art critic Royal Cortissoz that he wanted to address both "the heart and

Fig. 3.9. Henry Bacon. East elevation of proposed Lincoln Memorial, September 29, 1911. Scale 1/8". Ink on glazed linen. (Henry Bacon Collection, Wesleyan University Library, Special Collections & Archives)

the brain of the citizen."[10] Such aesthetic democracy, permitting the memorial to appeal in a direct, unmediated fashion to the "ordinary" visitor, was rooted in the late-eighteenth-century idea of *architecture parlante*—an architecture that could "speak" empathetically to the body of the beholder.[11] Bacon proposed doing this in two ways, primarily. One was to have the parts of the building represent the anatomy of the Union in a literal way. A drawing of September 29 shows his intent to have the memorial hall stand on a platform of thirteen steps with

their faces inscribed with the names of the first states to ratify the U.S. Constitution (Fig. 3.9). The metaphorical structure of the Republic and the nation reunited after the Civil War stood on the foundation these had laid. Further, the number of columns in the peristyle, thirty-six, equaled that of the states reunited in 1865. Here Bacon saw the hand of Providence at work, writing on the plan in Figure 3.5, "It is a curious coincidence that I happened to draw 36 col's around the building without counting them though I had an idea after making the drawing of having them represent the States. At that time I didn't know the number of States at the close of the War." Those states are named in the frieze above, between intertwined pairs of wreaths, but the thought of engraving the names of all forty-

63

eight states of the Union as it was by 1911 did not occur to him until later in the fall.

Second, Bacon proposed appealing to the ordinary visitor by incorporating signs of Lincoln's warm humanity inside the shell of the memorial hall. Cortissoz wrote to him, "Lincoln was the most human great man we ever had, not simply a man with a constructive genius for government but a tender, gentle being. . . . I am strongly in sympathy with your aim, which I take to be the making of a popular shrine that will kindle the popular imagination, not overpower it with a cold stateliness."[12] One reason the memorial in the first scheme was overloaded with iconography was that Bacon wanted to incorporate narratives of Lincoln and the war. Eventually, perhaps after reviewing the plan with the more austere French, he decided to do away with some of these and leave the statue to represent Lincoln the human being, and the elevated architecture and the words of Lincoln's addresses to communicate his ideals. In the end, Bacon did incorporate murals in the side chambers. High on the end walls, where they would be less obtrusive than the panels shown in Figure 3.6, these proved in fact the least successful part of the decorative system. Bacon was most effective where he was simplest.

On December 9, 1911, he presented his design to the Lincoln Memorial Commission in a display of drawings and models in a room of the National Museum, now the Smithsonian Museum of Natural History (Fig. 3.10). He had made some of the drawings himself, and some had been made by the gifted Sym-

bolist painter Jules Guérin.[13] The show was accompanied by a printed report.[14] Since Bacon's stated mandate was to give the memorial commissioners grounds to determine a site, the heart of his presentation was a defense of Potomac Park as a home for the memorial. He invoked the McMillan Commission's vision of a Mall "stretching in one grand sweep from Capitol Hill to the Potomac River," with the U.S. Capitol, the Washington Monument, and the Lincoln Memorial mingling their "associations and memories" and "forever free from proximity to the turmoil of ordinary affairs, . . . distinguished, isolated and serene." A "large lagoon" from the grounds of the Washington Monument to the circle of the Lincoln Memorial would "introduce . . . repose and beauty," and a memorial bridge to Arlington would "add . . . meaning and solemnity." To counter Cannon's objections to building in Potomac Park, he pointed out that a streetcar line would soon make a Lincoln Memorial there "readily accessible . . . to all classes."

Visible from the four cardinal directions and at oblique angles from the projected bridge and riverfront parkway, the memorial would stand on a series of concentric terraces crowning in a central "plateau" 750 feet across, equaling the length of the U.S. Capitol (Fig. 3.11). The topmost terrace, on which the memorial would seem to stand, would be sixteen feet high and five hundred feet in diameter, "surrounded by a wide roadway and walks." The apparent baseline of the memorial, twenty-seven feet above the existing grade, would be at the same level as that of the Washington Monument, asserting equal-

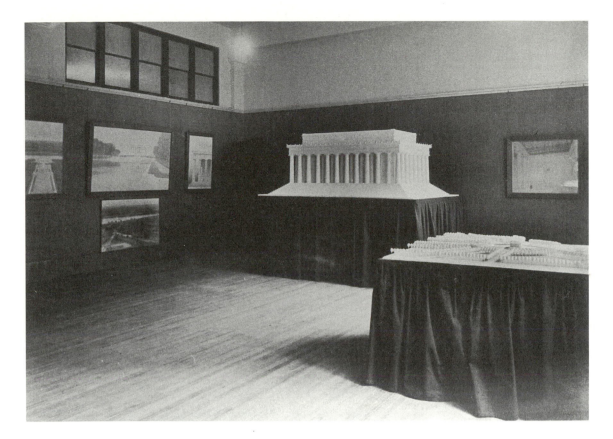

Fig. 3.10. Exhibition of Henry Bacon's preliminary design for Lincoln Memorial, December 1911–January 1912. (Henry Bacon Collection, Wesleyan University Library, Special Collections & Archives)

ity and kinship. Bacon imagined his Lincoln Memorial as a great teacher of democracy (Fig. 3.12), symbolizing "the Union of the United States of America" and housing in its "sanctuary" three memorials to Lincoln himself: "a statue of heroic size expressing his humane personality, the others, memorials of his two great speeches; one of the Gettysburg speech, the other of the Second Inaugural address, each with attendant sculpture and painting telling in allegory of his splendid qualities." These qualities, "Devotion,

Integrity, Charity, Patience, Intelligence and Humaneness," would find "incentive to growth" in the memorial; so would Americans' "just pride . . . in their country." So, Bacon envisioned the memorial as a gigantic ethical and pedagogical instrument.

Though all its visible parts, including the steps, would be of white marble, the memorial would actually rest on a "granite rectangular base" anchored to bedrock below the spongy soil by deep concrete foundations. The "colonnade of the Union," employing the Greek Doric order, would rest on thirteen "plinths or steps." Bacon himself had rendered a stunning elevation in ink and wash, now known only from photos (Fig. 3.13), of the southeast, or "Delaware," corner, so-

Fig. 3.11. Henry Bacon. Perspective of Lincoln Memorial as seen from cross-arm of reflecting basin. Mounted photo. (Henry Bacon Collection, Wesleyan University Library, Special Collections & Archives)

called because the states were listed by order of admission to the Union, starting at that corner with Delaware. The splendid drawing makes his ornamental system clear and shows exquisite sensitivity to the jointing and mottling of the marble. On the "main" frieze (to distinguish it from the upper frieze of the attic), between the names of the reunited states, appear wreaths interwoven of Northern laurel and Southern pine. The states admitted to the Union between 1865 and 1911 are named on the east front of the attic, below a frieze of wheat garlands and immortelles (perpetual flowers) bound by ribbons and punctuated by fierce, rampant eagles. The ornament is simple and dignified, scaled to the angles and distances from which it will be seen, and the carved serif lettering has beautiful understatement. Defensively, the Commission of Fine Arts feared that cultured Europeans would laugh at American excess and bombast if the wrong architect or design were chosen.[15] Bacon gave them no cause for anxiety.

Having enlarged the memorial earlier in the fall, he had later, on account of cost, shrunk it again by 10 percent. The savings realized would allow costly, extensive refinements to be incorporated in the structure, following the custom of Greek temple builders, especially those of the Parthenon.[16] Barely noticeable, these would give the building "an appearance of great stability and strength." In reviving such refinements, his example, besides ancient Greek masons, was his men-

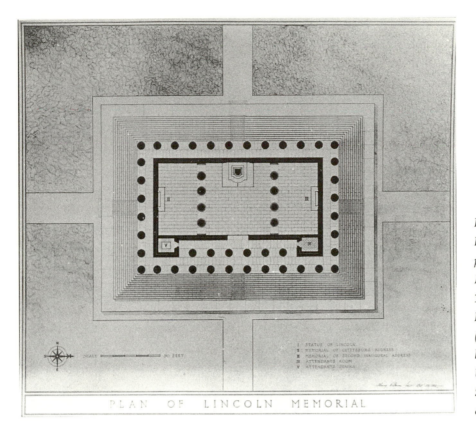

PLAN OF LINCOLN MEMORIAL

Fig. 3.12. Henry Bacon. Plan of proposed Lincoln Memorial, October 12, 1911. Scale 1/8". Ink on glazed linen. (Henry Bacon Collection, Wesleyan University Library, Special Collections & Archives)

tors McKim, Mead & White, who had subtly enriched some of their most luxurious and scholarly building designs by reintroducing Greek refinements. They had done so in consultation with a world specialist on the subject, Professor William H. Goodyear of the Brooklyn Institute of Arts and Sciences, for which McKim, Mead & White (assisted by Bacon) had designed a new building in the 1890s.[17] In the Lincoln Memorial, all vertical surfaces of the walls, columns, and entablature would lean inward slightly, adding dynamic character by causing the memorial to become, in effect, the base of a pyramid, rather than a uniform block. In addition, the floor of the memorial hall and outer walk and the steps would crown toward the center, a

detail with aesthetic and practical (water-shedding) value.[18] Drawings Bacon had made earlier in the fall suggest that he also considered varying the intervals between columns in the "colonnade of the Union," contracting the outer ones in the Greek way for an appearance of compactness, but he seems not to have entertained the Greek practice of thickening the corner columns for still greater compactness. Fabricating the marble for the memorial would clearly be demanding and expensive.

As noted earlier, Bacon planned a fully closed memorial chamber (see Figs. 3.11 and 3.13). To light the statue of Lincoln adequately from the front and have him seem to gaze toward the Capitol, the symbol of consti-

Fig. 3.13. Henry Bacon. Preliminary design for Lincoln Memorial. Elevation of southeast ("Delaware") corner. Mounted photo. (Henry Bacon Collection, Wesleyan University Library, Special Collections & Archives)

tutional government, the chamber would have a large doorway, eighteen feet wide by thirty-six high, glazed to its full height. Bronze grilles across the lower part of the door would be supplemented in winter by a bronze-and-glass vestibule. He also planned to heat the memorial hall. The central statue hall would be a cube (considered ideal in a set-ting for figural sculpture), sixty feet to a side, and evocatively lit from above by skylights. Bacon's description and Guérin's dusky perspective (Fig. 3.14) suggest that the architect visualized a dim, richly colored sanctuary, a subdued version of the garish cellas nine-teenth-century Néo-Grec architects and archaeologists had re-created for Greek tem-

Fig. 3.14. Henry Bacon. Preliminary design for Lincoln Memorial. Perspective of interior, rendered by Jules Guérin. (National Archives, Cartographic Division. Photo: author)

ples.[19] The memorial's walls and floor would be of colored marbles; colonnades of the Greek Ionic order would articulate the rooms; and "massive bronze beams gilded, colored and laquered" would frame the skylights in the ceiling. The gleaming white-marble statue would show against a tinted backdrop: the pedestal is shown as pink. The statue would be of heroic size (twelve to sixteen feet high) and, though Figure 3.14 shows a seated figure that is a miniature, introspective version in modern dress of the awesome colossus of Zeus at Olympia, we know Bacon was already debating whether Lincoln should be shown standing (see chapter 4). The near emptiness of the cavernous hall in Guérin's perspective adds to the air of awe, and on close inspection the pair of figures huddled in the corner appears to be African-American, perhaps elderly freedmen, shown gazing reverently up at their emancipator. It is the only reference

69

to race in the design, and only a mild departure from the consistent presentation of Lincoln as Savior of the Union.

Even more inside than out, the memorial was to be a didactic place teaching Americanism: "The visitor, entering through the great doorway, the only approach, will find himself directly facing the portrait statue, which through subtle interpretation of personality must dominate the hall, and later may pass to the right or left beyond the stately columns to read and consider the words of this inspired man who 'though dead, yet speaketh.'"[20] Of the still dimmer side chambers, Bacon said simply, "Large tablets bearing the full text of Lincoln's two great speeches, combined with adjacent allegorical figures will form imposing memorials." The screens of Ionic columns were placed between the statue hall and the side chambers "[in] order . . . that even these profound utterances of the great statesman may not be confused with his personality, but pondered in seeming seclusion."[21]

Though the Greek temple was Bacon's primary inspiration, it was by no means his only source. Ancient Roman and modern neoclassical models also played roles. In general, Greek inspiration is stronger in the details than the overall character of the memorial. If the white marble, stepped *crepidoma* (platform), columnar order, some external ornament, and skylit statue hall with a seated figure framed by colonnades, reminiscent of *Athena*'s setting in the Parthenon, recall features of Greek temples, the building's stern majesty, elevation on a masonry plinth, width, frontality, and climactic axial position are qualities one associates more often with Roman buildings.

The Greek temple was normally approached from end on, whereas the need to terminate the Mall axis emphatically caused Bacon to turn his temple sideways and cut the doorway in the side wall. Width, in turn, prompted the use of a triple interior and a square-cut Roman attic to replace the Greek gabled roof, which would have looked awkward viewed from the side. The Roman theme is strong and old in American public architecture. Thomas Jefferson had looked to the Romans for models for American public buildings, considering that their civilization had the gravitas required to symbolize the new form of government that was being brought into being and to inspire virtue in the Republic's citizens.[22] Bacon followed suit, alluding not only to the Roman temple but also to the basilica, a civic and imperial form.[23]

The Roman temple was a stern affair with knit brows, raised on a podium and approached by a flight of steps across the front. In a Roman or Romanized town the state temple, or *capitolium*, typically stood at the head of the civic square, or forum, framed (as at Pompeii) by colonnades. It would have a raised triple cella dedicated to the state divinities Jupiter, Juno, and Minerva. It is possible Bacon had a specific model in mind: the Temple of Concord, rebuilt under Augustus to celebrate the unity and prosperity he had bestowed on Rome and its empire, the so-called Augustan Peace, an appropriate association for Bacon's temple to Lincoln, American reunion, and postwar prosperity under Republican rule.[24] Known to us mainly from impressions on coins, the temple was in the

Greek taste Augustus championed, with a cella, like Bacon's, roughly twice as wide as it was deep, and occupied a site, analogous to that of the Lincoln Memorial, at the northwest corner of the Roman Forum, at the head of a wide, steep flight of steps. Through the central doorway in its long side, which faced the Forum, ascending votaries could catch glimpses of a seated statue of the goddess inside. Above all, the dedication to Concord, deity of Unity or Harmony, would have recommended it to Bacon as a source.

By contrast, the basilica was an official building type found throughout the Roman world that combined the functions of public meeting hall, commercial exchange, and courts of justice. It, too, had a hierarchical character. On one of its long sides would be placed a tribunal, sometimes raised and set in an apse, for the magistrate's throne, the symbol of his office. The audience halls and throne rooms in which Roman emperors met dignitaries and staged epiphanies (state appearances) were a grandiose development on the basilica type, and it may be no coincidence that, during his student travels twenty years before, Bacon had studied the remains of the Basilica of Constantine, or Maxentius, in Rome (306/10–13 c.e.). Consisting of three huge, barrel-arched bays of the basilica's original north aisle, the remains have a breadth and symmetry that reappear in his design for the memorial (Fig. 3.15). Metaphorically, then, Lincoln's memorial would be both a temple where his votaries could meet the American god face-to-face and a basilica where justice, mercy,

and infusions of patriotism would be dispensed.

Strong as Bacon's connections were to ancient archaeology, however, he filtered ancient models through a screen of neoclassical precedents of the eighteenth and early nineteenth centuries. For him, as for the neoclassicists, especially of the German cultural sphere, emulating the Greeks was the basis for forging a modern national expression.[25] While earlier Greek Revivalists, especially in America, had tended to replicate temple forms whole, Bacon, several generations later, tended to meld and modify the ancient sources to suit modern needs in keeping with current ideas of architectural fitness or "character." He was especially skilled at tempering large, grave building masses with deft, lightly detailed ornament of Graeco-Roman origin.

Although he considered the design just discussed superior to any other, Bacon also submitted sketches for seven alternatives, prompted to do so, perhaps, by the knowledge that he was competing with the more colorful and dramatic Pope. All showing memorials of predominantly horizontal character, these were labeled A to G.[26] Alternative A is similar in outer appearance to the building in his preferred design, but it is wider and squatter (fourteen columns across by six deep), with entries in both fronts opening into a long chamber with a statue of Lincoln at one end and a freestanding tablet with the Gettysburg Address at the other (Fig. 3.16). It answered a potential objection to his main design, that in it the memorial turned its back on Virginia, and it avoided the need to include a pendant text to the pithy, moving Gettysburg

71

Fig. 3.15. Henry Bacon. Drawing in pencil and water-color, mounted in scrapbook, of Basilica of Constantine (Maxentius), Rome, April 1890. (Henry Bacon Collection, Wesleyan University Library, Special Collections & Archives)

Address. Alternative C, more appealing, shows an open memorial with a statue of heroic size at the front of a broad, elevated terrace, with a backdrop of Ionic columns and a closed wall behind and outside it (Fig. 3.17). It alludes to the classical altar, specifically the Pergamene altar of Zeus, which he adapted with his usual light touch. With some of the advantages of McKim's portico, it nevertheless lacks the power and mystery of his main design. Alternative D shows a massive, simple Egyptoid mastaba, a type often associated with death and the afterlife (Fig. 3.18). The outer walls are closed, and colonnades line the walls within. The memorial may be hypaethral (unroofed), something we know he did not favor. Opposite the entrance, facing the Mall, is a large apse with a raised platform to hold the statue of Lincoln, and address tablets are set into the end walls behind the column screens. But the mastaba, though possessed of brute power and funereal associations, lacked refinement and would be less inspiring as a memorial to living ideals than the other forms. All in all, the alternatives lack the conviction of Bacon's main design.

Fig. 3.16. Henry Bacon. Alternative A for proposed Lincoln Memorial, fall 1911. Elevation (above) and plan. Pencil and color crayon on tissue mounted on board. (Henry Bacon Collection, Wesleyan University Library, Special Collections & Archives)

POPE'S DESIGNS

Pope showed the Lincoln Memorial Commission through his exhibition nine days after Bacon opened his.[27] Whereas Bacon, following McKim, conceived of the memorial as a symbol of the Union and Lincoln as its providential agent, Pope stressed Lincoln's humanity. He argued that the great man's memory should be enshrined "not in the form of a monument, a tomb, an arch or any form of building . . . *but in a figure of the man him-self, alone, serene, above us, in a setting of simple memorial dignity . . . in which the man is always felt.*" To him the statue was so vital that he had collaborated with sculptor Adolph Weinman in developing his schemes. Emphasizing the statue responded to popular feelings of affection for Lincoln and was also practical, for it allowed Pope to spread his architecture relatively thinly across the sites. At the same time it was a matter of architectural ideology, rooted in the ideal of collaboration among artists that was a hallmark of

73

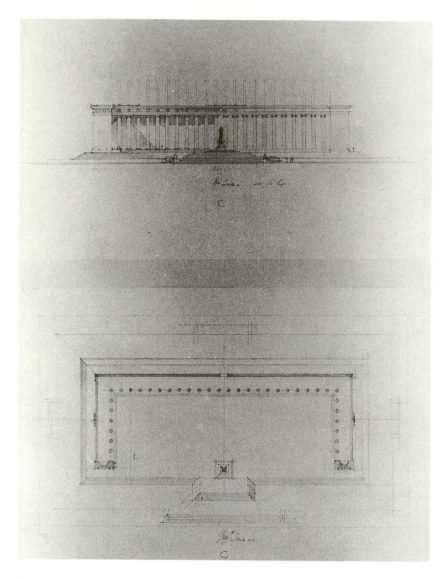

Fig. 3.17. Henry Bacon. Alternative C for proposed Lincoln Memorial, fall 1911. Elevation (above) and plan. Pencil and color crayon on tissue mounted on board. (Henry Bacon Collection, Wesleyan University Library, Special Collections & Archives)

the Beaux Arts tradition, to which Pope subscribed. Both sites he had been assigned, Meridian Hill and the grounds of the Soldiers' Home, were hilltops rising to about two hundred feet that offered commanding views of the city and lent themselves to terraced compositions. "Elevation has always added dignity, grandeur and loftiness of purpose to beauty," he noted, and the memorials he showed were as high as, or higher than, the

colonnade on the dome of the U.S. Capitol. After the dome and the Washington Monument, the Lincoln Memorial should be, he thought, the "*third* dominating vital feature in Washington."

For Meridian Hill he proposed a memorial with the envelope, silhouette, and raw primitivity of a massive early Greek Doric temple (Fig. 3.19). His models included the

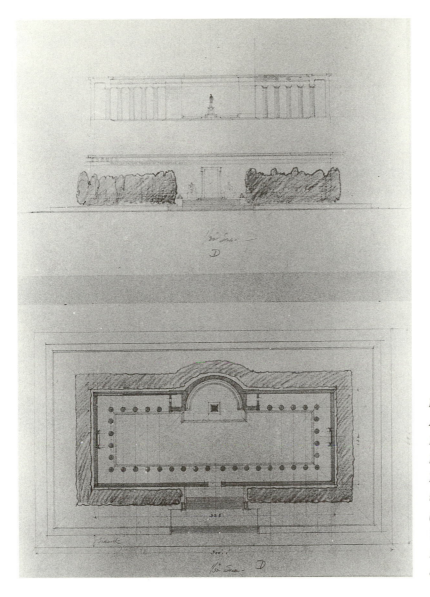

Fig. 3.18. Henry Bacon. Alternative D for proposed Lincoln Memorial, fall 1911. Elevation (above) and plan. Pencil and color crayon on tissue mounted on board. (Henry Bacon Collection, Wesleyan University Library, Special Collections & Archives)

Temple of Demeter at Paestum, Temple "FS" at Selinus, and the Temple of Concord at Acragas, remains of which he had studied in Italy and Sicily.[28] The temple to Lincoln, however, would be a roofed portico without a cella and would stand on a platform at the head of broad flights of steps rising from plazas at the north and south ends of the sliver lot dividing Sixteenth Street. Trans-parent enough to draw the eye when seen from the city below, the structure would also be solid and chunky enough to hold its own against the sky. Within the portico, a colossal statue of the seated Lincoln would occupy the center of the platform (Fig. 3.20). From Mary Henderson's point of view, one shortcoming of the design lay in the fact that Pope's dramatic memorial would

Fig. 3.19. John Russell Pope. Design for memorial on Meridian Hill. Perspective, rendered by Otto R. Eggers. (Collection of Commission of Fine Arts. Photo: author)

require the razing of the French embassy, the crown jewel in her diplomatic hilltop tiara.

Pope, however, favored the site on the grounds of the Soldiers' Home, to the northeast, which offered much more space to work with. Here, his platform alone could be six hundred feet square, to the one hundred by two hundred possible on Meridian Hill. This, he said, was "a location in the biggest, finest sense for a great memorial, and the finest in Washington for that purpose." He exploited the advantage with a design as titanic as those of eighteenth-century revolutionary classical architects in France. Great flights of steps would rise to the memorial from an enormous court on the south, city side (Fig. 3.21). He envisioned, again, a seated statue on a pedestal at the center of a vast, circular terrace ringed by a dual colonnade of Doric "sentinel columns" punctuated by porticoes at the cardinal points (Fig. 3.22). The porticoes recalled McKim's design of 1901 and the porticoes of his own recently finished Lincoln National Birthplace Memorial in Kentucky. A dedicatory inscription to Lincoln the man would appear on the attic of the main portico, overlooking the city.[29] Again, the design emerged from a long pedigree of Greek, Roman, and neoclassical sources. It was an enlarged version of the circular pantheon in which Robert Mills had hoped to rest the base of the Washington Monument (see Fig. 3.8) and a modification of a design of 1909 by Pierce Anderson for a Lincoln

Fig. 3.20. John Russell Pope. Design for memorial on Meridian Hill. Perspective of interior, rendered by Otto R. Eggers. (Collection of Commission of Fine Arts. Photo: author)

memorial near the Capitol. The design was bound to appeal to Elliott Woods, Pope's patron in Washington, who called it "a stunner,"[30] and perhaps even to Daniel Burnham. Pope's impressive schemes, combining the scale of imperial or baroque Rome with French neoclassical composition and classical Greek detail, were presented in spectacular colored renderings by his assistant and eventual successor, Otto R. Eggers. (The nocturnal perspective of the Temple of the Scottish Rite in Figure 2.9 was also Eggers's.) For the Lincoln Memorial, Eggers created huge drawings with dynamic raking viewpoints, strong contrasts of value, dramatic sky effects, and engaging detail.

Fig. 3.21. John Russell Pope. Design for memorial at Soldiers' Home. Perspective, rendered by Otto R. Eggers. (Collection of Commission of Fine Arts. Photo: author)

A SECOND STAGE

The architects' exhibitions of rival designs for the Lincoln Memorial attracted great attention in the American press, and Bacon, the leading choice of the art establishment, generally received better treatment from critics.[31] The *New York Sun* praised him for having "adhered, as he always does, to the classical in inspiration and execution" without "copying

the ancients and their successors." His "magnificent but solemn temple" would be "American in all its significance." Royal Cortissoz, critic for the *New York Tribune* and a close friend of Bacon's, observed that there was "nothing theatrical" or "fanciful" about his presentation, indirectly criticizing Pope and Eggers. In the genteel monthly *The Century*, Leila Mechlin called Bacon's memorial "so simple in its design as to seem almost

Fig. 3.22. John Russell Pope. Design for memorial at Soldiers' Home. Perspective of interior, rendered by Otto R. Eggers. (Collection of Commission of Fine Arts. Photo: author)

obvious . . . the one and only solution. . . . That this site and design will not be accepted is beyond belief."[32]

The drama of Pope's designs, especially that for the Soldiers' Home, made them popular with a wider audience, however. *Harper's Weekly* reported: "There seems to be a general sentiment . . . that the public will be more in sympathy with Mr. Pope and his desire to show in the open his Lincoln, his free, great Lincoln, alone and dignified, as an example to all the people, for all the people."[33] "Everyone likes that Soldiers' Home design," wrote Pope to Elliott Woods gleefully. "Have even had inquiries why it could not go on the Potomac site."[34] Suddenly Pope, whose appointment was an afterthought, was threatening Bacon's position.

Support for Pope did not, however, much penetrate the artistic establishment nor most newspapers and magazines. Typical was a comment by a writer for the *Washington Star*, who thought Weinman's seated statue of Lincoln "very unpleasant and undignified" because it portrayed the president with bowed head and "arms upraised in alarm, warning or consternation."[35] Lack of support for Pope stemmed largely from a concerted publicity campaign launched by Glenn Brown to press the undependable memorial commissioners to reject both the building of a highway in Lincoln's honor and the choice of any site except Potomac Park.[36] He first quelled a revolt against his position in the ranks of the Washington Chamber of Commerce and then, in November 1911, with Mechlin's help, mailed a circular to his alliance, which included artistic societies and the editors of major newspapers. He urged that resolutions be passed in favor of "the site recommended by the Park Commission" and sent directly to senators and congressmen, bypassing the Lincoln Memorial Commission, which he continued to mistrust. A second mailing in early 1912 followed, enclosing a clutch of new press clippings supporting his position. All told, by April 1912 seventy art societies and more than twenty chambers of commerce had endorsed the building of the memorial in the park. Brown even drew halfhearted support from the white South. The Art League of Waco, Texas, wrote: "[W]e Southern people can *exist* if there is no memorial, but if there

is to be one we prefer that it should be . . . an ornament to our capital city." Regrettably for Pope, his designs, despite their considerable merits, were buried under Brown's avalanche.

The Commission of Fine Arts was convinced that Bacon's design vindicated the choice of Potomac Park as the site for Lincoln's memorial, but the memorial commissioners remained divided. On January 22, 1912, Shelby Cullom, wanting action of some kind, moved a resolution to build the memorial in Potomac Park, but Joe Cannon moved a substitute to build it at the Soldiers' Home, and Champ Clark, known to favor a highway memorial, moved yet another for the site on Meridian Hill. When Clark's substitute was defeated, he joined "Uncle Joe" in supporting the site at the Soldiers' Home. The meeting ended deadlocked, the only concrete action being a decision to consult the art commissioners about building another obelisk on the Mall, an unlikely idea indeed.[37] Even when a final vote was taken, on February 3, Clark and Cannon voted against Potomac Park, though the five votes in favor were enough to carry the resolution. Cannon's defeat, however, was tempered by the commissioners' diplomatic decision to invite Pope as well as Bacon to refine their designs (in Pope's case, the rotunda at the Soldiers' Home) for the site in the park. The architects were given until March 26 to revise their designs, for Taft hoped to put a definitive design before Congress in that session, the last before the presidential election and what, it was becoming clear, would likely be his last, lame-duck session the next winter.

The campaign for a highway was not dead, however; nor were Mary Henderson's ambitions for Meridian Hill. The second was easier to quench than the first because support for it was shallower. Knowing Taft's reputation for evenhandedness, Henderson sent him a last-ditch appeal to have the question of a memorial on the hill reconsidered. She coyly alluded to the strength of the drive for a highway memorial. She had gone so far as to commission a design of her own for a Lincoln memorial at the crest of the hill, less expansive than Pope's. Her architects, Frederick V. Murphy and W. B. Olmsted, envisioned a triumphal arch terminating the "Gettysburg Boulevard" and tiers of steps and water stairs descending to a plaza and circular basin below.[38] She also tried to reach Taft through his secretary of the Treasury, Franklin MacVeagh, who lived on the hill.[39] But Taft thought her a meddlesome nuisance and was learning to listen selectively. He pushed the decision to build in Potomac Park, effectively eliminating Meridian Hill, but not the pressure to build a highway as a memorial.

Knowing that with enough support in Congress he could win passage of Borland's bill to revise the enabling act and substitute a highway memorial for the one in Potomac Park, Champ Clark, the day after the Lincoln Memorial Commission decided on the site, promised a fight on the House floor to save "the Gettysburg road plan."[40] Thanks to the temporizing of Taft and his memorial commission, support for Borland's bill had grown to huge proportions. It was the subject of a public-relations campaign that dwarfed Brown's and had the support of motor compa-

nies, automobile clubs, and McCleary's Lincoln Memorial Road Association. In the fall of 1911 the association had mailed out a quarter million brochures asking recipients to lobby their congressmen and petition the memorial commission, on tear-out forms, "to adopt the Lincoln Road as the National Memorial to Abraham Lincoln." Borland and others spoke at Good Roads conventions, and the association lobbied veterans' groups, knowing their moral and financial influence. At its peak, over a hundred congressmen, including Speaker Clark, were behind Borland's bill, as were leading senators of both parties.[41] Again, political and ideological motives were mixed. Progressives, especially in the Democratic fold, smelled political blood and, convinced they held the balance of power in the election that November, fastened on good roads as a key issue. Their vehicle was the fight over the Lincoln Memorial. This put the memorial of the McMillan Plan in peril, Brown and his supporters realized, even though the Lincoln Memorial Commission had officially ruled in favor of an ideal memorial in Potomac Park. "We came near losing after being assured of our victory."[42]

At stake in the debate on Borland's bill were more than government finances and Lincoln's posthumous honor. More deeply, the debate concerned who controlled that memory—cultural and political conservatives, or Progressives. In favor of a highway memorial, besides those who stood to gain financially, were those who wanted to commemorate Lincoln as Man of the People by an improvement whose memorial character lay in novelty and usefulness. Whether the highway its backers envisioned would or would not be as useful and practical as they claimed it would is somewhat beside the point: the road would be a symbol of utility, a "living" memorial.[43] The legendary Lincoln would be used to promote automobility, which was, it was argued, America's way of the future. On the side of an ideal memorial in Potomac Park were realists and cultural traditionalists who sought to honor the nation's hero in abstract classical form and inspire the American public, which in reality they often deeply mistrusted, to moral and patriotic virtue. Each side considered itself, and in its own way was, progressive. That the debate over the Lincoln Memorial occurred in 1911–12 was to be expected given that it was an election year and that the debate over tradition versus change was white-hot throughout American society at that moment. A sure sense of modernity, that life was different from what one's parents and grandparents had known and that the rush of history required it to be so, ran high in some quarters during these years, before the disillusionments of the First World War.[44] Culturally, what Henry May christened The Liberation and The Rebellion arose among young Americans, who demanded that The New be embraced in every area of life.[45] "The New Freedom," "the new poetry," "the new woman," "the new marriage" were phrases heard everywhere. Modernity was not just a passive mental accompaniment to technological and economic progress but a conscious, active process of re-visioning all life.[46] "The rock of ages, in brief, has been blasted for us," wrote Walter Lippmann.[47] "History is more or less bunk. We want to live in the present," said Henry Ford in 1929, but he could have been speaking in 1912.[48] Before 1914, optimism and openness to the future were not just widespread traits of young Americans but positive moral imperatives. More widespread than political Progressivism, that mind-set demanded hope in the future and confidence in the people and in democracy's potential to renew itself. Even more than the split in Republican Party ranks, that mind-set swept Taft from office in 1912, replacing him with Woodrow Wilson and the Progressive Democrats. More widely still, it made the fluid, mobile "American way of life" of the twentieth century imaginable.

Naturally, the largest monumental campaign in the nation's history, to build a memorial to Abraham Lincoln, its greatest hero and (it was said) greatest force for good, crystallized the tension between Americans more oriented to the future and those more cautious ones who preferred to rely on tradition. So, the debate about the Lincoln Memorial was more than an expedient grab by Progressives at a handy brush with which to tar Taft and his administration dominated by party regulars and mild Progressives; it resonated throatily with the way younger Americans of 1912 viewed themselves and their country.

The turning point was a two-day hearing, held in March, of the House Library Committee, chaired by James L. Slayden of Texas, the firmest friend the McMillan Plan had in the lower chamber.[49] William P. Borland orchestrated the first day's testimony and defended his own bill, speaking contemptuously of the plan to memorialize Lincoln by "some sort of Greek temple" and portraying the scheme for a memorial highway to Gettysburg as universally popular. Brown had secured estimates as high as $34 million to build the road the association had in mind; highway engineers testified that it could readily be built for the $2 million appropriated for the memorial, and one called Brown's estimate "extravagent, wild, ridiculous." The committee members were skeptical of McCleary's denial that anyone connected with his association had "any personal financial interest whatever in the result of this legislation." Brown and a colleague on his Committee of One-Hundred organized the second day's testimony, which was against the bill. Their witnesses questioned the fitness of dedicating a functional improvement as a memorial. One made the point that a highway grand enough to memorialize Lincoln would have to be grander than the macadamized strip of roadway the engineers had described the day before. Another witness questioned the plainness of the "plain people" who stood to benefit from the roadway. Major W. V. Judson of the Army Corps of Engineers produced evidence that the road Borland and McCleary had in mind would cost $20 million to build and $1 million annually to maintain. The financial argument proved decisive, and Slayden's committee reported the bill back to the House unfavorably. The movement for a memorial highway had passed its high-water mark. Although the campaign for it was kept up for another year, support waned after the hearing. Architect Bacon credited Slayden personally with turning back the tide.[50] That may be, but what the

victory shows is that, though movements for change were strong in Congress, cultural conservatives still held sway there and on the Commission of Fine Arts.

THE REVISED DESIGNS

By affiliating himself with Cannon, whose power in Washington was now sentimental rather than real, and by presenting a viable and dramatic alternative to Bacon's serene design for the Lincoln Memorial, John Russell Pope had managed to secure a true competition, if one limited to two architects. The architects had their revised designs ready for inspection in late March 1912. As he had been instructed, for Potomac Park Pope presented a revised version of the scheme he had developed for the grounds of the Soldiers' Home (Fig. 3.23).[51] In it he drew attention to the kinship of his plan with McKim's of 1901 (see Fig. 1.4), whose viewpoint he adopted, and the superiority of his own. He borrowed McKim's columned portico facing the Mall but used it to preface an open rotunda, removing the three other porticoes of his first design. Again, his conception had hugeness and rude simplicity. With a diameter of 320 feet, his rotunda would occupy substantially more space than McKim's 250-foot colonnade, and its shape would harmonize better with the traffic circle enclosing it than a rectangular form would.

All his life, Pope would allude to early American sources when he worked in the capital; here, his open rotunda especially recalled Mills's for the base of the Washington Monument (see Fig. 3.8). Pope considered that his

Fig. 3.23. John Russell Pope. Perspective of design for Potomac Park, February–March 1912. (Collection of Commission of Fine Arts. Photo: author)

design's "independence of customary building forms and its individuality . . . forcibly challenge the eye and mind," but in revising it he had fallen back on the model of Saint-Gaudens's serene standing figure in Chicago, remembering how unpopular Weinman's titanic, tormented seated *Lincoln* had been. He also presented a series of dramatic but somewhat menacing sketches in graphite of alternate memorials. One showed an Egyptoid pyramid with classical pedimented porticoes in its four faces.[52] Another, still more extreme, had a colossal brazier blazing away at the summit of a stepped Mayan pyramid, shown silhouetted against a livid sunset (Fig. 3.24). Other sketches showed a hypaethral replica of the Parthenon, a Doric gateway framing a statue of Lincoln on its approaches, a stepped ziggurat with a statue at the summit, and a conical mound or tumulus, also lifting a statue into the sky. In these alternatives, Pope tapped both his own penchant for the sublime and the American public's taste for novelty and gigantism. He admitted in his report, though, that he did not favor these gigantic and fanciful schemes.

Bacon, in his three schemes, also released his imagination, if less freely.[53] The only original drawing for his revisions that has survived is a site plan for scheme A (Fig. 3.25), a modified version of his previous design, but it and his verbal report are enough to show the changes he had made.[54] Typical of him, these were subtle and aimed at reducing complexity. He had eliminated the wide but shallow vestibule and row of columns *in antis* (between wall spurs) of his first design in Figure 3.12. The change simplified the memorial's exterior and added ten feet to the depth of the statue hall, giving the visitor a more sudden meeting with the statue and making the hall no longer a perfect cube but a more dynamic oblong volume. Then, by thickening the front and rear walls of the side chambers, he reduced their size fractionally, created service space within the thickness of the

Fig. 3.24. John Russell Pope. Graphite sketch for a Lincoln Memorial in form of a stepped Mayan-like pyramid, February–March 1912. (Photograph courtesy of the Photographic Archives, National Gallery of Art, Washington, D.C., Dunlap Society Collection)

walls, and gave the whole interior a more elastic cruciform plan with subtle cross-axes. The new plan, he said, gave "greater prominence" to the statue hall. He had also changed the memorial's entourage, or surroundings, in an important way, substituting for the circular setting of the first design a markedly smaller but slightly higher rectangular terrace, which lifted the memorial fractionally for better lines of sight. The changes made the building appear marginally bigger and more imposing than it had, while smoothing the awkward junction of a rectangular memorial with a round terrace. The circular terrace had been 500 feet in diameter; the new rectangle

was 380 feet across by 310 deep, and the memorial would stand 5 feet higher than before. His studies of sight lines from the Mall of the building, especially its friezes, show how concerned he was that they be seen to advantage. Finally, to reconcile the square of roadways to the angled lines of the river-bank, bridge, and parkway, he created a concourse behind the memorial with a small monument in its center, providing a viewpoint over the river and diverting some distracting traffic from the front of the memorial to the rear.

The popularity of McKim's and Pope's open-air designs caused Bacon to study similar ideas more seriously than he had before. His schemes B and C showed, in striking drawings, forms of open-air memorials with Doric colonnades as backdrops to large statues of Lincoln. In the altarlike scheme B, the colonnade terminates in monumental "tablets

Potomac River

Design for Lincoln Memorial · Scheme A · ·
Scale 1 inch = 100 feet

Fig. 3.26. Henry Bacon. Perspective of scheme B. (Henry Bacon Collection, Wesleyan University Library, Special Collections & Archives)

inscribed with the two great speeches," framing on three sides a statue on the upper terrace (Fig. 3.26). The more austere scheme C shows a portico four columns deep, without returns, behind a statue set well forward on an intermediate terrace (Fig. 3.27). The strong, "masculine" Doric order would give the colonnades a solid appearance when seen against the sky. In both designs the statues are twenty-two feet high, the size eventually

Fig. 3.25. Henry Bacon. Site plan for scheme A, proposed Lincoln Memorial, February–March 1912. (Photograph courtesy of the Photographic Archives, National Gallery of Art, Washington, D.C., Dunlap Society Collection)

adopted. Bacon argued against building an open memorial, however, ending his report with another vigorous defense of his closed design that reused the passage "[t]he power of impression by an object of reverence and honor . . ." (mentioned earlier). Probably echoing French, he stressed the importance of showing the statue under controlled conditions.

The architects presented the two commissions with a clear choice, between the closed building Bacon favored and Pope's open, expansive schemes. The Commission of Fine Arts expressed satisfaction that the design exercise proved that "the Potomac Park site . . . promises the best results" and was clearly fixed on seeing Bacon appointed as the memorial's architect.[55] It warned the Lincoln Memorial Commission against being unduly influenced

*Fig. 3.27. Henry Bacon. Perspective of scheme C. (*American Architect *118 [October 27, 1920]: 532. Photograph courtesy of the Photographic Archives, National Gallery of Art, Washington, D.C., Dunlap Society Collection)*

by the draftsmanship of Pope's scheme and expressed reservations about its cost, since "such a scheme depends for success largely on the manner and character of its execution." Pope's supplementary graphite sketches were virtually ignored. The art commission called Bacon's design for a closed memorial "the best of all the designs presented" and seconded his plea for a closed "shrine," which would be comfortable for visitors, especially in winter, and would "shelter the statue and other reminders of Lincoln's greatness." A closed hall would "afford conditions of comfort and sentiment conducive to quiet contemplation" and permit the statue to be seen under ideal light at all times. While the commission liked the "breadth" of Bacon's scheme B, "which makes it a better termination of the Mall . . . better compos[ing] with the Washington Monument," it believed his closed design, scheme A, could be restudied to the same effect. The art commissioners rapped the memorial commissioners' knuckles for conducting a competition at all and not following their original advice to select an architect directly. Here a note of impatience can be sensed: "Skillful execution; the care and knowledge to be exercised in working out details and in the choice of materials; the proper supervision of the construction; the study required during the entire progress of the work—these are considerations of almost as much concern as the original conception. . . . Much, therefore, depends on the experience, ability, and temperament of the artist to whom the work is committed."

Even after two meetings, though, Clark and Cannon remained resistant to appointing Bacon. Besides the fact that Clark had joined the highway movement, he, along with Cannon and some critics, appreciated the large scale, drama, and openness of Pope's design. Cannon, whom Pope later called "the leader of the minority opposition," fought stubbornly for him, calling him in private "too modest."[56] The Commission of Fine Arts anxiously sent Burnham to put its case before the memorial commission and planned to have the golden-tongued Millet do the same. Millet never appeared, however, for at the height of all this he traveled home from England on the *Titanic*. The delays permitted Pope to mount a behind-the-scenes campaign to defend his design's "appearance of bigness" and produce evidence that it could be built within the congressional appropriation.[57] Former clients wrote testimonials on his behalf. Henry White, for whom Pope had designed a house on Meridian Hill, told Taft, "I have never had an architect to deal with so accurate in his estimates and who has never exceeded those originally given."[58] Rightly or wrongly, Taft and the others on the two commissions who wanted to hire Bacon formed the impression that Pope was insinuating himself into an otherwise straightforward process and creating needless dissension. The normally even-tempered Taft had a rare outburst on the

subject, and, however they had begun, Pope and Bacon fell out over the competition.[59] Taft's rage was surely all the greater in that Clark and Cannon, from opposite ends of the political spectrum, were using the debate over the Lincoln Memorial to take political revenge on him, for, by spring 1912, Taft was so unpopular he could hardly have been elected county dogcatcher. Nevertheless, when the votes of the memorial commissioners were tallied on April 16, Bacon received four to Pope's two.

Ending anticlimactically, the two-stage design competition had in fact achieved a great deal. Pope's goal of becoming better known in Washington was realized: whatever legacy of bitterness remained, he went on to distinguished service on the Commission of Fine Arts in 1917–22 and design in the capital, building some of the principal federal buildings and monuments of the twenties, thirties, and forties.[60] For Bacon, the contest with Pope had served to strengthen his design, loosening his strict adherence to the model of the Greek temple and giving his memorial a degree of command, breadth, and openness it would not otherwise have had. For the commissions and the federal government, the pseudo-competition and limited competition had drawn massive publicity to the project of building a Lincoln memorial. The young Commission of Fine Arts, in particular, grew in prestige by successfully arguing its case. Finally, American architects as a profession and their umbrella body, the American Institute of Architects, benefited from the exposure of middle-class American readers of

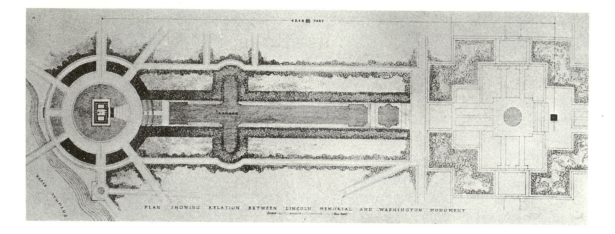

PLAN SHOWING RELATION BETWEEN LINCOLN MEMORIAL AND WASHINGTON MONUMENT

Fig. 3.28. Henry Bacon. "Final" design for Lincoln Memorial, June 1912. Site plan. (Lincoln Memorial Commission Report. Photo: author)

newspapers and magazines to architectural issues, which in turn created a new degree of architectural culture and literacy in the country.

Having eliminated Pope, the memorial commissioners had Bacon restudy his design yet again before presenting it to Congress. At the end of June 1912, he presented what may be called his "final" design, though in fact he continued to revise it for some time afterward.[61] All his restudy was encapsulated in the sentence "The structure has been enlarged, the design of the approaches, terraces and steps has been revised, and the front of the Memorial has been made more open." The sentence alone suggests the value of Pope's involvement and the appeal of a bigger, simpler, and more accessible memorial to Lincoln than Bacon had first planned. He had reverted to the idea of clasping the memorial within a circular ring road (Fig. 3.28), which, though it would draw traffic—not expected to

be heavy, anyway—to the perimeter of the memorial precinct, would also increase the casual passerby's awareness of the memorial without much marring the experience of the visitor inside. The scheme also left the treed margins of the precinct and riverbank to pedestrians and pleasure vehicles. Again and again, Bacon had most difficulty when dealing with the memorial's surroundings, a result both of the hybrid character of the structure and of his discomfort in working at an unfamiliarly large scale. This discomfort might well have been less had he received his architectural training in the Beaux Arts tradition, which emphasized entourage of a sculpted, modulated type.

His final design for the base of the memorial fused the wide terrace of his open designs to the compact, stepped podium of his closed one (Fig. 3.29). His study of open alternatives had added richness and subtlety to his preferred design. For the earlier thirteen "plinths," or steps—an outrageous expense in masonry—he had substituted three, each eight feet high, forming a platform that would appear to rest on a grass terrace enclosed in turn, by a verti-

Fig. 3.29. Henry Bacon. "Final" design for Lincoln Memorial. Perspective from east, rendered by Jules Guérin. (Henry Bacon Collection, Wesleyan University Library, Special Collections & Archives)

cal fourteen-foot retaining wall. Seen from ground level, this terrace would create largeness of effect while inflecting the memorial's profile in a satisfying way.

In addition, the building was slightly larger in most dimensions than it had been, though the central chamber retained its harmonic interior proportions of sixty feet deep by seventy across (Fig. 3.30). Instead of flights of low climbing steps in the center of each face of the podium, a single wide, regal flight would rise in several runs on the east front only, from the end of the reflecting pool. While climbing, the visitor would catch

glimpses of the statue in the memorial chamber through an enlarged entrance doorway, forty-five feet wide (three intervals between columns) by forty-four high, with two Doric columns *in antis* (Fig. 3.31). Nowhere did Bacon explain this crucial change, but he did agree with the observation that it "gives more light and a finer approach."[62] A rendering by Jules Guérin of the memorial seen from the reflecting basin suggests that the statue was now to be seen not just from inside but also from some distance (see Fig. 3.29). The new and wider opening also allowed the visitor, once inside, to turn and gaze at the reciprocal vista of the reflecting basin, the Washington Monument, and the Capitol dome (Fig. 3.32). An apparently minor design change actually constituted a reimagining of the memorial as a porous, indoor-outdoor structure, a formal

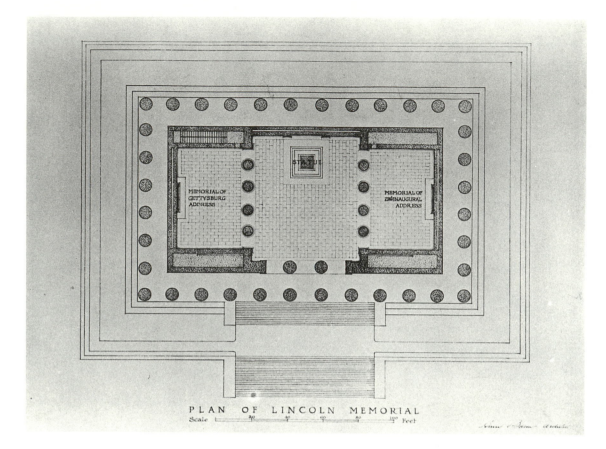

PLAN OF LINCOLN MEMORIAL
Scale ┃   30   40   50   100 Feet

*Fig. 3.30. Henry Bacon. "Final" design for Lincoln
Memorial. Floor plan. (Lincoln Memorial Commission Report. Photo: author)*

analogue to democracy. The word "light" also
suggests that Bacon hoped the widened
entrance would illuminate Lincoln's statue
better than before. Certainly, he was concerned about the lighting of the side chambers, which in another perspective he showed
strongly illuminated from above (Fig. 3.33).
Guérin's distant perspective also suggests—
though nothing confirms it—that because of
the larger opening Bacon was beginning to
think of a larger statue than he had until
then, one more like the twenty-two-foot fig-

ures of his open schemes. Under the influence
of his own and Pope's schemes for open
memorials, then, he had decided to combine
the advantages of open and closed architectural forms. For security and comfort when
necessary, the entrance opening would be fit-
ted with "sliding bronze grilles, filled with
plate-glass," which would roll back out of
sight, and, in winter, "a temporary bronze
and glass vestibule." The memorial would also
be heated.

A firm decision on Bacon's design was
deferred until Congress reconvened in
December 1912. Senator Money was ill and
could not come to Washington; the delay was
intended partly to accommodate his wish to

*Fig. 3.31. Henry Bacon. "Final" design for Lincoln Memorial. Charcoal perspective of entry and statue, probably by Bacon's assistant William Berg. (*Lincoln Memorial Commission Report *Photo: author)*

Fig. 3.32. Henry Bacon. "Final" design for Lincoln Memorial. Charcoal perspective of view eastward from memorial floor, probably by William Berg. (Lincoln Memorial Commission Report. *Photo: author)*

have his voice heard. In any event, the memorial would not get much attention in the midst of what promised to be an extremely heated and divisive presidential election campaign.[63] When the commissioners met again on December 4, Money had died, and the Republicans, split between Taft's party regulars and Roosevelt's Bull Moosers, had been trounced by the Democrats under Woodrow Wilson. He would take office in March 1913, giving the Republicans no time to lose in getting a serious start on the memorial. The memorial commission approved Bacon's design and forwarded it to Congress, recommending it be authorized for construction. Since the hearing before Slayden's committee the previous March had fatally weakened the highway campaign, and since other sites, as

well as Pope's designs, had been eliminated, the building of Bacon's design for a closed memorial in Potomac Park seemed sure. What could stand in its way?

AN "AMERICAN" MEMORIAL?

At the eleventh hour, another hurdle appeared, which, like the others, manifested the power of Progressivism in Congress, in this case reinforced by Midwestern regionalism. It, too, profited from Democrats' control of the House during Taft's lame-duck session, with Wilson in the wings. The hurdle was a sentiment, which crested in the winter of 1912–13, that a less classical, more home-grown and "American" design should be adopted for the memorial to the most American of presidents. Though strongest in the Midwest, especially Chicago, its cultural capital, that feeling was expressed in some quarters everywhere. The *Independent* of New York called all the designs "a public confession of architectural insolvency" and modern architects mere copyists, not true "architectural alchemists."[64] Washington architect F. W. Fitzpatrick compared the adherents of "Art Commission classicism" to a fawning religious sect: "The elect have gone into raptures over the Bacon design for that Lincoln Memorial—a few columns and an entablature for a lid. . . . Of course there is a lot of purity and all that, and no end of symbolism to it. Those columns represent the States we had in Lincoln's time, and no doubt the flutings of the columns likewise typify the number of counties in each State, and the proportioning of the details is most perfect and strictly according to the Hoyle of classicism. We do so love the ruins of antiquity, the broken columns!" What way was this to honor "a son of [the] Western prairies . . . [who] knows the heart of America"?[65]

Fitzpatrick and those who felt as he did lacked the official standing enjoyed by the traditionalizing artists of the Commission of Fine Arts and failed to fasten on a viable alternative to the Bacon design. Their arguments, however, resonate deeply in American culture. These arguments expose a vital vein that surfaces from time to time in a conviction that the forms in which Americans embody their culture should be more rugged, honest, and pure—less refined and more original, somehow—than those of allegedly effete European culture. That conviction was espe-cially understandable in 1912, after several decades of "American Renaissance" during which cultured urban elites had captured or copied countless specimens of European art and architecture as emblems of national maturity and uplift.[66] It was perhaps particularly understandable in the Midwest, which claimed Lincoln as its own and was then experiencing cultural self-consciousness and rebirth. (Cultural historians speak of a "Chicago Renaissance.")[67] Here the tensions between old and new, eastern and western, vital and moribund, were at their most intense. Here the shapeless search for new, native forms found shape in the naturalism of Dreiser, Lewis, and Anderson, in Louis Sullivan's facades for tall office buildings—themselves an American invention—and in Frank Lloyd Wright's near-mythical "Prairie-style" houses. To the young intellectuals of Chicago before the First World War, the past was, in Carl Sandburg's words, a bundle of ashes.[68] Yet there, they felt, was a cultured New York architect in swallowtail and corsage set to honor the arch-American Lincoln with a modern version of a Greek temple. It was the post–Civil War battle for the ownership of Lincoln's memory all over again, heightened and freshly colored by Midwestern political Progressivism, with its faith in the People and hopes for renewed democracy.

Corresponding exactly to the political election that removed Taft as president, a minor cultural rebellion, which included architects, arose, especially in Chicago, against the Bacon design and the work of the Lincoln Memorial Commission. The reason is not hard to find. For many Progressives, the classicizing Lincoln Memorial had become, far from the shining emblem of honest, dispassionate leadership envisioned in 1901, a symbol of tired, old eastern millionaire Republicanism. In January 1913, on the eve of the vote in Congress on Bacon's memorial, the Illinois chapter of the AIA, defying the position of the national body, passed a resolution criticizing Bacon's design as "purely Greek and entirely un-American."[69] Led by one of Wright's assistants, Walter Burley Griffin, the protest drew in other cultural progressives in the city, such as author Hamlin Garland. George W. Maher, a Prairie School architect and chair of the chapter's committee to review the Lincoln Memorial, proposed an alternative design:

> A colossal statue of the Great Emancipator, standing forth in all his backwoods ruggedness, approached by tier upon tier of granite steps.
>
> A semi-circular wall, 60 feet high, as a background, picturing in heroic bas-relief the stirring episodes of the time of Lincoln.
>
> A scheme of hidden lights to illuminate the picture at night. . . . I would advise perhaps a building at each end of the "back drop"—one housing, let us say, the log cabin in which the Emancipator was born; the other containing bronzes of his speeches.
>
> Here, in epitome we would have, the spirit of America in the crisis of its history, with the great, silent figure of Lincoln dominating it all.[70]

The outrage at Bacon's "Greek temple" design, however, was weakened by a lack of alternatives; Maher's was one of few concrete proposals for a less objectionable type of memorial. So, the protest had an inchoate quality, which a cartoon in a Chicago newspaper lampooned: to be truly American, what would Lincoln's memorial have to be? A log cabin? A skyscraper? A tipi? (Fig. 3.34). The Lincoln birthplace association, we saw, had sidestepped the contest for his memory by building a hybrid—a log cabin inside a classical reliquary. (One wonders where Maher planned to lay hold of *his* cabin.) McKim, Bacon, and the Commission of Fine Arts were, precisely, not interested in the specifics of Lincoln's life and legacy but in what he could be made to symbolize. For them, as for Saint-Gaudens (see Fig. 1.3), classicism diffused, idealized, and universalized his aura, avoiding historical ambiguities and embarrassments.

The zeal for novelty, nativism, and gigantism in commemorating Lincoln that the protest embodied was distilled in purest form in sculptor Gutzon Borglum, best known today for his suite of herculean carved presidential heads on the face of Mount Rushmore in South Dakota's Black Hills (1924–41).[71] Though Borglum was excluded from direct involvement in building the memorial in Washington, his views on Lincoln and the memorial epitomized those of many Americans, especially in the West and Midwest, views that colored the way the memorial was received in 1912–13 and again when it was finished. Raised in the West of Scandinavian stock, Borglum subscribed to an utterly mythologized version of Americanism that he was convinced Lincoln embodied. (He named his son, who finished the work on Mount

Fig. 3.34. "To Laugh or Not to Laugh!" Cartoon, Chicago Inter-Ocean, January 17, 1913. (Henry Bacon Collection, Wesleyan University Library, Special Collections & Archives)

Rushmore, Lincoln.) Around 1900 he had begun to sculpt a series of colossal and, in other respects, unconventional images of Lincoln, especially of his head, making himself the sculptor of Lincoln much as Sandburg became his poet. He kept an eagle eye on the campaign to build the memorial in Washington, hoping to receive the sculptural commission for it. Since August 1911, he had been pressing the Lincoln Memorial Commission, through Wetmore, with whom he was on cordial terms, to incorporate sculpture—his own—in the memorial, specifically "a colossal figure of [Lincoln] in Greek marble . . . a seated figure . . . on the scale of my large head." Conducting a vendetta against the modern classical designs of Pope and Bacon, he objected to both the old-world quality of the designs and the abstraction of architecture as opposed to narrative art: "In heaven's name, in Abraham Lincoln's name, don't ask the American people to associate a Greek temple with the first great American."[72] As he wrote to Wetmore, "Is it possible this [project] can beget nothing in a nation of ninety millions of the stoutest hearted world builders ever known but a colonnade, torn from the pages of little Greece. . . . The story

97

must be wrought in great friezes and groups, including the great actors with Lincoln."[73] Unsolicited, he proposed a memorial in the form of a three-sided enclosure at the summit of a great flight of steps, with wall friezes depicting events connected with the war—exactly the sort of narrative realism Bacon and the Commission of Fine Arts were bent on avoiding. Idealizing, traditionalizing artists dismissed Borglum as a crude upstart and enthusiast. Went one jingle, "Down in New York there dwells a man, and sculpture is his trade. He says right out whate'er he thinks, he calls a spade a spade. . . . His name is Gutzon Borglum—with the accent on the glum."[74] Enraged at this reception, Borglum challenged Bacon, in person, to define the memorial's sculpted and painted program. To Borglum's charge that his monument was nothing but "a Greek temple with the Lincoln Memorial on the door-mat," Bacon replied that his building was a modern and American evocation of an antique temple, by no means a servile copy. Anyway, said Bacon, Lincoln's speeches meant more to Americans than "guns or battle scenes."[75]

While Bacon and the commissioners thought Borglum an irritating nuisance, and one can indeed dismiss him as a crank and producer of kitsch, the cultural current he represented is crucial to understanding the Progressive period. It demanded of American art, especially American public art, that it depart from earlier, European precedents and embody a new "American spirit" of gigantism, formal simplicity—even crudity—and unsophisticated directness. It was poles apart from the refined sensibility of the American

Renaissance that Bacon, Pope, French, and the Commission of Fine Arts shared.

During the congressional debate over the Lincoln Memorial in the lame-duck session of winter 1912–13, vague yearning for a more "American" memorial than Bacon's combined with revived demands for a highway memorial created a substantial revolt against the Commission of Fine Arts and the Lincoln Memorial Commission. The memorial commission's recommendation handily passed the Senate, in which Republicans still had a majority, meeting only one dissenting vote. The senators took to heart Root's advice that "[t]o reject the conclusions of this commission apparently would prevent the erection of any Lincoln monument whatever."[76] The recommendation, in the form of a Senate resolution, met heavier weather in the Democrat-controlled House, and Glenn Brown, inoculated against minimizing danger, was convinced that all might be lost, even at that late date. As good as his promise to support a memorial highway, Speaker Clark used his procedural power to fight the Senate resolution. He directed the resolution first to the hostile Appropriations Committee, rather than to Slayden's sympathetic Library Committee, and let Borland revive his highway bill and canvass their colleagues fiercely. This was an ideal, distracting, yet flamingly symbolic issue to occupy the House in a lame-duck session, and lobbying became frantic on both sides. For the defense, "Uncle Shelby" Cullom was perhaps the most useful lobbyist. He cajoled hostile and undecided representatives into voting for the Lincoln Memorial on the grounds that it signified "a sort of monument to himself as well as to the martyred President."[77] When the resolution at last reached the Library Committee, it endorsed it strongly, reminding congressmen of the mercenary interests behind the plan for a memorial highway.[78] By about January 22, the committee's argument, the frenzied lobbying, and Brown's public-relations campaign had caused opinion in Congress and the press to swing away from the highway supporters, despite the strength of automobility. In the end, the vote in the House a week later all but unanimously supported the memorial commission's recommendation.

Some read deep cultural significance in the conjunction of the authorization of the Lincoln Memorial and the recent election of a Virginian to the White House, forty-eight years after the Civil War ended.[79] To most white contemporaries, the events jointly signaled definitive reconciliation between the sections. Today we may read the conjunction differently, seeing in it evidence of the erasure in official, national memory of the actual issues fought over in the war and the racial politics it inaugurated. In a narrowly partisan sense, however, Wilson's election meant that the memorial now had to be built in a political climate lukewarm to Lincoln and hostile to his votaries. Battle was soon rejoined.

CHAPTER 4

Constructing the Memorial

STANDING REGALLY IN gleaming white marble at the end of its long reflecting basin, today the Lincoln Memorial appears inevitable and eternal. Who can imagine Washington without it? Yet the historical record shows that the memorial was not easily built. Party politics, inflated costs, problems of design and construction, wrangling among the artists, and interruptions during wartime protracted its building to more than nine years. In particular, the choice of marble for the exterior was politically controversial, but that was later forgotten amid paeans to Lincoln and Nature. The modernity of the building and its construction, behind the mask of allegedly timeless classicism, is also overlooked. In addition, the decoration, especially the murals inside, encodes ideological assumptions that are easily missed in the seamless, reassuring whole the memorial became.

During early 1913, the fastidious Bacon restudied his design for the memorial in detail, presenting it to the Commission of Fine Arts in May in the form of new models and a set of working or contract drawings. He had decided to thicken the exterior columns slightly, to seven feet, five inches, from seven feet in diameter at their bases, for an appearance of greater solidity. He had also worked more to ensure the legibility of the ornament and inscriptions of the attic from various distances. Of the building stone to be used, he stipulated only that it be a "white marble containing a minimum amount of veining."

The building's design being already highly refined, its landscape and surroundings concerned the fine arts commission most at this stage.[1] Cass Gilbert recommended omitting the "large glass panels at the entrance" and building "a low surrounding wall" at sidewalk level around the circular grass mound; it never appeared. Gilbert's suggestion to omit the glass proved to be the death knell of the memorial as a closed building. Bacon followed his suggestion but unwillingly, for in December 1915, when supplementary funding was sought, he tried to reintroduce bronze screens with hinged doors between the columns to prevent condensation from forming inside the memorial. He was not successful. Frederick Law Olmsted Jr., heir to the family's celebrated practice in park and landscape design, wanted to reduce wheeled traffic along the river, eliminate unnecessary formal masonry and terracing, and generally preserve the parklike air of the memorial precinct. He urged that the outer of the two concentric roadways around the memorial be reduced in diameter to withdraw it from the riverbank and save expensive terracing. A Rock Creek Parkway Commission was struck in that same year, 1913, to develop a scenic drive along the creek and the Potomac riverfront, and Olmsted feared this might draw too much wheeled traffic into the ring around the memorial and necessitate elaborate terrace-works where the parkway met the planned memorial bridge to Arlington. Ever the park planner, he wanted nothing more than a simple path laid out along the shore but was up against the Army Corps of Engineers' Office of Public Buildings and Grounds, specifically Colonel Spencer Cosby, who served as executive officer for the Lincoln Memorial Commission, the Rock Creek Parkway Commission, and the Fine Arts Commission. Cosby had ideas for the back of the memorial that required more masonry, and Olmsted lost his contest eventually.

The Lincoln Memorial Commission approved Bacon's revised design on June 9, 1913, and called for tenders to build it. In late September, the memorial commission recommended to the secretary of war that he contract with the George A. Fuller Company, of New York and Chicago, to build the superstructure, but that all bids for the foundation be rejected and new ones, based on revised specifications, called for. A bidder for the foundation, the Underpinning & Foundation Company, of New York, had proposed a method of sinking it simpler and cheaper than that specified by Bacon and his engineer, the aptly named L. J. Lincoln,[2] and they became convinced that an amply strong foundation would be produced for $50,000 less than anticipated. That method will be described. Since all the bids, in whatever combination, were running perilously close to the $2 mil-

lion appropriated for the project, Bacon and the memorial commissioners had to save money wherever possible, particularly given that Democrats, many of them hostile to the project, were now in the saddle in Congress and the White House. But, knowing they could not risk seeming to favor one bidder, they recommended that all bidders on the foundation be allowed to resubmit tenders based on the revised system.

One reason the budget caused Bacon and the memorial commissioners anxiety was that, although, to avoid overt favoritism, he had not specified a particular marble for the superstructure, he in fact wanted to build it of an exceptionally pure white marble called Colorado-Yule. This was quarried, in larger blocks and aggregate quantities than could be obtained from older eastern quarries, under difficult conditions at high elevation in the Elk Range of the Rockies, near Aspen.[3] Eastern architects who had seen it in use in the West, particularly in buildings in Denver, raved about the stone; and Bacon, who thanks to his Greek connections was considered an expert on marbles, had visited the company's quarries and shops at Marble, Colorado. He thought the stone's "whiteness with delicate veining" placed it "above any white building marble in appearance that I have seen here or abroad." "I remember one block in particular," he reported, "that was about 15 feet long, 5 feet wide, and 2-1/2 feet thick—I never saw a block of marble as beautiful as that one."[4] He naturally wanted to use the most perfect marble available for Lincoln's memorial, often said to be the largest marble building ever constructed;[5] but extreme quarrying conditions and high shipping costs meant that Colorado-Yule cost more than eastern marbles. Using Colorado-Yule might cause the project to exceed the appropriation. Two bids on the memorial's superstructure specified its use. One came from the large, reputable construction firm of George A. Fuller Company, which as a precaution filed a second, lower bid to build in a less expensive marble from Georgia called Amicalola. Bacon clearly favored the Fuller Company as builders and proceeded to identify features of his design that, if dropped or modified, would save enough money to allow the company's bid to build in Colorado-Yule to be accepted. A grass mound could be substituted for the terrace and masonry retaining wall at the base of the memorial; the ceiling beams inside could be sheathed in painted plaster rather than bronze; and the memorial's foundation could be sunk by the cheaper method to be described.

Most of the memorial commissioners were prepared to follow Bacon's advice, but, knowing this might raise controversy, the commission held a public hearing on the tenders on September 26, 1913. There appeared competing bidders, spokesmen for marble companies, congressmen from marble-producing states, and other architects familiar with marbles. Hostile witnesses questioned the stability of a pile foundation in the soft landfill of Potomac Park and queried the gravity of "dry cracks" turned up in some samples of Colorado-Yule. Borland, still hoping to derail the plan for a memorial in Potomac Park, had introduced a bill in the House two days before to require the memorial commission to answer charges that its budget was inadequate to permit "a

safe foundation" to be sunk. (It did not pass.) The objections were dismissed, however, and, except for the parsimonious Cannon, the memorial commissioners voted to follow Bacon's advice and recommend that the secretary of war contract with the Fuller Company to build the memorial's superstructure in Colorado-Yule. At the same time they decided to call for new bids for the foundation. When Congress saw the memorial going up, they reckoned, it would loosen the purse strings to allow items dropped from the design to be replaced.

Questions about the fairness of this course of action hung over the hearing and remained. The jilted local builder who had filed the second bid to build in Colorado-Yule accused Bacon of colluding with the Fuller Company to fix the result.[6] Judging by the business ethics of his time, more relaxed than those of our own, Bacon was probably not guilty of the direct charge, but he did consistently show favoritism to the Fuller Company. After the hearing he called Fuller "a splendid company" and the result of the hearing "simply glorious."[7] To be sure, the company had done some of the best large-scale construction in the country—railroad stations, skyscrapers, and the like[8]—and Bacon's concern for quality was legendary. In this he followed the example of McKim, Mead & White, which would not tolerate competitive bidding when artistic quality was at stake.[9] Still, he and the memorial commissioners may have been too cozy with the company's executives. He was on friendly business terms with the company's vice president, James Baird. Baird told the hearing he had met with the commissioners on the previous day and, after the meeting, obtained authorization from his superiors to reduce the company's estimates on certain items. Suggesting how desperate Bacon and the commissioners were to save money in order to be able to use Colorado-Yule marble, such conduct, while not strictly a breach of ethics, was questionable and opened them all to charges of collusion. There is one small piece of collateral evidence. In 1921, when the memorial commission was seeking additional money from Congress to underpin the memorial's retaining wall and approaches, its executive officer, in a memo exploring the background to the problem, spoke of "consultation with the Architect, Mr. Bacon, and his engineer, Mr. Lincoln, and Mr. Baird of the Geo. A. Fuller Co., to use a slab foundation for the terrace wall."[10] The context of the remark makes clear that the consultation had taken place in July 1913, two months before the sealed bids were opened. This suggests at least the expectation that Fuller would win the bidding. It may be no coincidence that the company was jointly owned by Standard Oil, United States Steel, "and a number of large railroad corporations"[11]—interests generally allied with the Republicans. Washington in 1913 was not the place, however, for a Republican-dominated memorial commission to conduct business that way. For two years, Democrats and insurgent Republicans in Congress—even some of the commission's own members—had been gunning for Taft's commission, and anything with a whiff of conspiracy gave them ammunition. Wilson was in the White House, putting the executive

branch in the hands of Progressive Democrats, to whom old-style millionaire, cronyist Republicanism was the enemy. Wilson cared little about Washington's appearance: so far as we know, he never visited the building site of the Lincoln Memorial, a mile from the White House, although it was active throughout his administration. But his secretary of war, Lindley M. Garrison, was the consummate Progressive jurist and public official, "methodical and efficient, judicial and impartial. . . . [H]e steadfastly resisted all political pressures and considerations, even necessary ones, and pursued his course regardless of the consequences."[12] Zealous in his first year in the cabinet, Garrison heard charges that Colorado-Yule marble was inferior to cheaper eastern marbles and that the Lincoln Memorial Commission had shown partiality. He felt responsibility in the matter because the memorial's enabling act gave the secretary of war authority to sign building contracts and put construction under his "supervision." (This is why the memorial commission had framed its decisions as recommendations.) But the act also put construction "under the direction of said [memorial] commission," a formulation intended not to create conflict but to give the memorial commission the benefit of the Army Corps of Engineers' expertise in executing monumental building projects in the capital through its Office of Public Buildings and Grounds.[13] The fastidious Garrison, however, fastened on the ambiguous division of authority to conduct his own investigation, which held up construction. He would never have admitted it, but politics and political geography played a role, for Wilson drew much of his strength from the "solid South" of the Democrats, which included the marble-producing states of Tennessee, Alabama, and especially Georgia, whose marbles had been passed over in favor of the stone from Colorado. That state had also gone for Wilson in 1912, but we know that "certain Representatives from Georgia" asked the secretary not to act on the Lincoln Memorial Commission's recommendations until a protest could be filed, "presumably on behalf of certain of the bidders."[14] Hewing to the letter of the law, Garrison asked the attorney general for a legal opinion as to the extent of his jurisdiction over the memorial's construction, and the federal Bureau of Standards for exhaustive scientific data on the strengths and properties of all competing marbles. The tests proved inconclusive, showing only that Colorado-Yule marble absorbed more water than some of the others, and hence might stain. Nevertheless, they cost several more aggravating months of delay.

At this, Taft again grew apoplectic, and Shelby Cullom, who had only a few months to live, feared his dream of building a memorial to Lincoln would again evade him. Arguing that the act gave the memorial commission clear precedence in artistic matters, Cullom told the attorney general the commission had "selected the Colorado-Yule marble as the whitest, prettiest, and all things considered, the best marble" and had accepted the Fuller Company's bid because it was the lowest using it.[15] Convinced at last that the choice of one marble over another was an artistic, not a factual or scientific, matter, Gar-

rison stalled more by asking the government's statutory aesthetic arbiter, the Commission of Fine Arts, a niggling question about the grounds on which such a choice should be made. Taft countered with a broader question, and in late January 1914 the art commission answered, surely to no one's surprise: "The artistic qualities of the Colorado-Yule marble . . . fit it preeminently for a structure of the character of the Lincoln Memorial."[16] At this, Garrison met with the commissioners to agree on a division of authority over the project and finally signed building contracts with the Fuller Company to build the superstructure in Colorado-Yule marble, and the M. F. Comer Company, of Toledo, to build the foundation. Nearly six months had been lost.

CONSTRUCTION AND DETAIL DESIGN

Ground was broken for the memorial, in a ceremony of what one newspaper called "Lincolnian simplicity," on a frigid Lincoln's Birthday, 1914.[17] Senator J. C. Blackburn of Kentucky, a former Confederate cavalry officer who had replaced Cullom as special resident commissioner, spoke briefly on the reunion of North and South, of which he viewed the memorial as an emblem.[18] He, Bacon, and the contractor for the foundation then turned over spadefuls of frozen earth.

The following month, the first cylindrical steel tubes for the piers of the subfoundation began to be sunk.[19] Since the site in Potomac Park was landfill—even a mile to the east, on what appeared terra firma, the soil was too soft to support the terracing at the base of the

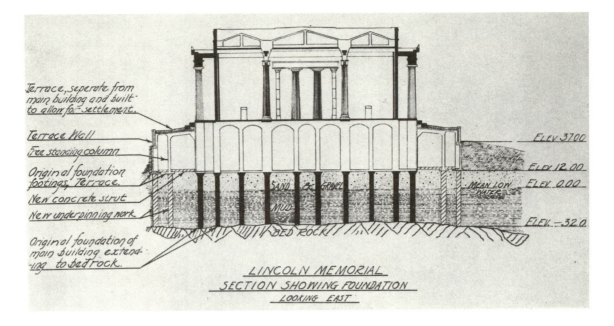

Labels on drawing:
Terrace, seperate from main building and built to allow for settlement.
Terrace Wall
Free standing column
Original foundation footings, Terrace.
New concrete strut
New underpinning work
Original foundation of main building extending to bedrock.

SAND & GRAVEL
MUD
BED ROCK
MEAN LOW WATER

ELEV 37.00
ELEV 12.00
ELEV 0.00
ELEV -32.0

LINCOLN MEMORIAL
SECTION SHOWING FOUNDATION
LOOKING EAST

Fig. 4.1. Henry Bacon. Section through Lincoln Memorial and its foundations, looking east. (Edward F. Concklin, Lincoln Memorial, *opposite p. 56. Photo: author)*

Washington Monument that the McMillan Plan had proposed—the memorial's foundations had to be sunk to bedrock, below the level of the river channel. They would be in upper and lower sections (Fig. 4.1), and Bacon and engineer Lincoln had planned to sink the lower piers in the usual way, by men working under atmospheric pressure in caissons. The Underpinning Company proposed instead to sink the foundation from the surface, without costly excavation and caisson work, by a method that, though novel for the foundations of a building, had been used in bridge construction. Hollow steel cylinders would be driven to bedrock; the soil and debris inside would be pumped out; and anchor rods would be driven from the surface down the length of these cylinders into the bedrock. The company did not win the second round of bidding for the subfoundation, but the method was followed nevertheless. One of the army engineer-officers described it: "A hole is dug 10 or 12 feet deep in which [wooden] frames are placed for [sinking] the cylinder. A section of 20 feet [of cylinder] is placed vertically in these frames, held in place by the frames, and then 10 to 20 tons in weight composed of concrete blocks are placed on the upper edge, sinking it through the soil with the aid of a water jet. When the cylinder has ceased to sink, the interior is cut out . . . and the weight again applied."[20] When one twenty-foot section of steel was buried to full length, another was attached to its top end, and the weighting and sinking continued. When a cylinder finally met resistance, signaling bedrock or the layer of soft rock overlying it (Fig. 4.2), "The hole was . . . carried two feet deeper by blasting that depth into the bedrock itself. . . .

105

Fig. 4.2. View downward
through cylinder of
lower foundation, Octo-
ber 1, 1914. (Edward F.
Concklin, Lincoln Memo-
rial, *following p. 71.*
Photo: author)

Fig. 4.3. Progress photo of Lincoln Memorial under construction, September 1, 1914. Piles of blocks are weighing down sections of cylinder for subfoundations. (Henry Bacon Collection, Wesleyan University Library, Special Collections & Archives)

A cage of reinforcing rods was inserted reaching below the tube two feet, to the bottom of the bedrock excavation. . . . Concrete was poured and tamped in. . . . The piers are spread at the top and tied together by reinforced concrete grillage one foot thick."[21] Thus, the subfoundation, consisting of 122 cylinders, became a monolithic mass of concrete and steel. Work proceeded generally from north to south, creating a forest of cylinders and stacks of blocks of various heights, which delighted journalists and sidewalk superintendents and turned West Potomac Park into a "place of great popular vehicular resort."[22] Images such as that in Figure 4.3 convey the—literally—underlying modernity of the Lincoln Memorial. It is, in effect, a modern classical temple standing on twentieth-century bridge or skyscraper foundations, a contrast seen again in the fabrication of the marble.

By midsummer 1914, the subfoundation for the north half of the building and the steps was all but complete, and the first pier of the upper foundation was being raised. Figure 4.3, a photograph of the site taken on September 1, shows the first of the upper piers rising in the background. Of reinforced concrete and oblong in footprint, these rose to flat arches, which would support the floor of the memorial hall. A catwalk called a gallery was built inside the perimeter of the upper foundation. Today these upper piers can be glimpsed, exposed in a high, open basement, through a porthole in the memorial's apron wall. The upper foundation was complete by March 1915, barely a year after construction had begun.

Meanwhile, Bacon and his staff continued to review the design of the visible superstructure, in part to make its details as classically pure as possible. He had planned to travel to Greece after building contracts were signed "to study some of the Greek details which I have in mind,"[23] but the conflict with Garrison made the trip impossible. Instead, his brother Frank may have "taken off" details of classical buildings for him during a visit to Greece in 1914, completed just as war broke out in the Dardanelles. The Greek refinements in the design took definite shape at this time.[24] Bacon planned the taper, entasis (slightly bulging profile), and inward inclination of the outer columns to have them match exactly those of the Parthenon, except that his were forty-four feet tall to the Parthenon's thirty-four. The walls of the memorial hall, like those of a Greek temple, had a base course of orthostats, six-foot upright stones projecting slightly forward of the wall above. All the way up, the courses of the wall were of uni-

form height, just over two feet, but their blocks diminished in width almost imperceptibly toward the center of each wall. The outer faces of the walls battered inward very slightly—two inches in forty-four feet—as did the entablature over the columns, and the attic walls. The inward inclination is most noticeable at the foot of each column. Bacon also wanted every plane of the memorial, as in the most refined classical Greek temples, to swell subtly outward for an appearance of life, but he was forced to modify his plan, and drawings show only that the platform has a slight outward bow and crowns at the center, like a segment of a sphere (Fig. 4.4). He told Colonel W. W. Harts, then the memorial commission's executive officer, "I am sorry to say that I have finally been obliged to abandon the curving of the memorial, as I discovered it would necessitate the recutting of quite a number of the large stones at the corner and moreover Lincoln and I, after carefully considering the matter, decided we would get better stone setting, if we hold to the original plans."[25] Nevertheless, the refinements he did incorporate, especially the inward inclination of the verticals, give the memorial the appearance less of a static, rectilinear block than of the base of a pyramid, imparting to it a dynamism buildings in the neoclassical tradition often lack. This is especially true when the memorial is viewed from below and close up, most of all from a corner vantage point.

Bacon strove for flawless craftsmanship in every detail, even in the joints of the marblework. In Greek temples, the blocks of stone—on the Greek mainland, from the fifth century B.C.E. onward, these were usually marble—

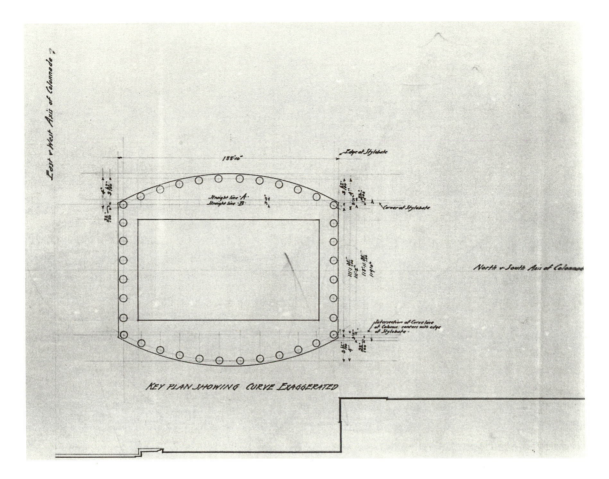

Fig. 4.4. Henry Bacon. *"Key plan showing curve [of platform] exaggerated" (detail of contract drawing for Lincoln Memorial), June 30, 1914. Draftsman, G. Beninati. (Henry Bacon Collection, Wesleyan University Library, Special Collections & Archives)*

were cut very precisely and laid up dry, without mortar. But, given modern techniques and labor and a climate prone to heavy frost in winter, this was impracticable, especially on a limited budget, for the federal Treasury of the United States could not be plundered as Athens had that of the Delian Confederacy. Bacon came as close as he could to the ideal, specifying narrow joints between the blocks,

an eighth-inch wide on vertical seams and three-sixteenths on horizontal beds, filled with white, nonstaining portland cement. The joints were reinforced in the Greek way, with bronze clamps. (Brass was substituted when the war in Europe made copper hard to obtain.)

With the aid of trusted sculptors, he refined previously sketchy ornamental details. Henry Hering modeled the wreaths of the main frieze (Fig. 4.5), and Daniel Chester French, the rampant eagles of the attic. French's protégée Evelyn Beatrice Longman, under his supervision, modeled the palms, eagles, and wreaths of the address tablets in the side

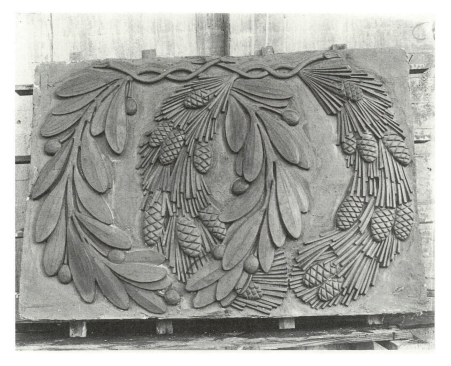

Fig. 4.5. Henry Hering (after design by Henry Bacon). Clay study model of paired wreaths of main entablature, made ca. 1915. (Henry Bacon Collection, Wesleyan University Library, Special Collections & Archives)

recesses (Figs. II, 4.14, and 5.2). (Earlier versions of the address tablets had shown sentry figures [Fig. 3.33], but these were eliminated.) Some details, such as the state names and dates of the main frieze and some floral ornament, were modeled in plaster at full size. A model for French's eagles on the attic is visible in the upper right-hand corner of the photo in Figure 4.10).

Ornamental and symbolic motifs were studied with special care. Over eighteen months routine neo-Roman tripod braziers on the parapets of the stairway took on heraldic American character (Fig. 4.6), with eagles, pinecones, and corncobs that evoke Latrobe's native columnar orders in the U.S. Capitol.[26] On the faces of the parapets below, the bundles of lictor's rods in relief, symbols of Roman consular authority, were Americanized by attaching eagle-headed tomahawks.

Bacon used splendid, large-scale drawings, such as that in Figure 4.7, to study the friezes. For the "medallion composed of a double wreath of leafs" of the main frieze (see Fig. 4.5),[27] during a vacation in North Carolina he sketched a cone of long-leaf pine, his chosen symbol of the South; presumably he did the same with Northern laurel. The symbolism of the wreaths is a little confusing, in fact, since both plants grow in both regions; associating laurel with the North was a subtle reference to the region's victory in the Civil War.

The details of the attic gave him most hesitation, since it was one of the least Greek and

Fig. 4.6. Lincoln Memorial. Detail of upper flights of steps, cheek wall, and tripod as seen from foot of second flight. (Photograph courtesy of the Photographic Archives, Washington, D.C., Dunlap Society Collection. Taken for the Dunlap Society by Richard Cheek)

Fig. 4.7. Henry Bacon. Design for Lincoln Memorial. Detail of main entablature and attic at southeast ("Delaware") corner, March 24, 1914. Pencil and blue crayon on tissue. (Henry Bacon Collection, Wesleyan University Library, Special Collections & Archives)

thus least familiar features of the design. The so-called final design for the memorial showed there a frieze alluding to the number of states in the Union at the time of construction. It had forty-eight festoons, supported at intervals and pinned at the corners by eagles, running above the state names. Perhaps because the birds' wings wrapped the corners awkwardly, Bacon decided in early 1914 to replace them with more decidedly frontal tripod braziers, echoing those of the parapets below (see

Fig. 4.7). More important, however, was the decision that fall to raise the height of the attic by three feet to make the ornament and inscriptions legible from a greater distance. This meant inserting an extra course of marble, and, since cutting and fabrication of the marble were then far advanced, the Fuller Company objected. Bacon insisted on the change.[28] Visibility was so crucial to him that when, in 1915, Olmsted proposed a slight drop in the level of the circular roadway, he objected: "[I]f the circular roadway, which affords some of the most important views, is placed below level plus 27 one will not see from there the bottom of the columns and the attic will disappear too much. Moreover the statue of Lincoln will partly disappear from the roadway directly in front of the memorial."[29] He changed the design of the memorial's interior less than that of the outside. Though forced temporarily to accept concrete or plaster ceiling beams in the memorial hall, he held to his plan to ornament their soffits with alternating sprays of oak and laurel. The correct wording of the Gettysburg Address was debated at length in 1914–15, since several versions of Lincoln's text had survived. In this, the memorial commission consulted with Robert Todd Lincoln, the president's eldest son, who took a keen interest in the project of his father's memorial.[30] The care Bacon gave to the memorial's decorative and symbolic detail was entirely in character and justified the recommendation of him by Burnham and Millet.

THE MARBLE

As the memorial's subfoundation began to be sunk in spring 1914, Bacon and his staff faced the urgent task of preparing detailed drawings and calculations for the marblework of the superstructure. The stone was quarried under exceptionally difficult conditions, inside a mountain: "That part of the white marble deposit which has been developed outcrops for a distance of 4,500 feet and is more than 240 feet thick. It dips into the side of the mountain at an angle of about 36 degrees and

to an unknown depth. . . . The canyon sides, rising more than a thousand feet perpendicularly, have been pierced near their tops, and openings driven in on the deposit of white marble."[31] Behind these "portals," shafts were drilled back and downward into the vein of marble, forming a vast, ghostly chamber inside the mountain, which grew steadily deeper.[32] Once cut free, the blocks were hoisted by crane through the portals and lowered on cables and pulleys to a loading station, where they were transferred to flatcars on a private electric railroad, which took them to the mills at Marble, a company village in the valley three and a half miles below. Since the blocks of marble in their rough state were extremely heavy—even finished, the largest ones in the memorial weigh twenty-three tons—the short trip by rail was very dangerous. The line had grades of up to 15 percent, and cars loaded with marble had been known to run out of control, killing employees of the company and even its founder. Since the quarry was at an elevation of nearly ten thousand feet, the area was also given to deadly avalanches, which could strike at any time without warning during winters that lasted nine months a year. Even normal snowfalls, which could exceed a hundred inches in three months, paralyzed the company's operations for days at a time.

The mill at Marble, built in 1910 and staffed by a force that included workers brought from the Carrara region of Italy, was said to be the largest of its kind in the world. Long and narrow—eighty feet wide by more than a quarter mile long—it worked on an assembly-line principle, with

113

Fig. 4.8. Photos, "At Work on the Huge Marble Columns of the Lincoln Memorial." (Scientific American, *March 20, 1915, 261. Photo: author)*

traveling cranes carrying the stone between workstations. First the stone was given a preliminary inspection, for the company saved money by shipping to Washington only pieces it was sure the government would accept. Then came the cutting, which required exceptional precision and special machinery (Fig. 4.8):

A large cylinder core barrel 7 feet 6 inches in diameter and 4 feet high was erected for the purpose of sawing out the large column drums. This core barrel was set with diamonds and was run at high speed making it possible to saw out one of these immense drums in four hours. After the drums were sawed they were transferred into Shop 4 which was especially equipped with overhead traveling cranes of large capacity, turning lathes and upright fluting lathes especially designed and installed for the turning of these drums and cutting the flutes. This work was all done with diamonds and carborundum. . . . With this equipment Shop 4 had capacity to turn two drums in eighteen hours. The barrel saw and fluting lathes were run continuously twenty four hours a day during the fabrication of the Lincoln Memorial. Other special machines were made for finishing the caps, ceiling panels and other parts of the building, the blocks being of such enormous dimensions that ordinary machines usually employed in the fabrication of marble for building work were not strong enough in capacity to handle these immense sizes.

Superlatives abounded in accounts of the process, such as this one in *Scientific American*: "These will be the largest columns of their kind in the world. Each block of marble as it comes from the quarry weighs about thirty-five tons, and twelve of these huge blocks are required for each column. . . . As the thirty-eight columns will require four hundred and fifty-six blocks of about 25 tons each, the total weight of marble will approximate 11,400 tons."[33] Since these figures apply to the columns only and do not include the marble of the walls and platform, concern for the stability of the memorial's foundations is understandable. At the marble mill, the finished blocks and drums were loaded onto cars on a short, standard-gauge rail line owned by the company and taken to a junction with a main line, seven miles away. The cars were then rolled cross-country to Georgetown, D.C., northwest of the construction site, and shunted onto a custom-built rail spur to Potomac Park. At the construction site, the marble was unloaded, given a second inspection, and stored in orderly piles, with the final position of each block or drum marked on it. (This was standard practice in important masonry building projects of the time.) Throughout, military precision marked the logistics and staging.

Rhetoric conflating state jingoism and praise of the idealized Lincoln, his memorial, the United States, and American nature gathered around the marble of the memorial. Senator John F. Shafroth of Colorado, who had lobbied for the use of Yule marble, expressed joy that marble from his state had been chosen to build "the greatest memorial of the Western Hemisphere. It is exceedingly fitting that the pure life of the great lover of human liberty should be typified by the purest marble taken from mountains which all history has shown to be the birthplace of freedom."[34] To mark the laying of the memorial's cornerstone, a Denver newspaper published an appreciative poem, ending:

> [C]ame a day when the hill was riven,
>   And white in the sun I gleamed,

The fairest thing from the mountains
    given—Gold but a bauble seemed;
Now shall I stand, while the world grows
    hoary, Builded to Lincoln's fame;
Gift of her heart—what greater glory
    Shall the state of the high peaks claim![35]

Both the efficient, industrial process of producing and delivering the marble and popular
fascination with that process evidence Americans' growing obsession with machinery in
the period. Machines, long an American
fetish, came to dominate middle-class life and
imagination to a high degree in the years
before the First World War. Indeed, Europeans
and many of its own citizens viewed America
as "the supreme altar of the new God," where
the coming way of life that machines would
make possible already existed in outline;
Henry Ford wrote of machines as "the New
Messiah."[36] Faith in machinery was an aspect
of the modernity mentioned earlier in connection with the memorial's massive, utilitarian concrete-and-steel foundations. Gigantic,
new construction gave material form to the
modernist sensibility and ideology that
underlay political Progressivism, and, just as
the memorial project and its backers occupied
an ambiguous place with respect to Progressive politics, so the building harbored ambivalence, too. Modernity literally underpinned it
and made its construction possible, yet the
design disguised this modernity behind a
facade of traditional, indeed antique, architecture, as in other historicist buildings of the
early twentieth century, placing modernity at
the service of loyalty to tradition. Dedication
to Lincoln, moreover, forged a link between

his memory, modernity, and values of Americanism. One recalls Le Corbusier's warning to
European modernist architects, "Let us listen
to the counsels of American engineers. But let
us beware of American architects."[37]

On Lincoln's Birthday in 1915, around the
time workmen began to set the marble of the
superstructure, a modest cornerstone ceremony was held.[38] This represented rapid
progress in just one year. The marble was set,
proceeding generally from north to south,
with the same order and dispatch as it was
quarried and fabricated. Columns and the
walls behind them were carried up in tandem,
the stone being hoisted into place by twin
derricks mounted on the platform. A photo
taken during the spring of 1916 shows a drum
being lowered to the platform, probably of the
south portico (Fig. 4.9). The limestone interior
walls and columns of the memorial hall were
raised along with the marble exterior, and the
marble floors were laid—Colorado-Yule on
the outside platform and Tennessee pink marble in the memorial hall. The setting of marble reached a peak in May 1916, when almost
ten thousand cubic feet were put in place.

Carving of the memorial's friezes and
inscriptions began as soon as the stone of the
upper parts of the building was in place (Fig.
4.10). This was done by Ernest C. Bairstow of
Washington.[39] Echoing Greek sacred building
practice, Bacon wanted the states' names to be
carved on the friezes in ritual order, but his
wish was not fully realized. He told the
Washington Post he intended to have the
names of the first thirteen states to ratify the
Constitution carved on the main frieze first,

Fig. 4.9. *Progress photo of Lincoln Memorial under construction, taken ca. May 1916. Drum of column being lowered into position. (Henry Bacon Collection, Wesleyan University Library, Special Collections & Archives)*

followed by that of Kentucky, to honor Senator Blackburn.[40] His attention, all along, to the Delaware corner had the same honorific flavor. Figure 4.10 shows, however, that even if Bairstow carved the names of the earliest thirteen states first, he did not proceed by order of their entry. The decision to carve the names of the forty-eight states on the attic after those below may likewise have had ritual significance, but it was partly a matter of practicality, for these, at slightly above head height when one is standing on the roof of the colonnade, could be carved from scaffolds or even step stools. The wreaths and states' names of the main frieze were carved in place, from raised bosses left on these stones, but the garlands and eagles of the attic frieze were probably roughed out in the workshop. Figure 4.10 shows an eagle roughed out in the center and a plaster model of the bird set up at the right, possibly as a test. The last of the exterior stone for the attic was put in place in November 1916, allowing the girders of the roof—representing the only substantial use of steel in the superstructure—to be inserted and skylights installed, to close the memorial

Fig. 4.10. The carving of the exterior friezes of the Lincoln Memorial in progress, probably in fall 1916. Plaster model of one of eagles of attic appears in upper right. (Henry Bacon Collection, Wesleyan University Library, Special Collections & Archives)

in for the winter. Then the ceiling beams, bronze-plated over a core of cinder concrete, were locked in place. Thereafter, most work on the building was interior, though much exterior carving still remained to be done.

Meanwhile, as Bacon and the commissioners had hoped, Congress made a supplementary appropriation of nearly $600,000 in February 1916 to replace items dropped from the budget three years before. The need for emergency funds was acute owing to inflation caused by the war in Europe, but the parsimonious, Democrat-controlled Congress was at first unsympathetic. The House turned down the request but, in conference with the Senate, agreed to it, swayed no doubt by Thomas S. Martin of Virginia, who besides serving as Money's replacement on the memorial commission, chaired the Senate appropriations committee. The extra money allowed the stone terrace wall and its foundations to be restored to the design; the ceiling beams would once more be of bronze; and the bronze screens across the entry were authorized, which Bacon thought necessary to prevent condensation from forming inside the memorial hall and causing structural damage. These, however, were never installed, an omission the documents leave unexplained. It owed perhaps to wartime shortages of metals, but possibly also to French's anxiety for lighting his statue, which will be discussed. With the fresh infusion of funds, construction proceeded at such a pace that the Fuller Company turned the completed shell of the memorial over to the government in October 1917, five months ahead of schedule.

Ironically, it was Joe Cannon who presented the Lincoln Memorial Commission's case for supplementary funding to the House. The sight of the memorial rising in Potomac Park had won over even him. Cannon, visiting the site to prepare his presentation, is reported to have said: "The farmer is the back-bone of the country; he works hard and lives frugally. His three meals a day cost him about 15 [cents] and he smokes a corn cob pipe. But he has no imagination! He cannot imagine a thing and it is [not] until he actually sees it that he can form a conclusion. . . . I guess you boys are all right."[41] To the House, he said:

> [L]ooking through the hindsight [sic], I am inclined to think the Art Commission and the majority of the Memorial Commission located this memorial where it ought to be located [applause], although I was somewhat worked up at the time. There it is, just across from Arlington, on the Potomac River: a beautiful park. . . . I am very glad that there has been a design for that park and for its extension. I am very glad that the park was

rendered possible by producing the elevation you have there . . . because the tide ebbed and flowed over that park for many years after I came to Washington.[42]

THE STATUE

Though he had the benefit of Daniel Chester French's advice all along, Bacon had not been sure what kind of statue belonged in the memorial hall. His first impulse had been toward a standing figure (see Fig. 3.6)—no surprise, in that the starting point for his design was the Parthenon, with a colossal standing figure of Athena enshrined in its cella. Furthermore, in 1911 he and French were collaborating on the design of a Lincoln monument for the grounds of the Nebraska state capitol that featured a figure of the president standing before a stone slab.[43] On the slab were incised the words of the Gettysburg Address; here, too, originated the idealized, rather verbal quality of the memorial in Washington. By the end of 1911, however, Bacon had decided on a seated figure, the time-honored way in Western sculpture to honor a dead statesman or philosopher.[44] (Enthronement also designates kingship, a less comfortable association for most Americans.) In the early Republic, Horatio Greenough had modeled a seated, godlike figure of George Washington, inspired by that of Zeus at Olympia, for the rotunda of the U.S. Capitol (Fig. 4.11), but its grandeur, heroic nudity, and literal classicism had made it controversial, and it did not remain in the Capitol long.[45] Bacon's first design for the memorial showed a less than commanding seated figure

Fig. 4.11. Horatio Greenough. Statue of George Washington, 1832–41. (Smithsonian Institution, National Museum of American Art Washington, D.C. transfer from the U.S. Capitol)

of Lincoln in modern dress, looking reflective but rather timorous in the cavernous memorial hall (see Fig. 3.14). It recalled a seated figure of him modeled for a site in Chicago's Grant Park by Augustus Saint-Gaudens, who was then, we saw earlier, considered the canonical sculptor of Lincoln.[46] While these prototypes confined Bacon's imagination, he was unhappy when a movement arose to have a replica of one of them, the better-known standing figure (see Fig. 1.3), installed in the memorial in Washington. "Several people have mentioned to me," he told a friend, "Glenn Brown and Mrs. Saint-Gaudens among the number—that they thought it would be a good idea to have the Lincoln in Chicago by Saint-Gaudens reproduced for the Lincoln Memorial."[47] Indeed, the sculptor's formidable widow, Augusta, descended upon Bacon in his office in spring 1914 and challenged him to explain his opposition to the idea:

> I told her there were several reasons; the first being that Saint-Gaudens modelled the Chicago Lincoln to be executed in bronze, whereas I wished to have the statue for the Memorial executed in marble. Moreover, the Chicago Lincoln was executed to be seen from a particular point of view, and if a replica of it was used for the Lincoln Memorial, it would have to be enlarged which would necessarily make the point of view . . . at a greater distance from the statue itself.
>
> I also stated that I wished to have the statue for the Lincoln Memorial a seated one instead of a standing one. I further stated that if the Saint-Gaudens' Lincoln was enlarged certain of the proportions would undoubtedly have to be changed, to which Mrs. Saint-Gaudens replied, that it was easy enough to get this done by living sculptors. In answer to this, I stated that it would be an outrage to modify this important work of Saint-Gaudens, and that I believed if he knew of it, he would turn in his grave![48]

Besides, Bacon was bent on having Daniel Chester French model the statue. Nearly a year before, he had told the same friend, Professor Franklin W. Hooper of the Brooklyn Institute of Arts and Sciences:

> The personal relations between me and the sculptor . . . will have an important bearing on the success of the combined work. . . . I have collaborated with a good many sculptors in the design of monuments, Saint-Gaudens among the number, and of them all, I have found the collaboration to be most congenial when working with Mr. French; and we each have given in to the other and stood out against each other on points that arose for discussion during our work with the result that each, at the end, has been satisfied with the combined efforts.[49]

He had Hooper, a leader in traditionalist art circles, mount a movement to draft French to counter the one to reuse a Saint-Gaudens replica, but, since French chaired the Commission of Fine Arts after 1912—he had succeeded Burnham, who died in that year—French could not ethically have accepted a sculptural commission of such magnitude from the federal government. To do so, French told Bacon, would be "a calamity" and "would arouse adverse criticism" of the Commission of Fine Arts and its principles. Bacon replied that it would be "a calamity" if he refused the commission, but French remained unmoved.[50] Bacon and Hooper kept up the pressure, however, although other sculptors, including Paul Bartlett, Bela Pratt, George Barnard, and, as we saw, Gutzon Borglum, wooed Bacon and the memorial commission. French was playing coy, however, and at the beginning of 1915 he offered Bacon his "unconditional surrender," having resigned from the Commission of Fine Arts, the minutes say, "to devote his time entirely to his profession."[51]

That spring, at Chesterwood, his summer home and studio in the Berkshires of western Massachusetts that Bacon had designed, French began sketches toward the statue of Lincoln. Twelve feet high, it would show him seated in a thronelike chair, dressed in a frock coat and gazing downward pensively.[52] That December, he formally contracted to furnish "in the best statuary bronze or marble . . . an heroic seated statue of Abraham Lincoln, not less than ten (10) feet in height."[53] By early 1916, he had prepared a model of the figure, three feet high, atop a high, square, molded base with eagles in relief at the corners. The plinth and throne were very simple; the eagles were soon eliminated, and all that remained of ornament was bound bundles of lictor's rods on the faces of the throne arms. Enlarging the figure to a height of seven feet that summer, French refined it further, especially the face and hands. This approximately half-size model was finished by October 1916, followed by another ten feet high the next spring. In April 1917, French and Bacon had the ten-foot plaster model of the figure set up to judge the effect. As Bacon wrote to Harts, "[W]e found it was too small; and after experimenting with enlarged photos of the statue, of varying sizes, it was determined that the statue should be nineteen feet high, and that it would be best to have it cut in white marble. . . . The unusually large scale of the interior of the Lincoln Memorial, becoming apparent as the building approaches completion, conclusively shows that a larger statue is necessary, than the one first planned."[54] Moreover, a figure ten feet tall would have little presence when seen from below, on the memorial's steps and terraces. French and Bacon probably suspected this: they had come armed with "enlarged photos . . . of varying sizes," and, three years earlier, Bacon had told Mrs. Saint-Gaudens he wanted a marble statue larger than those of her husband, which were nine and twelve feet high.[55] These were what sculptors call heroic size; he wanted a colossal figure. The claim to have only just discovered in 1917 that a ten-foot figure was inadequate, then, should not be taken at face value, though he and French may truly have been taken aback by the degree to which it was too small. Now, with the memorial hall finished and French involved in the project as an expert supporter, Bacon dared voice the need for a larger figure. Presented with his arguments, the memorial commissioners, knowing the additional $60,000 needed could be found within the existing appropriation, recommended that the secretary of war sign contracts to have carved a figure nineteen feet high—twenty-two, including plinth—and to alter the rear wall of the memorial hall, behind the statue, to accommodate it.

The statue was carved by the Piccirillis, a family of stone carvers and sculptors whose patriarch, Giuseppe, had emigrated in the 1890s from Massa-Carrara, in Tuscany.[56] Starting in starkest poverty, the Piccirillis had built the largest, most reputable marble workshop in America, a vast Italian-style *bottega* covering a city block in the Bronx. They owed much of their success to French's patronage, and he would not have entrusted the fabrication of the Lincoln statue to anyone else. Bacon also had them carve the marble tripods for the parapets of the outside stairway (see Fig. 4.6).[57] The task of fabricating the statue was immense, for, finished, it weighed 340,000 pounds.[58] The white Georgia marble for it had to be worked in twenty-eight pieces in order to pass through the memorial's doorway. The Piccirillis "pointed" the statue—transferred its forms from plaster into marble—and French worked the surfaces at the shop and, later, in the memorial hall. Delivered to the site in November 1919, the pieces were assembled over several months (Fig. 4.12). French admitted that he was "very much relieved to see that it was not too large for its surroundings. I got into rather a panic about this for it didn't seem that a statue that large could fit into any place without being too colossal."[59] In May 1920, he announced with pride, "The Lincoln statue, with its pedestal, is an accomplished fact . . . as nearly perfect technically as I can make it."[60]

The most compelling image of Lincoln yet devised, French's statue presents him as both man and god. Brooding and severe but also compassionate, he is depicted as Father of the People, a living personality (Fig. 4.13). This humanity accounts in large part for the statue's appeal. At the same time, gigantism removes him from earthly life, culminating his apotheosis as spiritual patron of the reunited nation. This is in keeping with the aim of the memorial's planners to emphasize Reunion over other themes and to avoid partisan, sectional, or racial embarrassments about Lincoln's presidency and the actual legacy of the war. "Work over, victory his," is how French characterized the statue's attitude.[61] The square throne in which Lincoln sits, though reminding us of chairs in Brady's and Gardiner's wartime photo studios, is eternal and abstract, representing the grandeur of the central government. His dress of vest and frock coat is modern, but the cape draped over the back of the throne, recalling a shawl Lincoln would throw over his shoulders on cold nights, has become a Graeco-Roman vestment of state. The facial features are the man's, but his gaze toward the Washington Monument and the dome of the U.S. Capitol is symbolic. It climaxes and terminates the apparently seamless, untroubled system of the Mall.

SIMPLICITY AND UNIVERSALITY

As the memorial's "kernel" of warmth and humanity, the interior of the hall is more colorful than the stark white exterior. Its walls are of buff Indiana limestone; the floor, dado, and statue pedestal, of Tennessee pink marble; and the ceiling beams, of bronze with relief ornament of rosettes and sprigs of foliage—oak and laurel on alternate beams. The statue, the address tablets in the side recesses, and the murals running above these were intended to sustain an air of universality and evenhanded neutrality, and implicitly to abstract high principles from the carnage of war and the conditions that caused it. The nation has evolved to a point, the memorial hall implies, where the suffering of history and the present, while still real, has taken on higher meaning within an enveloping destiny. In this sense the memorial hall echoed the Gettysburg Address itself, found carved in dignified lapidary lettering and heraldically

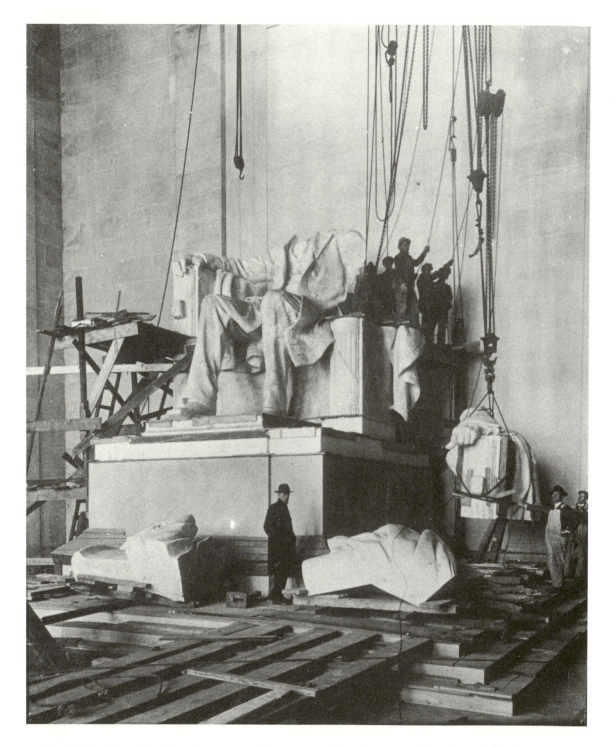

Fig. 4.12. D. C. French and work crew assembling statue of Lincoln in central chamber of Lincoln Memorial, early 1920. (Henry Bacon Collection, Wesleyan University Library, Special Collections & Archives)

framed in the left (south) chamber (Fig. II). The address called a series of military blunders on both sides a "new birth of freedom" and sought, rhetorically, to reinvent the war and the United States on the basis of high principles and purposes, without referring to actual conditions of war and slavery.[62]

Less important only than the statue and the address tablets were the murals above the tablets on the end walls of the side chambers (Fig. 4.15).[63] Because these were to be universalizing and uplifting, Bacon entrusted them

to Symbolist painter Jules Guérin, who had collaborated with him on the presentation drawings for the memorial in 1911 and 1912. (Guérin also decorated the soffits of the ceiling beams.) Sixty feet long by twelve feet high, the murals were to underscore the themes of the addresses in allegory. Their long, low shape inspired Guérin to paint compositions of symmetrically grouped clusters of idealized figures posed frontally. Above the Gettysburg Address in the left-hand chamber, Guérin painted the vaguely titled *Emancipation of a Race*. In the right, or north, recess,

Fig. 4.13. French and Bacon standing at the base of statue of Lincoln, May 1922. (Henry Bacon Collection, Wesleyan University Library, Special Collections & Archives)

Central Group above the Gettysburg Address, typifying Freedom and Liberty.

Central Group above Second Inaugural Address, typifying Unity.

Fig. 4.15. Jules Guérin. Murals in Lincoln Memorial: Emancipation of a Race *(above and)* Reunion *(below). Note that titles given in the printed captions are incorrect and evasive. (*Pencil Points 5 *[May 1924]: 66. Photo: author)*

over the Second Inaugural, he painted *Reunion*, the memorial's overarching theme. Fabricating the murals was, again, a logistical feat of a high order. For a studio large enough to work on them, Guérin rented the penthouse of an office tower in New York. Unassisted, he painted each mural on a seamless roll of canvas, devising a system of pulleys to lower first one and then the other into place so that he could develop them together and ensure that their tones matched. To accommodate the memorial's indoor-outdoor character, he mixed weatherproof paints of pigment, white wax, and kerosene, imitating the wax-based paints used in ancient Egyptian tombs. (He had a long-standing interest in technique.) Bacon did manage to have a heating system installed in the memorial, but it was abandoned in the 1940s, and the murals suffered more than other features from moisture that built up in the memorial hall. As part of a renovation campaign in the 1990s, the murals have required extensive restoration and can now be seen as they were intended.[64] Because they were formerly badly faded, visitors have tended hardly to be aware of them, particularly since they are so high on the walls.

All three—the statue, the address tablets, and the murals—elevate Lincoln and the war to the empyrean, contributing to the erasure of actual historical memories of the war, Reconstruction, and Jim Crow. While allegedly discouraging taking sides by emphasizing national reunion, the design in fact took sides by underlining what white Americans, North and South, had in common and omitting the experience of African-Americans and others. In keeping with the ideology of the mainly Republican political and cultural elite that built it, the memorial excluded from its design any reference not strictly avoidable to slavery, emancipation, or the contemporary situation of American blacks and other disenfranchised groups.

By 1916–20, when the memorial hall was under construction, conditions for these people were in some instances very bad. The situation of African-Americans before 1912 has already been discussed. Though military service in the war represented an improvement for some, and huge numbers of blacks escaped agricultural peonage in the South by migrating to the industrial cities of the North, the war period gave them little cause to rejoice.[65] In *Birth of a Nation* (1915), filmmaker D. W. Griffith romanticized the Ku Klux Klan of the Reconstruction era and depicted African-Americans as utterly degraded. The film's celebrity led to the refounding of a contemporary Klan, which at first directed its bigotry indiscriminately at blacks, Catholics, and Jews. The year 1915 alone saw seventy-nine lynchings across the country. In the domestic tension that followed the armistice of 1918, the orgy of racial rioting and lynching continued.[66] In Washington, on the memorial's doorstep, African-Ameri-

cans' position was generally deteriorating as the memorial was being built. Since Wilson drew much of his support from white Southern voters, the federal service became less hospitable to blacks, and segregation became the rule in federal parks and office buildings.[67] "Separate but equal" lunchrooms and rest rooms and "Jim Crow corners" in offices were already found in federal government buildings under Theodore Roosevelt; under Wilson, they became the norm. Conditions did not change significantly until Franklin Delano Roosevelt's time. During the Second World War, the Pentagon, located in northern Virginia, was built with segregated rest rooms; FDR insisted they be integrated.

No such grim realities receive attention in the memorial hall. In his Gettysburg Address, Lincoln referred, somewhat misleadingly, to liberty as the principle on which the United States was founded, yet he avoided emancipation and other controversies in his funeral oration over the dead.[68] The tablet's solemn serif lettering and framing seem to give the transcendental text standing as the war's official interpretation. In his Second Inaugural, given as the war dragged to an end, Lincoln outlined a clement program to rehabilitate the white South. This text is found in the opposite (north) address chamber (Fig. 4.14). Here, Kirk Savage observes, Lincoln "matter-of-factly affirmed that everyone had known the slave interest 'was somehow the cause of the war' and proposed that the war might be God's way of scourging the nation for allowing slavery to persist."[69] Otherwise, the design treats slavery and race as something abstract and in the past, without present meaning or importance for visitors. In the murals the evasion seems especially gross. *Reunion* is represented as a spiritual ideal, without acknowledging the price African-Americans had paid so that the whites of Northern and Southern states could be reunited. Even many white Southerners did not feel restored to full citizenship in the national whole. The mural sidesteps these jarring experiences. *Emancipation of a Race*, the only allusion to Lincoln as Emancipator, keeps the whole matter of African-American servitude ethereal and unnamed, as if choosing to deny the snail-slow progress—indeed, actual regress—in relations between the races since the war and Reconstruction. One would hardly expect disappointment and double cross to be celebrated on the walls of a national memorial, but it is hard to study the murals without sensing bad faith behind them.

In keeping with the ideal of classic simplicity, Bacon fought hard to keep clutter in all forms out of the memorial. He did not even want a flagpole on the building, asking that a rule requiring every federal building to bear one be suspended for the memorial, since it was not a building, properly speaking.[70] Sometimes the battle for visual economy was hard because the Lincoln Memorial Commission was besieged with offers, some quite touching, of Lincolniana, and the distinction between a memorial and a museum was not well understood.[71] Lincoln's former servant, Joseph Christian, offered the commission the president's razor. A congressman introduced a bill to have the commission buy the suit Lincoln was wearing the night he was shot.[72] Mrs. A. C. Hewitt pleaded with the commis-

sion to carry out her husband's dying wish by accepting for display his unique collection of Lincoln medals—"medallic Lincolniana." Such offers were generally forwarded to the Lincoln museum in the Petersen house on Tenth Street, Northwest, where the president had died. Some suggestions were bizarre. The Order of the Sons of Temperance ("A Live, Progressive, Non-partisan, Total Abstinence Society for All") asked leave to place a tablet in the memorial "telling of Mr. Lincoln's connection with our organization and any facts of public interest." One proposal would have disturbed the iconography. It envisioned hanging in the memorial an enormous, ungainly painting, *The New Republic*, surmounted by a huge eagle, painted abroad during the Civil War by "a member of the Academy of Bruges and Dusseldorf." Showing Lincoln, Secretary of State Seward, and Henry Ward Beecher in the shadow of the goddess of liberty, it celebrated the theme of human liberty—"exactly the same," said the donor, "as that of the great edifice."

There have been recurrent efforts, in fact, to establish an archive or museum in the memorial's basement, or undercroft. The earliest of these were functional, to make use of what seemed waste space. About 1915, with the memorial still incomplete, the Lincoln Memorial Commission and Fine Art Commission were pressed to allow the undercroft to be used for temporary storage of government documents, since there was then no national archives.[73] In 1917, there were appeals, which were again resisted, to use the basement for document storage during the wartime emergency.[74] More recent suggestions for a museum at the memorial have been heraldic and patriotic in character. In 1961, Fred Schwengel, a Republican congressman from Iowa and later president of the U.S. Capitol Historical Society, called for "the largest and the best Lincoln museum in the world" to be installed in the memorial's basement.[75] Perhaps as a result, a small display was set up in the northwest corner of the basement in 1976 in preparation for the droves of visitors expected at the Bicentennial. Calling the memorial's undercroft the "largest manmade empty space in the world," Schwengel resurrected his idea for a museum in the early 1990s, when it took on the theme of civil rights (see chapter 5).[76] The idea was not realized, but in the restoration of the same decade the display in the undercroft was renewed and enlarged to encompass that subject.

The most serious temptation to add an iconographic feature arose from a request by Judge Henry B. Rankin of Springfield, Illinois, who had studied law under Lincoln, to include in the memorial the text of the Farewell Address Lincoln made to the people of Springfield as he left to take up the presidency in 1861. Rankin had heard Lincoln give the speech, which was as taut and classical as the Gettysburg Address in expressing his sense of the historic burden facing him.[77] Bacon and French succumbed to Judge Rankin's blandishments largely, one suspects, as a tribute to him and his recently deceased townsman Shelby Cullom. First Bacon planned to have the text carved on the wall behind the statue, but in 1916 he told Rankin that he and French had decided to place it on the pedestal of the statue, believing the Get-

tysburg Address and Second Inaugural ample for the walls.[78] Three years later, when the statue was about to be installed, he reassured Rankin that the Farewell Address would appear on one side of the pedestal, with, on the other, the text of Lincoln's moving letter to Mrs. Bixby, who had lost her five sons in the Union cause.[79] The Commission of Fine Arts overruled him, however, on the grounds that the Springfield address and the Bixby letter were not "among the classics of the English language."[80] Sheepishly, French admitted, "[I]nscriptions attract undue attention and distract the attention of the beholder from the main subject in the case of statuary."[81]

Besides the two addresses, the one other inscription that was permitted in the memorial hall is the dedicatory inscription on the rear wall above the statue. It was carved at the time of the memorial's dedication in 1922:

IN THIS TEMPLE
AS IN THE HEARTS OF THE PEOPLE
FOR WHOM HE SAVED THE UNION
THE MEMORY OF ABRAHAM LINCOLN
IS ENSHRINED FOREVER.

Composed by Bacon's friend, art critic Royal Cortissoz, in April 1919, when the dedication was first planned, the inscription captures several ideas at the heart of the memorial's ideological content. Because the inscription was contested, its ideas, unlike those behind the building's other features, were made explicit.[82] "TEMPLE" specifies Bacon's prototype and captures the sacredness the memorial's builders imputed to it. In "PEOPLE," Cortissoz sought "to affirm the alliance between Lincoln and the people . . . the deep and tender tie between them" that explains "our love of his memory." Use of the singular implies that all citizens of the United States form an organic unity, which, though temporarily divided, remained unsevered. For all Americans, North and South, not just Unionists, the inscription suggests, Lincoln saved the Union, and not as a mere political entity but as a spiritual compact. "HEARTS" underlines this. "FOREVER" captures the eternity and transcendence of that Union. There is no mention of emancipation or human liberty and no questioning of who precisely the People are—who is included and who is not. The People is an abstraction, and Union is the governing idea of the memorial. The inscription is a succinct expression of the memorial's dedication to the idea of reunion; both it and the building embody in stone the ideal Lincoln sketched in his Gettysburg Address.

In spring 1922, when the inscription was about to be carved, the Commission of Fine Arts considered it, and Charles Moore, especially, took exception. With other purists, chiefly classically educated Harvard men, he objected to calling the memorial a temple. Cortissoz leapt to the defense of his wording, and, in deference to his office, President Harding was invited to mediate the argument. Harding was a notoriously clumsy wordsmith, though, as H. L. Mencken never tired of observing.[83] Enraged at a change Harding proposed, Cortissoz demanded that the inscription be used as he had written it or discarded altogether. The diplomatic Bacon defended the inscription to Taft, who arranged to have it carved, unchanged, before the dedication. Some, however, were never reconciled

to it. Moore was one of these; his friend William DeLancey Howe called it "that poor, cheap, sentimental, erroneous, disfiguring inscription." In the 1930s, the two led an unsuccessful campaign to remove it.[84]

APPROACHES

Although the Lincoln Memorial itself was under construction, its surroundings were not, and by 1915 the general scheme for West Potomac Park shown in the McMillan Plan needed to be given definite form. The Commission of Fine Arts addressed the question of the approaches to the memorial, with Olmsted naturally taking the lead. The size and shape of the reflecting basin and the width of the allée between the lines of trees flanking it received most attention. Olmsted, again emphasizing the parklike character of the grounds, favored a bucolic arrangement of grassy banks lining the basin and lines of trees raised several feet above these. Cass Gilbert wanted to see a more formal treatment suiting the zone between "two great monuments," and his point of view prevailed with the commission.[85] Because these matters impinged on his design of the memorial, Bacon was consulted on them but not directly involved. Based on comparison with the *bassins* of French formal gardens, the commissioners agreed that the basin—Olmsted preferred "canal"—should be 160 feet wide; and the avenue between the trees, twice that.[86] They wanted to dig the cross-arm of the basin shown in the McMillan Plan in line with Twenty-first Street (see Fig. 3.28), but Bacon, gravitating as usual to the simple solution, thought eliminating the cross-arm would cause the basin to "gain in scale" and "form a more appropriate link between the Washington Monument and the Doric architecture of the Lincoln Memorial."[87] The art commission took his advice and decided to extend the pool to a point slightly west of the one Bacon had considered, closer to the memorial's "great circle." The commissioners, however, decided to landscape the grounds in such a way that the arm could be dug later if it seemed desirable. The world war intervened, however, and the reflecting basin was not excavated until 1919–20. At that time the question of the cross-arm came up again. Cass Gilbert defended it eloquently, basing himself on a different reading of scale from Bacon's; but the cross-arm was never dug, for the presence of the temporary government buildings along the basin, discussed later, prevented it.[88]

Discussions like these showed the Commission of Fine Arts that the members could not be their own architects and debate every feature of West Potomac Park. They decided to consult with an outside expert, and, when William E. Parsons, of Chicago, turned them down, they retained Clarence E. Howard, a specialist in city planning known for his work at the lush Panama-Pacific Exposition in San Francisco, of 1912. Bacon came to regard Howard, even more than Olmsted, as a nuisance and a threat to his design for the memorial. As we have seen, he first skirmished with them in the fall of 1915 over a plan to drop by seven feet the grade of the "great circle" around the memorial. That proposal was quashed, but soon another appeared—a plan by Howard for a rectangular setting for the memorial, something Bacon himself had considered but dismissed long before. That December, he persuaded the Commission of Fine Arts to accept his scheme for a circular ring road, narrowed to sixty feet and built on the higher level he favored. The outer of the two circular roads would be replaced by a path through the trees. Howard did not like this scheme; nor did one of the art commissioners, architect Thomas Hastings, of the prominent Beaux Arts architectural firm Carrère & Hastings. When the commission next met, in January 1916, Hastings sketched an elaborate rectangular scheme for the memorial, cross-axial in the Beaux Arts manner, with stepped viewing platforms, fountains or statuary, and a concourse surrounding the memorial with dual carriageways. On the basis of this sketch, the commission instructed Howard to prepare detailed studies for both circular and rectangular settings. Bacon countered with drawings of his own circular scheme. Howard's rectangular scheme (Fig. 4.16) would have emphasized the memorial's main front, especially the corners, more than Bacon's circular one (Fig. 4.17), leaving the rear spacious and the roadways less crowded. But this would have cost Bacon his stepped watergate and viewing platform beside the river, the one survival from McKim's original open scheme. Moreover, Howard's and Hastings's elaborate concourse across the front would have been expensive and distracting, especially from views of the statue. They imagined a New York–style Beaux Arts urban plaza; Bacon, an island or acropolis in a park. The meeting in May 1916 at which

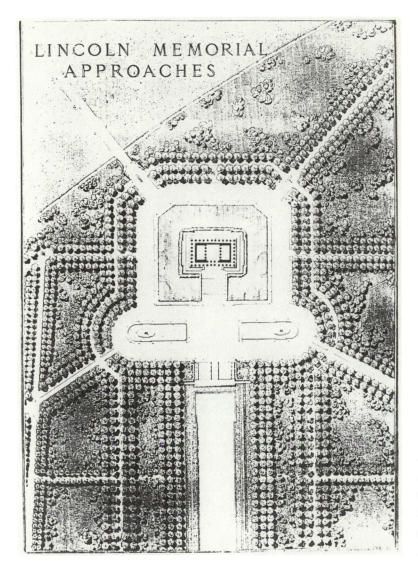

LINCOLN MEMORIAL
APPROACHES

Fig. 4.16. Clarence E. Howard. Alternate plan for approaches to Lincoln Memorial, May 25, 1916. (National Archives and Records Administration, RG 66)

the rival schemes were debated finally accepted Bacon's scheme and allowed work on the memorial's pink granite steps, platforms, and terrace wall to proceed.

FRUSTRATION AND DELAY

After mid-1917, construction activity on the memorial slowed, causing Bacon and members of the Lincoln Memorial Commission to wonder whether they would ever see the monument finished. Bacon was growing frustrated at the unfavorable terms of his contract with the government, what he viewed as unwarranted intrusion on his design by fellow artists, and the arrogance and lack of sympathy of some government officials. When French chided him two years later, "I hear you have made half a million out of the Lincoln Memorial!!!" he exploded:

· PLAN OF APPROACHES TO LINCOLN MEMORIAL ·

Fig. 4.17. Henry Bacon. Plan of approaches to Lincoln Memorial, January 14, 1916. (Henry Bacon Collection, Wesleyan University Library, Special Collections & Archives)

Of all the works I have ever engaged in, this Memorial has been the most unprofitable financially. It is over eight years since I started on the drawings, the Government does not allow my travelling expenses to Washington, which have been on an average, I should say, once every ten days for the eight years, the cost of the drawings and models has been abnormally high, furthermore the red tape and officiousness of some of the bureaucrats in Washington has been incalculable to my temper, and finally I wish to have nothing more to do with any Government work whatever under present conditions. . . . The total commission I will receive will be less than $150,000, the larger portion of which has been spent in drawings, models and supervision. Selah![89]

Bacon's dedication to the project was unquestionable. In 1918, a comparatively slow year on the project, he went to Washington thirty-two times, normally for one day, traveling by overnight sleeper to and from New York at his own expense.[90] Despite his famous tact, his personal relations with some collaborators, especially certain of the army engineer-officers, were strained. His nephew, who worked for a period on the project, called the engineer-officer Captain O'Connor "an SOB,"[91] and tension can be sensed in several exchanges between Bacon and Colonel C. S. Ridley, who was in charge of the site from 1917 to 1921, a difficult period.

In April 1917, the United States went to war with Germany and its allies. Although the project of building the memorial was nominally military and not officially curtailed by the emergency, the contractor was civilian and so ran short of men and materials. Had the administration in office been more determined to see the project through to completion, the pace of work might have quickened, but, with Wilson in the White House, that was not the case. Signs of a slowdown on the site can be detected as early as August 1917, when the Fuller Company was permitted to stop filing monthly progress reports and documentary photographs. The few photos and reports submitted thereafter show how irksomely slow progress was. It did not help that the winter of 1917—18 was unusually severe in Washington, and work on pouring the memorial's concrete approaches stopped

entirely at the end of December, until warmer weather allowed it to continue, and the company was given an extension of its contract date to complete the approaches past March 15, 1918. Real progress was not, in fact, seen on the site until well after the armistice of November 1918; even then, work slowed to a crawl until spring 1919 because of a postwar carpenters' strike. This and another strike of steelworkers, which had little effect because not much steel was used in the structure (and this, early on), were the only ones that affected the project. The memorial site itself was not a "union shop."[92]

The war did affect the memorial's environs, however, in a way that became practically permanent. Two colossal, utilitarian ranges of three-story concrete blocks, faced with stucco, were built in Potomac Park, between B Street (Constitution Avenue) and the muddy trench that would become the reflecting basin, to house the Navy Department and the munitions branch of the War Department for the duration of the war. Catching wind in early 1918 of the plan for these behemoths, Cass Gilbert prophesied accurately and gloomily that the buildings, once erected, would not be budged quickly.[93] Out of loyalty to the war effort, he and his fellow commissioners did not object publicly to their erection, but at war's end Glenn Brown mounted a campaign, in which the fine art and memorial commissioners joined, to banish the "obtrusively ugly and brutal" structures from the Mall.[94] As Gilbert had predicted, though, they survived, to be greatly enlarged early in the Second World War by the addition of similar "tempos" south of the basin, joined to the

Fig. 4.18. View from top of Washington Monument, probably during Second World War, of government "tempos" to either side of the reflecting basin. (Collection of Commission of Fine Arts. Photo: author)

original group by catwalks spanning the pool (Fig. 4.18). Similar structures were shoehorned, crosswise, between the mound of the Washington Monument and the transverse pool (or Rainbow Pool), east of the main basin. The *W.P.A. Guide to Washington*, in its 1942 edition, counted no fewer than ten wings on the Navy Department and eight on the Munitions Building, calling the buildings "crowded" and "factorylike" and voicing a hope that they would soon be demolished. The Department of Defense had too much power in postwar Washington for that to happen, however, and the last tempos on the Mall

were not removed until 1970, making way for the building of Constitution Gardens before the national Bicentennial.[95] Photographs like that in Figure 4.18 show how fragile is the illusion of the McMillanized Mall. It can be maintained only when everyday material conditions are carefully kept at bay.

The spring of 1919 saw construction on the memorial going again at full tilt. Guérin's murals were hung in the side chambers in March, and, that summer, the upper terrace and granite retaining wall were finished and the floor of the central chamber was reinforced to carry the weight of the enlarged statue. Dedicating the memorial in the fall seemed possible. The date kept being moved back, however. Only in May 1920 did French and the Piccirillis finish work on the statue, and, even then, French was aghast at the statue's appearance. His daughter reported melodramatically:

> Dan climbed the steps of the Memorial almost with bated breath. . . . As he mounted the steps he saw the head of the statue first. It had a strange and startled appearance. He hurried a little, with a new, wild pang of apprehension at his heart. There was something wrong. Terribly wrong. It had never looked like this in the studio. The solar prints hadn't looked like this. The face looked flat and white and frightened. Almost grotesque. And the knees loomed up large and white, looking out of proportion to the rest of the figure. Dan was appalled. . . .
>
> And then with a heavy heart, he realized what it was. It was the lighting. . . . The sunlight, coming through the columns to the east, reflected on the statue from the light floor so strongly as to counteract entirely the light that came from the ceiling above. . . . [This cast] all the shadows in reverse. The reflecting basin of water . . . caught the sunlight on its shimmering surface and added to the terrific glare that hurled itself upwards and into the Memorial.[96]

The problem is easy to explain. In the studio, a sculptor has light fall on his statue from above, usually at a raking angle; here, most light came from in front and below. Had Bacon's original design for a closed memorial hall been followed, with glass skylights and a monumental but relatively narrow entrance, more ideal conditions would have been obtained. When the decision was made to widen the entrance substantially and fit the skylights with translucent marble instead of glass, light entering from the top and front was reversed in intensity; the murals in the side chambers became hard to see, and far too much light fell on the statue from the front. Elbert Peets, a sensitive observer, reported in 1925: "I could not easily read the statue or feel the disposition of masses and the relative position of planes and projections"; inside, "[t]he principal source of light was back of me. I thus lost all but the fringes of shadow, and . . . the concentration of light which you get when you have a tangential view of an illuminated surface."[97] French agonized over the problem long after the memorial was dedicated.[98] He had photos taken of the face of his statue, wraithlike as it appeared and as it should have looked if lit from above and at a raking angle (Fig. 4.19). Before the dedication, he tinted the statue, hoping at least to soften the problem; later, he had Bacon experiment with replacing some of the marble ceiling panels with glass. All this was to no avail. In 1926 Congress, with Republican majorities, heeded French's repeated appeals and voted funds to have an up-to-date system of artificial lighting installed in the memorial. At the same time, experiments were conducted in floodlighting the exterior, a fad of the 1920s (Fig. 4.20). Finally, the statue's appearance satisfied the fastidious French. The lights installed in 1927, concealed behind unobtrusive metal louvers in the ceiling and kept on even during daytime, operated until the early 1990s, when the system was updated.[99]

Dedicating the memorial was delayed until 1922 mainly because the foundations of the approach steps and decks and of the wall that

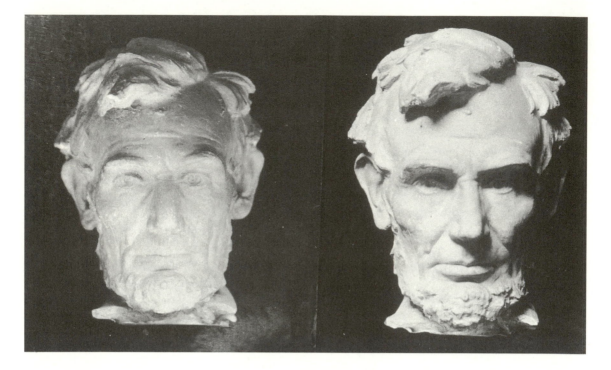

Fig. 4.19. D. C. French. Plaster model of head of Lincoln statue as seen in natural light (left) and as French wished it to be lit (right). (Collection of Commission of Fine Arts. Photo: author)

retained the upper terrace were found to be sinking.[100] Originally, these were "floated" or "rafted" on spread-slab foundations, not carried by piles to bedrock like those of the memorial itself. The intention was to save money, particularly since in 1916, when funds were appropriated to build the wall and approaches, the country was readying itself for war, and labor and materials were in short supply. Everyone connected with the project hoped that spread-slab foundations would prove adequate for these. Some settling of the ground was to be expected, but by 1919 the rate of settlement under the terrace wall had the engineers gasping.[101] When it continued,

though reluctant again to delay the dedication, already pushed back to spring 1920, they recommended that the wall and approaches be anchored to bedrock, like the memorial itself. But the country was in a troubled state with strikes, inflation, and the Red Scare; another presidential election loomed; and the Democratic Congress remained unsympathetic to the project. In spring 1920 it denied a request for $100,000 to grade and pave the roads around the memorial, and Taft believed that the hostility to the project still evident in Congress "stem[med] in large part from our choice of Yule marble."[102] After the election that November, which put Republican Warren Harding in the White House and gave party conservatives a majority in Congress, Bacon and Colonel C. S. Ridley, of the Office of Public Buildings and Grounds, advised the memorial commission to request the funds needed

Fig. 4.20. View of floodlit Lincoln Memorial from the northeast, probably late 1920s. (Collection of Commission of Fine Arts. Photo: author)

to underpin the foundations, cannily tagged an "appropriation required for the completion of the Lincoln Memorial."[103]

An appropriation of $345,720, to bring the memorial's total cost to $2,957,000, was passed in March 1921, and a contract for the underpinning was signed in June. By this time, damage to the retaining wall, the deck of the terrace, and the main steps was extensive. Much of the eight-inch-thick concrete deck of the terrace had to be removed and replaced. A thousand cubic feet of granite in the wall and walks were damaged beyond repair, and four times that amount had to be removed and

reset. The job of underpinning was cumbersome and dangerous. The periphery of the barely completed memorial had to be torn up; existing concrete columns below the steps and terrace, shored up with massive timbers; access pits, dug between existing footings; and shafts, angled down from these pits to align with the footings and turn and drop vertically for forty to sixty feet to bedrock. The shafts, less than three by five feet in section, were dug by hand, a job the discomfort of which in Washington's hot, humid summer can be imagined. When each shaft met solid rock, it was inspected and filled with concrete, and the timbers were removed to create a monolithic pier. To provide lateral bracing, horizontal reinforcing struts were inserted between the memorial's foundation wall, the columns under the deck, and the terrace wall. A slightly different method was followed below the steps and platforms of the approaches. Here, a grid of steel I beams was inserted at the feet of existing concrete uprights, and from there, two-by-four-foot concrete piers were sunk to bedrock. Damaged concrete, stone, and paving were replaced, and portions of the cobblestone paving of the lower terraces removed and reset. The work was performed so efficiently, however, that the dedication was rescheduled for May 30, 1922.

The Republican-dominated Congress released the funds, refused by the Democratic Congress in 1920, to finish the memorial's surroundings and the roads around it. By dedication day, the ring road was ready, as were Twenty-third Street, meeting it from the north, and the diagonal drives from the northeast and southeast (named, since then, after Bacon and French, respectively). Neither Arlington Memorial Bridge nor the entrance to Rock Creek Drive had been begun. These were completed by about 1932, and the statuary at their entrances was added later.[104] Landscaping of the memorial's main front and along the basin was also complete (Fig. 4.21). Only mature plants were used within the great circle of the memorial because the building was to look ageless, but finding enough of these proved a problem, even though parks and gardens in the Washington area were scoured for the best examples.[105] As a result, the other fronts were left until later to plant. Geometrically clipped hedges flanked the main stairs and terraces; elsewhere, the landscaping was marked by "easy formality," with evergreen species such as yew, boxwood,

holly, and southern magnolia (*Magnolia grandiflora*) used to signify heroism and set the memorial off to advantage in all seasons. When dedicated, the snow-white memorial seemed to be living in a Platonic world of its own.

Attention was given earlier, at several points, to dualities between tradition and modernity and between classicism and Americanism that the memorial embodied. When the building was completed, its critics tended to divide between those who were delighted by its traditionalism and those who felt disappointed by its failure to realize their aims for new and native forms of aesthetic expression. Critical response was highly polarized, in fact, leaving little room for objective commentary. And, since this was not just any monument, but the national memorial to the much-loved Lincoln, aesthetic and patriotic responses tended to mix quite freely and to intensify the feelings expressed. On one side were American idealists and artistic traditionalists who, as they had when the design was presented in 1911–12, saw the memorial's pristine classicism as perfectly expressing the transcendence they attributed to American history and government and, in particular, to Lincoln. The *Washington Post*, ignoring the controversies of a decade before, called the end of the Mall the "predestined site" for the memorial and said its isolation typified "the eminent and isolated position Lincoln occupies in our history."[106] For Grace Phelps of the *New York Tribune*, "There is not an unnecessary line, not a fault in proportion. Line and mass combine to make . . . the unity that is perfec-

Fig. 4.21. The Lincoln Memorial from the northeast, dedication day, May 30, 1922. (Library of Congress, Division of Prints and Photos. LC-USZ62-58706

tion."[107] The *Christian Science Monitor* said the "mass of stone" expressed "an ideal in universal language."[108] More extreme, still, was the response of architect Electus D. Litchfield, who told the 1922 convention of the American Institute of Architects that "truly under the providence of God" had Bacon and his collaborators "built a memorial—a shrine—worthy of that greatest American and of the place that his character holds in the hearts of the American people."[109] Litchfield's panegyric was uttered during a noctural ceremony in May 1923, in which the AIA, for only the third time in its history, awarded Bacon its Gold Medal for his achievement in

the memorial. The ceremony, which incorporated eerie floodlighting and included a Wagnerian torchlit procession in which the honor party was towed to the memorial on a barge along the reflecting basin, was itself an expression of the otherworldliness imputed to the memorial and Lincoln (Fig. 4.22).[110]

Not everyone agreed that the design should be adulated in these terms, however. As in 1911–12, some still nursed reservations or outright dislike toward it but expressed their feelings in measured tones, for the Republican reign of the twenties was a period of ultrapatriotism, and they did not wish to be heard detracting from what immediately became a national icon. Some objections were subtle; others, thoroughgoing. Glenn Brown later expressed regret that Bacon had chosen not to execute Charles McKim's design for a trans-

Fig. 4.22. Pageant at the Lincoln Memorial for the presentation of the Gold Medal of the AIA to architect Henry Bacon, May 18, 1923. (Library of Congress, Division of Prints and Photos. LC-USZ62-58280)

parent open portico to Lincoln;[111] and the architect and specialist in modern Gothic, Ralph Adams Cram, praised the design as "absolutely right in form" but unsuitable in style.[112] One who, true to form, did not whisper his doubts was Louis Sullivan. In virtually the last passage he wrote, he passed bitter, resigned judgment on the Lincoln Memorial and the state of the architectural profession that produced it: "Architecture, be it known, is dead. Let us therefore lightly dance upon its grave, strewing roses as we glide. Indeed let us gather, in procession, in the night, in the rain, and make soulful, fluent, epicene orations to the living dead we neuters eulogize."[113] For Sullivan, an organicist and vitalist with roots in nineteenth-century architectural "realism," the memorial was a footnote to the detestable academic classicism of the World's Columbian Exposition, which had dashed his hopes to see emerge new, living, American forms of architectural expression. Sullivan's disciple Frank

Lloyd Wright echoed his *Lieber Meister.* Using the rhetoric for the memorial that had formed in modernist circles in Chicago in 1911–13, Wright never tired of mocking its Graeco-Romanism. "[D]epravity," he said, "sees a Greek temple as [a] fitting memorial to Abraham Lincoln. He is the Greek antithesis. Nothing is Greek about his life or work or thought."[114] In the twenties, Lewis Mumford was just embarking on his long career as a critic of art and society. For him, the memorial was a metaphor for a turn-of-the-century politics he reviled:

> In the Lincoln Memorial . . . one feels not the living beauty of our American past, but the mortuary air of archaeology. The America that Lincoln was bred in, the homespun and humane and humorous America that he wished to preserve, has nothing in common with the sedulously classic monument that was erected to his memory. Who lives in that shrine, I wonder—Lincoln, or the men who conceived it: the leader who beheld the mournful victory of the Civil War, or the generation that took pleasure in the mean triumph of the Spanish-American exploit, and placed the imperial standard in the Philippines and the Caribbean?[115]

The political terms in which Mumford framed his critique form a bridge between prewar Progressivism, which had died in the war, and the renewed Populism of the thirties, when similar ideas resurfaced amid economic hardship. The Lincoln Memorial found itself in a different cultural world than the one in which it had been begun before the war. It was already a sacred relic. Almost no living Americans could remember the Civil War or Lincoln at first hand; he was at most a distant memory, available for still greater idealization and symbolism. The controversies around building his memorial now seemed distant and irrelevant. It was simply there, beyond question, and possible to experience as a pleasing (or displeasing) aesthetic object and tourist destination. It flavored the ideal air of the Mall, which was recast between the wars in McMillan-like terms. In a time, such as Harding's in the early twenties, of extreme patriotism and isolationism, it was tempting to idealize America and everything about it. In one way, the memorial came into its own at such a time. Yet the classical aesthetic and respect for tradition it embodied were under attack from Art Deco and other forms of modernism, in a period of still more determined modernity than that before the war. In the twenties, it was easy to forget how the memorial had dramatized tensions between Progressives and standpatters and between artistic traditionalists and modernists.

CHAPTER 5

The Memorial in American Life

LITTLE THOUGHT SEEMS TO have been given, in advance, to the uses the Lincoln Memorial would serve. Almost the only allusions to use found in the official record present it as a house of solitary or nearly solitary meditation. Yet the builders must have had in mind some role for the memorial in public ritual. What else explains its stagelike design, frontal character, and formal approaches? But if they had public uses in mind, the artists and planners felt no need to articulate them. Why?

Sometimes the purposes a building is to fulfill are considered too obvious to need specifying. That may be the case here, for, despite minor differences among them, the Lincoln Memorial commissioners, the competing architects, and the fine art commissioners shared essentially common views on national symbolics and ceremonial. Perhaps it went without saying that official rituals would be held at the memorial to mark Lincoln's Birthday, Memorial Day, and other major national holidays.[1] Though unspoken, such an intention seems likely. In addition, the memorial's planners and supporters viewed the very act of building it, apart from using it, as an act of homage to Lincoln and the Union. Simply by building the memorial, they believed, they were discharging the nation's moral debt to the slain president. And since the artists and architects, who largely promoted the project, framed it almost exclusively in aesthetic terms, for them it hardly mattered what the memorial was used for provided it was built. It was a piece of patriotic urbanism. In any event, the memorial's planners *could* not anticipate all the uses to which it would be put because, in large measure, these emerged from later historical developments. These uses need to be viewed against the shifting background of collective American life in the twentieth century.

Whether public or private, all acts performed at the memorial are forms of ritual, defined by one writer as "action wrapped in a web of symbolism."[2] This is true whether we are speaking of meditating in solitude on the address tablets, photographing friends or family in front of the statue, attending a Memorial Day ceremony on the steps, or participating in a vigorous mass demonstration. Widely viewed as above the political fray, the Lincoln Memorial is an example of what Pierre Nora calls a "memory-site"—a phenomenon, not always a place, that marks and celebrates collective, usually national values, said to be shared by all who make up the collectivity.[3] Yet ritual, which we associate with churches, kings, and tribes, is not supposed to matter anymore; we are supposedly too modern, rational, and functional to take it seriously. That, of course, is not true: we have

144

only to think of some ways in which ethnicity and religion have determined recent events in history. And, in fact, cultural anthropologists have attended a great deal to symbolism and ritual in recent decades, as promises of liberation through modernization have faded.[4] They stress the crucial role ritual plays in promoting cohesion in communities, whether African tribes or postwar European democracies. In modern America, civil religion has developed patriotic symbolism and insignia to a high pitch, as reciting the Pledge of Allegiance and practicing flag etiquette, more elaborated than in many countries, exemplify. Ritual is alive and well. Typically, it has been viewed as mainly conservative in intent, designed to strengthen and safeguard established values of loyalty and nationality.[5] But ritual can also help transform values and, even when not overtly revolutionary, ease the sense of disturbance brought on by sudden change.[6] At the Lincoln Memorial, public ceremonial and ritual have most often underlined stabilizing, conservative values; on the other hand, the most dramatic, memorable uses of the monument, especially ones connected with demanding civil rights, have been transformative in character. That idea will be pursued.

As behavior that links us over time and tends to be repeated, ritual overlaps processes of remembering. Like ritual, the pasts we construct bind us to larger communities, which in part cohere through sharing memories. Public memory is never neutral, a simple laying hold of what is already there. Rather, what and how we choose to remember as communities justify and give energy, direction, and meaning to present choices and actions. They help

shape "agendas" for future action. Nor is memory random and unmotivated. Like ritual, memory can be propounded either by official agents, especially the nation-state, or by smaller-scale communities lower on the social hierarchy, less concerned to maintain conditions as they are. John Bodnar, a social historian, emphasizes that public memory, like ritual, tends to be conservative when it originates in the state or a social upper crust.[7] That is largely true of the official ceremonial, sponsored by the government or by the GAR or like bodies, that is held on major national holidays at the Lincoln Memorial. Generally, such ritual promotes values—patriotism, self-sacrifice, awe, and so on—that cement participants' loyalty to the state. They support what may be called civil religion.[8] In these cases, public memory tends to play a reassuring, stabilizing role by reminding participants of events and heroes that official memory has cast as representing fixed values and loyalties. Where memory and ritual emerge from more popular settings, however—ethnic or religious communities are examples—vernacular culture may work to more radical ends. Chapter 1 presents examples of both in the conservative, or classical, and the populist portrayals of Lincoln after his death. In the period that opened with the dedication of his memorial, both images of Lincoln reemerged, and both types of rituals were practiced.

PRIVATE VISITATION

When the Lincoln Memorial was being planned and built, we saw, emphasis was put on private visiting and contemplation. Here, this will be considered before the monument's often more dramatic public uses. From the beginning, the Lincoln Memorial was a popular and symbolically charged destination for informal visiting by Washingtonians, tourists, diplomats, and guests of the government. Fifty-five thousand visits were logged in April 1923, a year after the memorial was dedicated, suggesting (since, in that period, tourism reached its peak in the spring) a total of one-third to one-half million visits for the year.

Beginning in 1929, when the memorial was permanently floodlit, visiting it at night became possible and popular. Floodlighting, as vignettes of early Hollywood premieres show us, was one of the many crazes of the racy twenties, and General Electric saw the new Lincoln Memorial as a conspicuous place to advertise its wares. Experiments with floodlighting the exterior conducted in 1927–29 were controversial, however, because the effects were garish and the Commission of Fine Arts, following Bacon's express wish—he had died in 1924—wanted the memorial floodlit subtly.[9] A balance was found, and opening the memorial to visitors after dark began in 1929. This was a welcome innovation in a city of nine-to-five office workers whose homes were often uncomfortably hot, and, even today, the Lincoln Memorial is reputed to be the most romantic spot in nighttime Washington.

The new automobility, a taste for spectacle, and the growth of travel and tourism in the consumerist twenties help account for the stunning success of the Lincoln Memorial with visitors. This is another instance of the paradox explored earlier: that the monument's genteel, idealized traditionalism was only made possible by apparently antithetical forces of modernity, forces that intensified with a vengeance in the Roaring Twenties. But modernity set up conflict in the visitor's experience of the memorial that is felt even today. It arises from colliding emotions of sacred awe and mundane irritation when one tries to experience the awe in the midst of a crowd. The effect is made worse today by the thunder of jets dropping, every sixty seconds or so, toward the main north-south runway of Reagan National Airport, across the river to the south. Only modernity, in the form of mass tourism, made visiting the memorial possible for large numbers; yet the numbers weakened the profundity of the experience some visitors had. On the other hand, it is remarkable how hushed and apparently moved most visitors become as they enter the echoing, cavernous memorial, especially the first time. Many experience Lincoln's memorial as a "threshold" or liminal space, where they move beyond the limits of everyday life and perception and contact higher, spiritual realities.[10] We have seen the care with which Bacon and his collaborators orchestrated the design to foster that experience. They were wise, in particular, to set the features that require the most sustained attention, the address tablets, behind column screens in the dim side chambers.

A sense of the sacred derived from American civil religion pervades most early descriptions of the memorial. Edgar R. Harlan, Iowa state historian, reported to Bacon that, during the dedication ceremony in May 1922, "By sheer accident if not through divine guidance,

I stood at the western end of the [pool] . . . and rose with you into a plane of spiritual elation I shall not ask providence to grant again."[11] Another who had a liminal experience but was jarred from it was Daniel Chester French's niece Mary P. Webster, who visited the shrine on Memorial Day 1924. So moved by this first visit that she copied Lincoln's addresses word for word, she could barely tolerate her fellow visitors' crass behavior: "There were some twenty-five persons in the Temple, most of them tourists—Americans. Four of them stood in a row just in front of the statue, in smiling array, a family group waiting to be snapped by a friend's camera—utterly unconscious of the impertinence of such a juxtaposition, mindful only of themselves and their sightseeing." "[T]he great monument" enshrining Lincoln's words, she thought more impressive than the dome of the U.S. Capitol, which represented only the "petty wrangles of the reactionary politicians," a sentiment often heard during the "normalcy" of the Harding-Coolidge period, especially after the activism of Teddy Roosevelt's and the idealism of Wilson's. Of Lincoln's words, she wondered, *Have our ears become atrophied so that we no longer hear their counsel?"*[12]

Miss Webster's reaction can be dismissed as the snobbism of a solemn daughter of Transcendentalist New England; and the civil religiosity induced by the Lincoln Memorial, cynically explained away—as, to a degree, earlier chapters have—as high-minded evasion of unpleasant features of American history and life. What I am attending to here, however, is the way her response juxtaposes reverence for history and tradition with dismay at modernity. It evokes a collision of cultural worlds that many experienced during the twenties, widely considered the first fully modern decade, when popular culture definitively supplanted traditional and elite custom in setting the tone of American life.[13] The introduction of radio, the maturing of the car culture, advances in cinema, the beginnings of civil aviation, and the adoption of seductive new fashions in dance, dress, and music, in what Fitzgerald called the "Jazz Age"—a general adulation of machinery and modernity—changed American life for good. Clearly, Miss Webster was out of sympathy with the changes. Not for her the mass tourism of buses and Kodak cameras. Beneath her disdainful, undemocratic hauteur we sense cultural panic and powerlessness.

She noted with distaste the custom of photographing friends and family members at the foot of the statue, a ritual commonly practiced today (Fig. 5.1). We often have ourselves or groups of which we are a part photographed in memorable, "important" places, as if to establish a link between ourselves and the numinous presence sensed there. The Lincoln Memorial, in addition, allows us to be photographed with someone important—Lincoln, as the statue remembers him. Technically, the statue makes a suitably outsize backdrop to a group, and its members appear to advantage facing into the light. While made possible by up-to-date technology, the practice embodies ancient ritual.

Tension between tradition and modernity, which Miss Webster's comments evoke, resurfaced in the critical responses to the

Lincoln Memorial cited at the end of chapter 4. Indeed, that tension and the symbolic significance imputed to Lincoln so dominated early commentary that hardly anyone stopped objectively to study how the memorial functioned in a bodily, material way to guide visitors' behavior. One who did so was Elbert Peets, a young landscape architect destined to have a significant impact on Washington, and he did not much like what he saw inside.[14] The building's role in the monumental civic plan as terminal of the Mall, he pointed out, forced distressingly wide, shallow proportions on its interior. The large frontal opening caused the statue to be caught sight of in an unfortunate way and then practically pushed into viewers' faces as they entered. He studied the responses of some tourists who had just arrived by bus. The harshly lit statue of Lincoln, he observed,

> did not hold them long. In the unfavorable light the statue could not compete with the attraction of the dark rooms behind the colonnades. Before they had been in the hall twenty seconds, most of the crowd had turned and discovered one of the inscriptions. And the moment they saw it, they moved toward the columns and took their stance where they could see the first panel. I could sense the relief with which they turned away from the statue, not very expressive at best and quite meaningless to them, and began to read the familiar words of the inscriptions. . . . The result is that half a minute after a group of people enter the Memorial, they are all standing with their backs or shoulders toward Lincoln—

which is as if at the king's coronation everyone ran to the windows to watch the fire engines go by.

Peets did not much like the "inscription halls," either, and would have preferred having the long inscriptions eliminated altogether: "There is no good reason for mixing up architecture with literature." "The interior of the Lincoln Memorial," he concluded, "is like a play written by a preacher. . . . It is a series of speeches rather than a beautiful dance that has the power to draw crowds of men into its overpowering rhythm."

The most sustained analysis ever written of how the memorial actually effects bodily responses, Peets's critique merits attention. Bacon and French might even have agreed with some of it. We know how conscious French was of problems in lighting his statue, largely the product of the huge entrance door. And, without doubt, the design is weakest where Bacon departed most from the classical temple, which he revered, with its dimly lit cella. But he could not let himself design a literal temple for fear of deifying Lincoln, an extreme he had to avoid at all costs. At a deeper level, Peets was right to observe that the two artists were idealists to the quick, unable to design a sensuously rich interior. In this, they precisely captured the puritanism, descended from Transcendentalism, of turn-of-the-century American official culture and of the way in which Lincoln himself, at Gettysburg, had spiritualized the war, made it a contest of words and ideas, rather than of blood and gore.[15] In this respect, the design is perfectly in tune with what it honors; Peets

Fig. 5.1. Group of tourists being photographed in the Lincoln Memorial, April 1999. The author is fourth from the left. (Photo: author)

missed that. In this context, though, what matters is that he published the only critical, objective analysis of the memorial, refusing both to be cowed by its exalted status as a patriotic icon and to take sides in the stylistic conflict over it.

For many Americans, the private visits to the Lincoln Memorial that left the deepest impression were those they saw in the movies. Especially memorable were the visits of Senator Jefferson Smith, played by Jimmy Stewart, in Frank Capra's film *Mr. Smith Goes to Washington*.[16] Released in 1939, at the end of the New Deal era, as the prospect of war in Europe loomed, the film is a morality play about virtue, national values, and the ability of an individual with integrity to stand against apparently overwhelming odds. Capra called the movie "a ringing statement of America's democratic ideals."[17] Lincoln is the

great hero of Smith, who represents a western state. During a whirlwind tour of the monuments after he arrives in the capital to take his seat, he becomes enthralled with Lincoln's memorial, then not twenty years old. "Mister Lincoln—there he is," Smith gushes. "He's just lookin' straight at you as you come up those steps." In creating a special relationship between his starry-eyed hero and Lincoln as the memorial represents him, Capra both responded to and catalyzed a ritual, which had already developed, of communing with the dead president in the statue. The ritual resonated with many Americans during the Great Depression, as the image of Lincoln as Man of the People, crafted for the birth centennial of 1909, reached its zenith of popularity.[18] Gutzon Borglum was then at work on his pantheon of colossal rock-cut presidential heads, giving Lincoln pride of place, on

Mount Rushmore in South Dakota.[19] This is also when Carl Sandburg was laboring over his herculean, poetically popularized life of Lincoln, on which generations were raised.[20] The populist, pioneering Lincoln came into his own in these years as the leading patriotic symbol of the political Left. American socialists and communists sent a Lincoln Brigade to aid the left-wing government in the Spanish civil war, and at home the Democratic Party under FDR claimed Lincoln's memory as its own, in a startling reversal of political symbolism. During his campaign to be reelected president in 1936, Roosevelt quoted Lincoln as an authority on "liberty" to argue in favor of his populist New Deal programs, which were being attacked by some buiness leaders.[21]

In these years, not surprisingly, the Lincoln Memorial rode a vast wave of popularity. By the late thirties, the annual number of visitors had more than doubled since it was dedicated.[22] One reason was the popular identification with Lincoln; another was the expansion of the federal government's and Washington's role under the New Deal; a third was the fact that fewer Washingtonians than usual could afford to travel away from the city. Visits to the memorial crested in 1937 at just over 1.2 million, dropped slightly, then set a new record, of roughly 1.5 million, in 1940, as the capital prepared for war. Awestruck communion with the metaphorical Lincoln embodied in French's statue had come to represent an accepted individual and cultural practice, giving Jefferson Smith's epiphanic moments a context in "real life." The memorial figures in the film twice. The first time, Smith listens in the side cham-

ber as a young boy, representing naive idealism, reads the Gettysburg Address to his immigrant grandfather and an elderly African-American man; the black man stands at a deferential distance behind the other figures (Fig. 5.2). The second visit occurs at night. Smith has uncovered a plot to divert public funds to nefarious private ends and is being pressed to resign his seat. In nocturnal contemplation of the statue of Lincoln, he finds strength to fight back; one would swear the statue cracks a smile toward him. Inwardly regenerated, Smith returns to the Senate to conduct an exhausting filibuster on the floor, and in the end he is successful.

Jefferson Smith's anguished exchange with the sculpted Lincoln is the most widely circulated example of a cultural topos, well established by 1900 (see chapter 1), of the patriotic American who seeks solace and counsel from the spiritual Lincoln, pleading, "What would you do about . . . ?" or "Father Abraham, help us." The heroically scaled marble statue in the memorial made the ideal place to enact that ritual, in reality and in popular culture. The issue was, which came first—life or art, actual practice or the cinematic use of the memorial? By the 1940s, it was hard to tell. A writer in the *Boston Herald* reported: "In the dark days of the war in 1941–43 . . . thousands of our men in uniform, stopping in Washington for a few hours, rather indifferently climbed the steps of the memorial and then, having stood silently before the fatherly Lincoln and communed, as it were, with him, came down the steps, their shoulders straight, their heads high, and their eyes shining."[23]

Private visits to the Lincoln Memorial con-

tinue to be hugely popular. Though numbers reveal nothing about the depth of visitors' experiences, they give a rough-and-ready idea of how resonant the monument remains. By 1950, visits had reached nearly 2.5 million per year, peaking again in 1966, 1975, and 1976—the year of the Bicentennial—at 4.3 million, a figure matched only once since, in 1987. The practice of communing with, or citing the authority of, the dead Lincoln has never altogether died, though in our more cynical times it tends to be carried off with less obvious sentimentality. The troubled Richard Nixon is said to have made at least one private pilgrimage to the memorial at night for solace during the Watergate crisis, a visit reenacted in the film *Nixon* (Hollywood Pictures, 1995).[24] At a ceremony held at the memorial to mark Lincoln's Birthday in 1974, a few months before he resigned, Nixon likened himself to his Republican predecessor when he observed, "No President in history was more vilified during his time in the presidency than Lincoln."[25]

As Nixon's example suggests, the Lincoln Memorial and its statue still make cameo appearances in contemporary films. Such appearances, we realize, are only illusionistically private, for mass audiences of moviegoers in fact look on. Public or private, however, such episodes establish a compelling type. In Oliver Stone's *JFK* (Warner Brothers, 1991), the memorial and its reflecting basin form the backdrop to the revelations by district attorney Jim Garrison's informant, code-named "X," on the plot to kill President Kennedy.[26] Connecting Kennedy with Lincoln was highly appropriate, though saying this veers off into consideration of the memorial's public significance. A cult of Lincoln had grown up around John F. Kennedy, a cult sharpened by the coincidence of his administration with the sesquicentennial of Lincoln's birth (in 1959) and the centennial of the Civil War, marked in 1961–65. Robert Kennedy, in particular, had a warm place for Lincoln and, to a degree, stage-managed the ceremonial around his brother's funeral in 1963 to emphasize parallels between the two assassinated presidents. These parallels were not lost on American newspaper cartoonists in the days after the assassination (Fig. 5.3).[27] The shootings had occurred almost a century apart, during periods of national crisis. After the funeral, Kennedy's body was taken in formal cortege to Arlington National Cemetery, which had begun (after Robert E. Lee abandoned the grounds) as a Union burial ground. It was car-

ried on the gun carriage that had borne Lincoln's corpse, along a route that circled the Lincoln Memorial before it crossed Arlington Memorial Bridge on its way to a hillside grave at Arlington. The grave is deliberately set on axis with the line of the bridge and the corner of the memorial, beyond. On returning from the cemetery, the Kennedy family stopped before the memorial, at Robert's request, to give family members a moment to gaze up at the statue of Lincoln.[28] In June 1968, his own less formal funeral procession, held at night and attended by crowds holding candles and singing "The Battle Hymn of the Republic," stopped at the Lincoln Memorial to give the temporary residents of "Resurrection City," a protestors' shacktown on the Mall, a chance to pay their last respects.[29] Imagery of Lincoln and the Civil War, in fact, was widely invoked to make sense of the crises of the 1960s and suggest that modern events were guided by Providence. An example is Norman Mailer's account of the March on the Pentagon in October 1967, which likened the protesters to a Civil War army.[30] Stone's sequence in *JFK* alluded to the parallels between Lincoln and Kennedy.

DEDICATION: A MICROCOSM OF AMERICAN LIFE

Though private meditation, solitary or in small groups, was the main use envisioned for the memorial in advance (see Fig. 3.14), its potential as a site for public ritual soon became apparent. We noted that this had likely been assumed but never articulated. Two rituals in particular, the memorial's dedi-

Fig. 5.3. Lincoln Mourning. *Cartoon by Bill Mauldin, originally published in the* Chicago Sun-Times/Daily News, *November 1963. (Reprinted with special permission of the Chicago Sun-Times © 2000)*

cation in 1922 and the ceremony, already described, of conferring the AIA's Gold Medal on Bacon a year later, immediately suggested a public role for the memorial. A reporter who witnessed the Gold Medal pageant (see Fig. 4.22) noted that it demonstrated the setting's potential "for national fetes and spectacles," with the "noble colonnade" as "a background . . . unsurpassed in the world for significant silent drama."[31]

The memorial was dedicated on May 30, 1922 (Fig. 5.4; see Fig. 4.21). Conducted at the highest level of government on the afternoon of Memorial Day, the ceremony drew a crowd, reliably estimated at thirty-five thousand, believed to be the largest in the city's history to that time.[32] The ceremony focused on the presentation of the memorial to the nation by Chief Justice Taft, as chairman of the Lincoln Memorial Commission, and its acceptance and dedication by President Warren G. Harding. Besides these official events, the dedication inadvertently set a trajectory for the powerful role the memorial would later play in unofficial, national symbolics.

Fig. 5.4. Dedication of the Lincoln Memorial. Chief Justice Taft (right) presents the memorial to President Harding (left). Dr. Robert Moton is shown walking at the extreme left. (Library of Congress, Division of Prints and Photos. LC-USZ62-107255)

The dedication was a microcosm of both the promising and the unfortunate in American life. Though focused on a classical temple, it celebrated the futuristic ideal of progress through technology that animated many Americans in the 1920s. Along with the crowds came the headache of parking ten thousand cars, a harbinger of things to come in Potomac Park. The speeches, delivered with classical rhetorical flourish by speakers in striped pants and swallowtail coats, were carried to the ears of the crowds by microphones and loudspeakers (seen on the rooftop in Figure 4.21). The speeches were audible because, though airplanes were allowed to fly over the memorial before and after the ceremony to take aerial photographs, a two-mile boundary on overflight was imposed during official proceedings. The pilot of a commercial plane got the time wrong, however, and flew over the memorial, "with its motor making a hideous noise . . . while the President was speaking"[33]—another hint of things to come. For the first time, the U.S. Navy "broadcasted" the ceremony over two frequencies simultaneously from its stations at Arlington and Anacostia, making its signal available to pioneering amateur radio operators. Since radio's "breakthrough year" was 1922,"[34] the dedication ceremony was on the cutting edge of the new technology. Here, however, modernity was at the service of conservative political and social values.

The dedication was a delicate balancing act requiring tact and diplomacy, a political ritual the politics of which needed disguise. A major national ceremony held on a public holiday six months before a midterm election of Congress, it should be viewed, in part, as a Republican Party rally to honor its founder. Unbounded optimism and self-congratulation, led by a former Republican president and a GOP successor, proclaimed pride at the party's achievements, which at that moment seemed substantial. Having united his formerly fractious party to win the greatest electoral victory in history in 1920, Harding as president was steering a middle course between conservativism and Progressivism, and the country was responding to his brand of "normalcy." It seemed almost a return to conditions under McKinley. America was materially better off and apparently more satisfied than at any time since before the war,

its postwar extremes of violence and hysteria apparently quieted. The scandals that would mar Harding's last year in office and contribute to his early death in 1923 were still far off. Taft and Harding felt there was much to boast of, yet the dedication must not be allowed, too transparently, to appear a party love feast; it should be an event of national rejoicing.

In an unabashedly patriotic and isolationist decade, when phrases like "100 percent Americanism" and "un-American" were bandied about without embarrassment, participants in the dedication draped themselves in Old Glory. Idealism and generality, ignoring actual material conditions, ruled the occasion. Mixing the language of Christian, classical, and secular (civil) religion, Taft presented the memorial to the nation through the intermediary person of Harding (see Fig. 5.4): "Here is a shrine at which all can worship. Here an altar upon which the supreme sacrifice was made in the cause of liberty. Here a sacred religious refuge in which those who love country and love God can find inspiration and repose." Harding responded in the same exalted, nineteenth-century tone: "This memorial, matchless tribute that it is, is less for Abraham Lincoln than for those of us today, and for those who follow after. His surpassing compensation would have been in living, to have his ten thousand sorrows dissipated in the rejoicings of the succeeding half-century." Harding spoke more truth than he realized: the memorial and the occasion *were* more about an idealized version of the war and subsequent American history than about Lincoln and historical reality. The person

155

whose absence from the dedication is most remarkable was Lincoln in his own times, though a proxy appeared in the form of his son Robert Todd Lincoln, now a lawyer and business executive. His absence was intentional. In his address, Taft distinguished between Lincoln the man and "the real Lincoln" that it had taken sixty years to distill. He paralleled the distinction between them to the one between the crude American art of Lincoln's time and the "real conception of art and beauty" at the time of the World's Columbian Exposition. Taft had a point: the inwardly noble but rather ungainly man with the high-pitched voice and stovepipe hat might indeed have felt out of place that afternoon. Not only might he have lowered the social tone, but he might have posed uncomfortable questions about the results of his war and the society it had produced in America. The memorial *was* "less for Abraham Lincoln than for those of us to-day."

For one thing, the dedication, like the memorial's design, avoided reference to any lingering division between the sections. For almost the last possible time, grizzled veterans of the blue and the gray were photographed bowing reverently side by side;[35] and overtly Unionist rhetoric that might rub salt into old wounds was carefully sidestepped. The only triumphalistic note in the impartial occasion was the presentation of colors by the Grand Army of the Republic, but that exception proved the rule. No other references to war and sectional differences were made, either in official rhetoric or in press coverage of the occasion. It helped that memorial ceremonies sponsored by the GAR

had been held in the morning at Arlington and other military cemeteries, and that the usual parade of Union veterans along Pennsylvania Avenue had also taken place that morning, leaving the dedication later to be a demonstration on a national scale of sociologist W. Lloyd Warner's idea that the function of Memorial Day ritual, in small American towns, was to bring diverse and often warring elements of the community into temporary harmony.[36]

On a second matter, the dedication, though it acknowledged Lincoln as Emancipator, set a poor example of relations between the races. An African-American speaker was in the platform party, but he was an ally of the Republican Party and an accommodationist, not a militant spokesman for black interests, such as Marcus Garvey or W. E. B. Du Bois. Dr. Robert Russa Moton was Booker T. Washington's successor as head of Tuskegee Industrial Institute in Alabama and president of the National Negro Business League.[37] He subscribed to Washington's "Atlanta Compromise," articulated in 1895, which declared that African-Americans should defer aspirations for racial equality for the time being in favor of economic progress.[38] Handpicked though he was, Moton gave a speech that harbored serious reservations about the success of American democracy. Using the image of two ships bound for America in 1619–20— the *Mayflower* making for Plymouth and a promised land of religious freedom, and a slaver en route from Africa to Jamestown with its cargo of human cattle—Moton observed that, ever since, two principles had been contending for the soul of America, liberty and bondage, a struggle that was far from over. While he conceded enough to the rhetoric of optimism to admit that American life, generally, had tended in an upward direction, the outcome of the battle of principles was far from clear, and the world waited anxiously for it. Courteous as it was, Moton's speech had been gotten off early in the ceremony, to allow speakers after him time to "correct" him if necessary. Taft and Harding proceeded to distract attention from his point, averring that Lincoln's greatness lay in saving the nation, not emancipating the slaves, an act that, though noble, was but a means to his salvific end of creating "peace and concord" between the two sections, by which they meant whites of the two sections. Apart from including Moton's speech, the proceedings served as a denial of real progress. Other African-Americans in attendance, even prominent ones, were abrasively directed by a marine to a "colored section," dubbed a "Bloc d'Afrique" by a militant black newspaper. Taken to task later for his rudeness, the soldier is reported to have answered, "That's the only way you can handle these damned 'niggers.'"[39] To deepen the bad faith, the colored section did not appear on the official plan of seating.[40] That the dedication ceremony in 1922 would be segregated was to be expected, given that parks and beaches in the District of Columbia were supervised by a cadre of white army engineer-officers drawn mainly from the South.

The ceremony was a microcosm of the strained race relations of its day, marked by the rhetoric of good intentions and the behavior of bigotry. One doubts whether many African-Americans agreed with Harding on the "rejoicings of the succeeding half-century" for, by any objective standard, the period had been a disaster for them, witnessing "the steady—and apparently accelerating—deterioration of the position of the Negro in American life."[41] Relations between blacks and whites, relaxed briefly until 1876 in the South and the 1890s in the North, had gotten steadily worse since 1900 and, after the First World War, as chapter 4 notes, sunk to a new low. Nationwide, the period from 1918 to 1927 saw over four hundred lynchings. During the early twenties, a time marked by extremes of novelty and conservatism, the revived Ku Klux Klan flourished, conducting "night rides"—campaigns of terror and mayhem against nonwhites, immigrants, Catholics, and others its members thought insufficiently "American."[42] Violence and discrimination against African-Americans were the most extreme aspects of a panicky revival of white nativism and widespread resistance to modernity in the period. For none was the postwar period more difficult than black Americans. Back home in the South, they were prey to violence and suffered penury as sharecroppers; migrating to cities in the North and West, they might find jobs but met new forms of poverty and hostility from poor or working-class whites, to whom their presence was a threat. If the black migration of the twenties brought jazz and the Harlem Renaissance, it also brought bigotry, exclusion, and worse.

The insult the dedication of Lincoln's memorial represented to African-Americans was made complete by mainstream newspapers, which hardly mentioned Moton or his speech and, when they did, reported it inaccurately. The *Washington Post*'s lead story of May 31, titled "Harding Lauds Lincoln as Nation's Savior . . . ," said, without naming Moton, "A representative of the race for which the great emancipator did so much likewise lifted his voice in gratitude for the freedom of so many in America from serfdom." On its third page, that same day, the *Post* carried another article, "Freedom to Negro Justified, He Says," which also fails to mention Moton's reservations. African-Americans saw the ceremony differently. The militant *Chicago Defender* said Moton's words fell "on ears closed and deaf to reason" and that Harding's hypocrisy was sufficient to "open" Lincoln's memorial officially but not to "dedicate" it. The editor urged a boycott until "juster and more grateful men come to power and history shall have rebuked offenders against the name of Abraham Lincoln" and uttered a remarkable prophecy: "With song, prayer, bold and truthful speech, with faith in God and country, later on let us dedicate that temple thus far only opened."[43]

THE MEMORIAL IN OFFICIAL AND VERNACULAR RITUAL

The dedication proved to set the tone for both official and vernacular ritual conducted at the memorial thereafter. The distinction is not very precise because all organizations, not just governments, have structure, organization, and politics; all, to a degree, are official. But it serves as a rough-and-ready dividing line between state-sponsored events and others initiated by private, particular groups, even large ones. National celebrations of Lincoln's Birthday and Memorial Day have officially and regularly been marked at the memorial. At one of these, as noted earlier, President Richard Nixon spoke. Such official ceremonial extended the appreciative, grateful rhetoric of the dedication, which played well, generally, to white American audiences between about 1930 and 1965, a period that, as also mentioned, corresponded to the height of Lincoln's popularity as Man of the People. To the "new era of nationalism" that was the thirties and to succeeding decades, he was a powerful symbol.[44] The vernacular uses of the Lincoln Memorial, however, especially those connected with civil rights, are the ones that have most captured the imagination. These, too, are rooted in the dedication, which from the start made of the memorial racially contested ground. Rededicating it as the *Defender* demanded, Scott Sandage argues, was accomplished between 1939 and 1963 in a series of events that deftly employed the monument as site and symbol in a "politics of memory." Exploiting a range of possibilities in the memorial's form and iconography, in the remembered Lincoln, and in American political ideals, protesters challenged the existing political order from within, turning its discourse upon itself to dramatize its internal inconsistencies and contradictions. The essence of the politics of memory was to bring "politics into the temple, but in a way that preserved the temple's holiness and conferred upon them its power as a national site."[45] They appropriated as their own the holiness of Lincoln and his memorial within

Fig. 5.5. Marian Anderson before the statue of Lincoln during her concert on Easter Sunday, 1939. (National Archives, Still Pictures Division, RG 306. Photo: Time-Life)

American civil religion. That is what is suggested by Theodore Horydczak's photo of two African-American children in the memorial, diminutive at the base of the Ionic columns and gazing up hopefully at Father Abraham (see Fig. I).

The appropriation was accomplished especially in Marian Anderson's celebrated concert at the memorial on Easter Sunday of 1939 (Fig. 5.5).[46] Since the world-famous African-American contralto was barred by reason of her race from singing in other large auditoriums in Washington, notably Constitution Hall, the city's premier concert hall, which the Daughters of the American Revolution owned, the organizers of her concert and officials of the National Association for the Advancement of Colored People (NAACP) hit on the idea of having her give an outdoor concert at the Lincoln Memorial to embarrass segregationists and remind Americans of Lincoln's role as Emancipator, which the dedication had singularly neglected. The plan worked better than they imagined. With firm support from Eleanor Roosevelt and Franklin Roosevelt's personal approval, his secretary of the interior, Harold Ickes, made the memorial available for the concert, which included Negro spirituals and, for ironic effect, stirring patriotic anthems. Many who attended the concert spoke of it in religious terms as a "spiritual experience" and a "beautiful awakening." Widely broadcast, the concert attracted the world's attention to the hypocrisy of America's continued tolerance of racial injustice and at the same time suggested a plan of action to bring about change. "With the concert, the civil rights movement began to develop a strategy of mass, symbolic protest that used ritual and appeals to memory to make race a national issue."[47] The most vivid product of that strategy was the March on Washington for Jobs and Freedom, of August 28, 1963, but it was only the largest and most widely publicized of a series of protest events staged at the memorial by the civil rights movement, under the leadership of the NAACP, between 1940 and the late 1960s. For these, says Sandage, a "standardized civil rights protest ritual" was perfected, "using mass rallies instead of pickets, performing patriotic and spiritual music, choos-

ing a religious format, inviting prominent platform guests, self-policing the crowds to project an orderly image, alluding to Lincoln in publicity and oratory, and insisting on using the memorial rather than another site."[48] In short, the events harnessed the authority and rhetoric of official discourse about Lincoln as Savior of the Union for an alternate and dissenting purpose.

The widely televised and publicized march in the summer of 1963 was the event in that series that drew the greatest attention of the white majority of Americans and thus did most to alter popular perceptions of the Lincoln Memorial (Fig. 5.6).[49] Held at a critical moment in the growing national crisis over civil rights, when John F. Kennedy's administration was seeking support from Congress for concerted federal action, the rally is believed to have drawn as many as four hundred thousand participants, making it the largest public gathering ever held in Washington. Like the other rallies, this one had a Baptist religious flavor and emphasized values of fairness and justice with which no American could take issue. The message the march communicated was that the restoration and enforcement of full civil rights for all persons, regardless of skin color, represented reform from within the central American tradition, which the memorial symbolized. The proceedings climaxed in the unforgettable, extemporized peroration Martin Luther King delivered from the memorial platform, incanting "I have a dream" and "Let freedom ring." Echoing Lincoln at Gettysburg, he called the memorial a "hallowed spot" and proclaimed his dream as "deeply rooted in the

Fig. 5.6. Speeches from the platform of the Lincoln Memorial, March on Washington, August 28, 1963. (National Archives, Still Pictures Division, RG 306. Photo: Corbis Bettman/MAGMA)

American dream." He intended these words as a coda, at an interval of almost exactly a century, to Lincoln's addresses carved on the walls behind him. The use of the memorial floor rather than a lower terrace, as in Anderson's concert, emphasized the rhetorical parallel and allowed Lincoln to loom in effigy from behind the speakers as implied supporter and critic.

Several motives lay behind the decision to bring the marchers to the Lincoln Memorial. Potomac Park could accommodate the huge crowds expected and contain them if they became unruly, far from the working centers of government. This was of concern to President Kennedy and his advisers, who supported the cause of civil rights and, reluctantly and belatedly, the march itself but were aware of its explosive potential to jeopardize both the administration and the civil rights movement. As with other rallies in the chain forged since 1939, symbolism within the politics of memory was foremost. The organizers chose the Lincoln Memorial over other possible sites to appropriate for their cause a symbol cherished by all Americans and to transform the memorial's meaning into an affirmation, again, that Lincoln was not only or even primarily Savior of the Union but, more important, was Emancipator. The March on Washington cemented the connection between his memorial and the ideal of freedom for all, reconstructing it as a metaphor in Americans' minds. Like Lincoln's speech at Gettysburg, this was a rhetorical and cultural exercise even more than a political one. Says Albert Boime, "[T]he marchers in Washington participated in a transformative ritual that reconstructed the site on which they stood in relation to the state."[50]

The metaphorical transformation initiated by a dissatisfied, challenging minority changed the way masses of Americans viewed the Lincoln Memorial. With it particularly in mind, architectural historian Vincent Scully said in the mid-1980s: "[T]he buildings of Washington have taken on much more intense meaning during the past generation than they had for my generation, when we hardly understood the ways in which we needed them, or what public sorrow might be."[51] For Scully, the dramatic, tragic events of the 1960s splashed with blood the memorial and, more generally, Washington's neoclassical and modern classical architecture, giving fresh resonance to what could otherwise be dismissed as bland, white, bureaucratic design. His assessment contributed to a renewed appreciation of classical and modern classical architecture that had set in about 1970, customarily attributed to postmodern culture.[52] More was at stake than a shift in aesthetic fashion, however: American classical

architecture was reappraised as the politics of memory overflowed into the politics of art criticism.

Since 1963, the Lincoln Memorial has continued to serve as a stage for events of both official and vernacular character, but with this difference: now, instead of vernacular events at the memorial deriving their sanction and authority from official ones, the reverse is true. Today, official events at the memorial draw strength from the building's association with vernacular, dissenting ones. Major rallies of protest and advocacy continue to be held there, but they refer less to meanings intentionally, officially inscribed on the memorial than to the chain of associations centering on the march of 1963. Because such assemblies are no longer the first of their kind, they lack the revolutionary force of the original, and their character as ritual is more transparent. This is partly because, Sandage observes, public memory has deprived King himself of revolutionary fire. Unitary official memory has captured him from dissenting vernacular memory, gelding, softening, and co-opting him.[53] Michael Kammen remarks, "There seems to be an American penchant for depoliticizing the past."[54] Nevertheless, the march of 1963 built a new metaphorical shell for the Lincoln Memorial.

Two ritual events of 1993, one at the Lincoln Memorial, the other held elsewhere but linked to it, illustrate how the politics of memory continues to engage several layers of association. As the principal event open to the public in the presidential inauguration of Bill Clinton in January 1993, a concert was held at

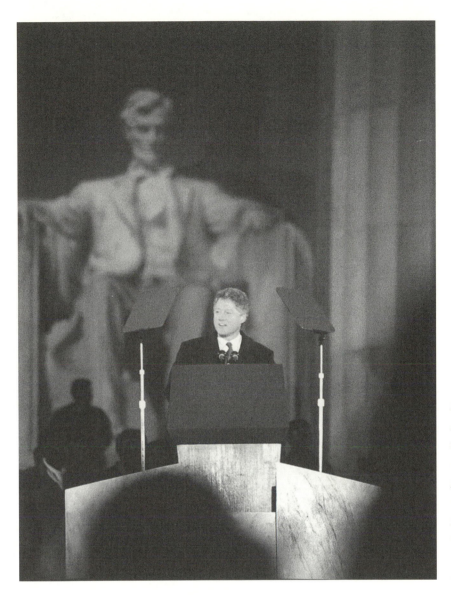

Fig. 5.7. "An American Reunion" concert for inauguration of President Bill Clinton, January 17, 1993. (Office of Printing & Photographic Services, Smithsonian Institution, Washington, D.C. Used with permission)

the Lincoln Memorial, with three hundred thousand in attendance (Fig. 5.7). Called "An American Reunion: The People's Inaugural Celebration," the concert was "a day of remembrance . . . filled with nothing but grand finales, all heralding a new beginning."[55] The retrospection was part fashion, part conviction. Sounding the note of liberalism the incoming Democratic administration hoped to set after twelve years out of office, vice president–elect Al Gore said the day marked a rededication to "the unfinished work of those who have gone before." His allusion to Lincoln's Gettysburg Address was matched by one to the inaugural address of John F. Kennedy, Clinton's great hero, given in 1961: Robert F. Kennedy Jr. proclaimed, "The torch has been passed to a new generation of Americans." Hymns, spirituals, and anthems, including "America the Beautiful," sung by Ray Charles, and "We Shall Overcome," by Kathleen Battle, filled the program, along with more popular music. These invoked memories of Marian Anderson's concert and civil rights rallies of the 1960s. The March on Washington, of 1963, loomed as a memory over the whole afternoon: video clips of King's speech and Kennedy's inaugural appeared on electronic screens in Potomac Park; and folksinger Bob Dylan, who performed at the original march, appeared, without advance warning, to sing a new arrangement of "Chimes of Freedom." For hours, a necklace of past events was strung, to herald the goals of the new administration and the president-elect's alleged populism, and to appeal to an audience of postwar baby boomers.

A campaign promise of Clinton's led to a second event the following April, not held at the memorial but linked to it, which again referred to 1963. While running for president, he had promised to support the cause of equal rights for sexual minorities, and to remind him of that, a huge springtime March on Washington for Lesbian, Gay, and Bi Equal Rights and Freedom was staged.[56] Though the Lincoln Memorial was not the destination of the march, which instead began at the grounds of the Washington Monument, passed the White House, and ended on the Mall at Seventh Street, the memorial's image and the memory of the rally there in 1963 were kept in view by a small early-morning prayer service on the steps. All day, the march was compared to the earlier one, whose name

it echoed, and the two were linked as events in a continuing struggle for equal rights for all. Again and again, speakers reminded audiences that "after 30 years, homosexuals are the last segment of the citizenry that still faces legally sanctioned discrimination." A judge from Detroit, who came to support his gay cousin, had attended the first march. "We believed in the march in '63," he said, "and we see this as an extension."

The March on Washington and the Lincoln Memorial's role as its stage haunt the building, and Washington, down to today. So durable a metaphorical shell did the rally put over the memorial that, when a memorial to King and civil rights was considered in the early nineties, many suggested placing it at the Lincoln Memorial. The suggestions ranged from a simple plaque, like the one set into a lower terrace to honor the entry of Alaska and Hawaii to statehood in 1959, to "a life-sized statue of King at the top of the memorial steps, where he gave his speech—a companion figure to Lincoln's,"[57] to a full-scale museum of civil rights in the undercroft, the empty space among the footings. When a major restoration of the memorial was planned in the early 1990s, talk of a museum revived, and a scheme, reverting to one of the midfifties, for a museum of Lincolniana at the memorial received public support from President George Bush's secretary of the interior.[58] Such a museum, proposed under a conservative administration, would have harmonized with the memorial's original dedication. But, mirroring the "culture wars" in the country at that time, an alternate plan for a museum of civil rights in the undercroft, advanced by a school class from Arizona, attracted more attention. The "I Have a Dream Museum" was even brought up in Congress.[59] All that has been done so far is the creation of a new, larger display on civil rights in the exhibit area below the memorial floor during the restoration of the 1990s, and, as this is being written, an anticlimactic site for the King memorial near the Tidal Basin is being considered.

Another kind of memorial to the events of the 1960s has been installed nearby, however. It is the national Vietnam Veterans Memorial, built in 1979–82 on a corner of Constitution Gardens, a few hundred yards northeast of the Lincoln Memorial.[60] The Lincoln Memorial's identification with antiwar protest marches and with national reconciliation led the veterans' committee to choose a site near it for their monument. As in the aftermath of the Civil War, healing the memories of national division over the Vietnam War was a goal.[61] Dedicated on Veterans Day in November 1982, the Vietnam Memorial consists of two long, polished, black granite walls, set at a shallow "V" angle. The tops of the walls are at ground level, while the wall bases drop gradually from the outer ends of the "V" toward the apex of the angle. The arms are so oriented as to point to the Washington Monument and the Lincoln Memorial (Fig. 5.8). On the hard reflective surfaces of the walls are inscribed, in relentless lines of small, dignified serif letters, the names of the nearly fifty-eight thousand Americans who died in Vietnam between 1957 and 1975. Once dedicated, the Vietnam Veterans Memorial immediately became the most visited site in Washington, outstripping the Lincoln Memorial as its most popular monument.[62] Constantly thronged, it is probably the most noteworthy war memorial of the past generation, anywhere. It achieved that standing by capturing the emotions of ordinary Americans toward the troubling, divisive war. Remarkably, the design, conceived by Yale undergraduate Maya Ying Lin, had been the object of widespread dislike and controversy when it was first shown. An "antimonument," with nothing celebratory or overtly patriotic about it—a flagpole and two gratuitous statuary groups in bronze were added nearby, to please the loyal opposition—the memorial was described by one disgruntled backer of the project as "a black gash of shame." That sentiment is seldom heard today because The Wall gives voice to countless people's emotions of grief and loss over the war. Even the process of building it largely circumvented official channels. Following nineteenth-century custom, the memorial was entirely paid for by private donations; an open design competition was held, the largest in U.S. history, producing fifteen hundred entries; and bureaucratic circuits of decision making were partly avoided. Whereas state-sponsored monuments generally celebrate the nation and patriotic ideals, this one, bearing nothing but the names of fifty-eight thousand individuals, honors their loss and the feelings of their families and of survivors. As nearly as it is possible to achieve in a modern nation-state, the Vietnam Veterans Memorial is a product of vernacular memory.

Proximity and orientation to the Lincoln

Fig. 5.8. Pilgrims at "The Wall," Vietnam Veterans Memorial, winter 1989–90. (Photo: author)

Memorial are crucial to its effect. The south arm of the Vietnam Memorial points to the older monument in apparent honor, yet accusation, too. Two things about the relationship between the newer, iconoclastic memorial and the older, classical one may be noted. First, the vitality the Lincoln Memorial achieved in twentieth-century popular culture was strong enough to draw the Vietnam Memorial, so to speak, under Lincoln's fatherly wing. Second, the symbolism of the Lincoln Memorial has, to a degree, been returned to its original,

explicit dedication, the ideal of national reconciliation after war—to Union—a theme not much emphasized since the 1930s. The official dedication is back, in what amounts to a return of the repressed. Allan Greenberg, an architect strongly identified with contemporary classicism who has pondered the architecture of Washington deeply, says, "Bacon's design is an exceptional example of a war memorial whose significance has grown with the passage of time. This capacity to absorb new meaning is the rarest and most important quality in memorial architecture."[63]

For a monument whose purposes, other than private reflection, were barely spoken of in advance, the Lincoln Memorial has proven a remarkably flexible and articulate vessel for experience. It presents the case of a commemorative site calculated to broadcast a nation's official view of itself and its history being turned to other, popular symbolic uses, foreign—perhaps opposed—to those intended. The memorial has been recuperated or recaptured by "ordinary" Americans, whose voices do not normally influence the trajectory of public memory.

Public memory, however, is never safe, neutral ground. It is always political in the broad sense. As Martin Luther King's memory has been recaptured from African-American civil rights fighters to weave it into a seamless narrative of national progress and "multiculturalism," so sites such as the Lincoln Memorial, because of their symbolic charge and resonance, are always metaphorical battlefields. Every generation must reconstruct them mentally; without absolutely fixed meanings, they require constant vigilance. Says John Gillis, "We have no alternative but to construct new memories as well as new identities better suited to the complexities of a post-national era."[64]

This account of the Lincoln Memorial ends where it began, in contestation. From the day after Lincoln was assassinated, or perhaps the day he was elected, his memory was a site of struggle between conflicting agents and forces that sought to determine the direction the nation would take. As chapter 1 shows, his image was so electric and controverted after the Civil War that commemorating him as an officially reunited nation was thought too dangerous a symbolic exercise until after 1900. Even then, officially remembering him in material form was possible only after his posthumous reputation had been pried free of messy historical particulars, to enter a realm of allegedly indisputable, harmless national ideals. Really, Lincoln could only be commemorated when he no longer mattered. But the ideals were not harmless to those who were sacrificed to reunion between the formerly warring sections. Henry Bacon, Daniel Chester French, their collaborators, and the supervisory commissions in the memorial they built shaped the consummate universal object, a self-contained sign with barely any earthly referent. Its true "signified" was a turn-of-the-century Republican vision of the nation-state and the federal government under the providential oversight of an imperial presidency. The struggle for Lincoln's memory continued through the period of his memorial's design and construction. For the mainstream Republican plan for an ideal Graeco-Roman temple, Progressive dissenters, especially Democrats, tried to substitute some more realistic sign of Lincoln's life and service, notably a memorial highway. Powerless as they were by 1913 to block the building of the memorial, Wilson's Democrats tried to curb what seemed to them idealist excesses in its design, particularly the use of Colorado-Yule marble in the superstructure. Metaphorically timeless and perfect, the memorial was in fact the product of path-breaking technology, a classical temple on skyscraper foundations. Disguised dualities abound. Memories of Lincoln as Emancipator were acknowledged but suppressed, especially in the murals and dedicatory inscription, beneath imagery of him as Savior of the Union. The rhetoric of old-fashioned, universalizing patriotism employed in the dedication of 1922 was beamed to a radio audience and concealed party politics. It also recognized but did nothing to change—indeed, helped preserve—blatant racial injustice. The cracks between competing sections and interests in American life, especially those along the lines of race and ethnicity, were papered over.

Once dedicated and effusively praised, the memorial again became contested ground, as it proved a potent site for public ritual, not all of it sponsored by the state. Like left-leaning Progressives early in the century, Populists, New Deal Democrats, and civil rights advocates emphasized Lincoln's symbolism as Emancipator and humanitarian, more than as Savior of the Union, his state-sanctioned version. The new emphasis affected how his memorial was seen and used; an early example was Marian Anderson's concert in 1939. The contest between the memorial's official and vernacular dedications was effectively decided in 1963 at the huge March on Washington, where Martin Luther King delivered his challenge to Americans from its platform. Since then, the triumph of vernacular over original, official symbolism has largely determined the trajectory of the memorial's use. It led, in particular, to the building nearby of Maya Lin's Vietnam Veterans Memorial.

A contested monument can always be recaptured by reassuring, conformist official optimism, however. This fact poses a threat to its continued ability to serve as a touchstone for national conscience, something, implies poet laureate Archibald MacLeish, that distinguishes the Lincoln Memorial:

And you,
Within there, in our love renew . . .
Renew the holy dream we were to be![65]

NOTES

INTRODUCTION

1. On the concept of the national icon, see Albert Boime, *Hollow Icons: The Politics of Sculpture in Nineteenth-Century France* (Kent, Ohio: Kent State University Press, 1987); and idem, *The Unveiling of the National Icons: A Plea for Patriotic Iconoclasm in a Nationalist Era* (Cambridge: Cambridge University Press, 1998), esp. 1–2.

2. The memorial has appeared on the reverse of the treasury note since 1928: Robert Friedberg, *Paper Money of the United States: A Complete Illustrated Guide with Valuations*, 8th ed., with additions and revisions by Jack Friedberg (New York: Coin and Currency Institute, 1975), 169. Frank Gasparro's engraving of the memorial replaced that of the wheat wreath on the penny's obverse to mark Lincoln's sesquicentennial in 1959.

3. The most expensive was the Capitol itself. Inevitability that discourages questioning and factual knowledge may be a mark of national icons: Jim Pomeroy makes almost the same point about the gigantic suite of carved presidential heads on Mount Rushmore, South Dakota (1924–41), in "Rushmore—Another Look," in *Critical Issues in Public Art: Content, Context, and Controversy*, ed. Harriet F. Senie and Sally Webster (New York: HarperCollins, 1992), 47–48. Main sources on the Lincoln Memorial are Edward F. Concklin, ed., *The Lincoln Memorial, Washington* (Washington, D.C.: Government Printing Office, 1927); Suzanne Gordon, *In This Temple: A Guide Book to the Lincoln Memorial* (Washington, D.C.: Museum Press, 1973); Michael Richman, *Daniel Chester French, an American Sculptor*, Landmark Reprint Series (Washington, D.C.: National Trust for Historic Preservation, 1976), 171–86; Christopher A. Thomas, "The Lincoln Memorial and Its Architect, Henry Bacon (1866–1924)," 4 vols. (Ph.D. diss., Yale University, 1990); idem, "The Marble of the Lincoln Memorial: 'Whitest, Prettiest, and . . . Best,'" *Washington History* 5, no. 2 (fall/winter 1993–94): 42–63. Like Rushmore, too, the memorial received attention during the 1990s for political reasons: Scott A. Sandage, "A Marble House Divided: The Lincoln Memorial, the Civil Rights Movement, and the Politics of Memory, 1939–1963," *Journal of American History*, 80 (June 1993): 135–67; and Boime, *Unveiling of the National Icons*, 253–306.

4. Perhaps others, too: the Chinese Communist government echoed the memorial's design in its mausoleum for Chairman Mao in Tiananmen Square; see Lothar Ledderose, "Die Gedenkhalle für Mao Zedong: Ein Beispiel von Gedächtnisarchitektur," in *Kultur und Gedächtnis*, ed. Jan Assmann and Tonio Hölscher, Suhrkamp Taschenbuch Wissenschaft (Frankfurt am Main: Suhrkamp, 1988), 327, 329–30.

5. Given in March 1997 at a symposium in Washington sponsored by the Latrobe chapter of the Society of Architectural Historians and the National Building Museum, the talk was titled "Lincoln as Theodore Roosevelt: The Politics of the Lincoln Memorial, 1901–1911."

6. Lewis Mumford, *Sticks and Stones: A Study of American Architecture and Civilization* (1924; 2nd rev. ed., New York: Dover, 1955), 141–42.

7. See Merrill D. Peterson, *Lincoln in American Memory* (New York: Oxford University Press, 1994).

8. Clifford Geertz, *The Interpretation of Cultures: Selected Essays by Clifford Geertz* (New

York: Basic Books, 1973), 5. For an introduction to semiotics, see Jonathan Culler, *Structuralist Poetics: Structuralism, Linguistics, and the Study of Literature* (Ithaca, N.Y.: Cornell University Press, 1975), 4–6, 16–20, and passim; and Terry Eagleton, *Literary Theory: An Introduction*, 2d ed. (Oxford: Blackwell, 1996), chap. 3.

9. See Terry Eagleton, *Ideology: An Introduction* (London: Verso, 1991), chap. 1.

10. Eagleton, *Literary Theory*, 207.

11. Benedict Anderson, *Imagined Communities: Reflections on the Origin and Spread of Nationalism*, rev. ed. (London: Verso, 1991).

12. See David Cannadine, "The Context, Performance, and Meaning of Ritual: The British Monarchy and the 'Invention of Tradition,' c. 1820–1977," in *The Invention of Tradition*, ed. Eric Hobsbawm and Terence Ranger (Cambridge: Cambridge University Press, 1983), esp. 108–134.

13. Eagleton, *Literary Theory*, 204–5. On postcolonial theory, see Homi K. Bhabha, "Postmodernism/Postcolonialism," in *Critical Terms for Art History*, ed. Robert S. Nelson and Richard Shiff (Chicago: University of Chicago Press, 1996), 307–22; and Bill Ashcroft, Gareth Griffiths, and Helen Tiffen, eds., *The Post-colonial Studies Reader* (London: Routledge, 1995).

14. See Robert D. Kaplan, *Balkan Ghosts: A Journey through History* (New York: St. Martin's Press, 1993), 33–41.

15. Though I use the phrase in a different sense, it comes from Van Wyck Brooks, "On Creating a Usable Past," in *Van Wyck Brooks, the Early Years: A Selection from His Works*, ed. Claire Sprague (Boston: Northeastern University Press, 1993), 219–26.

16. On postmodernity and postmodernism (its cultural equivalent), see Bhabha, "Postmodernism/Postcolonialism," which contains a basic bibliography on these controverted movements. Valuable in regard to national memory and heritage are Pierre Nora, "Between Memory and History: *Les Lieux de Mémoire*," *Representations* 26 (spring 1989): 7–25; and David Lowenthal, *The*

Past Is a Foreign Country (Cambridge: Cambridge University Press, 1985). For a résumé of new thinking in this area, see John R. Gillis, ed., *Commemorations: The Politics of National Identity* (Princeton, N.J.: Princeton University Press, 1994), esp. Gillis's introduction. Lowenthal's argument is found in a shortened version in the book edited by Gillis, as "Identity, Heritage, and History," 41–57.

17. On the distinction between official and vernacular memory, see John Bodnar, *Remaking America: Public Memory, Commemoration, and Patriotism in the Twentieth Century* (Princeton, N.J.: Princeton University Press, 1992), esp. chap. 1.

18. Michael Kammen, *Mystic Chords of Memory: The Transformation of Tradition in American Culture* (New York: Vintage Books, 1991), 12.

19. See William B. Rhoads, *The Colonial Revival* (New York: Garland, 1977); and Alan Axelrod, ed., *The Colonial Revival in America* (New York: Norton, with the Henry Francis du Pont Winterthur Museum, 1985).

20. Michele H. Bogart, *Public Sculpture and the Civic Ideal in New York City, 1890–1930* (Chicago: University of Chicago Press, 1989).

21. Kirk Savage, *Standing Soldiers, Kneeling Slaves: Race, War, and Monument in Nineteenth-Century America* (Princeton, N.J.: Princeton University Press, 1997), 4.

22. Wanda M. Corn, "Coming of Age: Historical Scholarship in American Art," *Art Bulletin* 70 (June 1988): 201.

23. On the context in contemporary public art, see the editors' introductions to W. J. T. Mitchell, ed., *Art and the Public Sphere* (Chicago: University of Chicago Press, 1992); and Harriet F. Senie and Sally Webster, eds., *Critical Issues in Public Art: Content, Context, and Controversy* (New York: HarperCollins, 1992).

24. Vivien Green Fryd, *Art and Empire: The Politics of Ethnicity in the United States Capitol, 1815–1860* (New Haven, Conn.: Yale University Press, 1992).

25. Dennis R. Montagna, "The Ulysses S. Grant

Memorial in Washington, DC: A War Memorial for the New Century," in Senie and Webster, *Critical Issues in Public Art*, 115–27.

26. Earlier, Kirk Savage published a historicizing study of the Washington Monument, "The Self-Made Monument: George Washington and the Fight to Erect a National Memorial," in Senie and Webster, *Critical Issues in Public Art*, 5–32.

27. Sandage, "A Marble House Divided," 135–67.

28. Boime, *Unveiling of the National Icons*, chap. 5.

29. For an introduction to the subject, see "Classicism," in James Stevens Curl, *A Dictionary of Architecture* (Oxford: Oxford University Press, 1999), 151–52.

30. On this movement see note 16; Diane Ghirardo, *Architecture after Modernism* (New York: Thames and Hudson, 1996), 7–42; and Charles Jencks, *Post-modernism: The New Classicism in Art and Architecture* (London: Academy Editions, 1987).

31. Though only in a handful of schools, notably, the University of Notre Dame (Indiana), the Institute for the Study of Classical Architecture in New York, and the Prince of Wales's Institute in London.

32. See Peter Katz, *The New Urbanism: Toward an Architecture of Community* (New York: McGraw-Hill, 1994).

33. See Allen Greenberg, "Lutyens's Cenotaph," *Journal of the Society of Architectural Historians* 48, no. 1 (March 1989): 5–23.

CHAPTER 1

1. James Russell Lowell, "Harvard Commemoration Ode," quoted in William W. Betts, *Lincoln and the Poets* (Pittsburgh: University of Pittsburgh Press, 1965), 33.

2. In a letter to Bayard Taylor quoted in ibid., 16–17.

3. From a sermon by the Reverend Henry Ward Beecher, quoted in Lloyd Lewis, *Myths after Lincoln* (New York: Harcourt, Brace, 1929), 102. On the "Black Easter" sermons, see also Peterson, *Lincoln in American Memory*, chap. 1.

4. On Lincoln and his achievement, see Abraham Lincoln, *Speeches and Writings, 1859–1865: Speeches, Letters, and Miscellaneous Writings, Presidential Messages and Proclamations*, ed. Don E. Fehrenbacher (New York: Literary Classics of the U.S., 1989); James M. McPherson, *Abraham Lincoln and the Second American Revolution* (New York: Oxford University Press, 1990); Mark E. Neely Jr., *The Last Best Hope of Earth: Abraham Lincoln and the Promise of America* (Cambridge, Mass.: Harvard University Press, with the Huntington Library and the Illinois State Historical Society, 1993); and Garry Wills, *Lincoln at Gettysburg: The Words That Remade America* (New York: Simon and Schuster, 1992). For recent critical perspectives on him, see Gabor S. Boritt, ed., *The Historian's Lincoln: Pseudohistory, Psychohistory, and History* (Urbana: University of Illinois Press, 1988); and, on his afterlife in American mythology, Peterson, *Lincoln in American Memory*.

5. Nathaniel Hawthorne, "Chiefly about War Matters, by a Peaceable Man," *Atlantic Monthly*, July 1862, and reprinted in Hawthorne, *Tales, Sketches, and Other Papers* (1883; reprint, Freeport, N.Y.: Books for Libraries Press, 1972), 309.

6. See Constance M. Green, *Washington: A History of the Capital, 1800–1950* (Princeton, N.J.: Princeton University Press, 1962); John H. Reps, *Monumental Washington: The Planning and Development of the Capital Center* (Princeton, N.J.: Princeton University Press, 1967); Lois Craig and the staff of the Federal Architecture Project *The Federal Presence: Architecture, Politics, and Symbols in U.S. Government Building* (Cambridge, Mass.: MIT Press, 1978); Frederick Gutheim, *Worthy of the Nation: The History of Planning for the National Capital* (Washington, D.C.: Smithsonian Institution Press, 1977); Richard Longstreth, ed., *The Mall in Washington,*

1791–1991, CASVA Studies in the History of Art, no. 30 (Washington, D.C.: National Gallery of Art, 1991); and appropriate sections of Pamela Scott and Antoinette J. Lee, *Buildings of the District of Columbia* (New York: Oxford University Press, 1993).

7. Pamela Scott, "This Vast Empire," in Longstreth, *The Mall in Washington,* 37–46. The part of the District of Columbia severed from Virginia was given back, or "retroceded," in 1849 and became Arlington County.

8. Quoted in Craig, *Federal Presence,* 82.

9. See Therese O'Malley, "A Public Museum of Trees," in Longstreth, *The Mall in Washington,* 60–76.

10. Ernest Samuels, ed., *The Education of Henry Adams* (Boston: Houghton Mifflin, 1974), 99.

11. See Margaret Leech's classic *Reveille in Washington, 1860–1865* (New York: Harper and Brothers, 1941).

12. Quoted in Craig, *Federal Presence,* 136.

13. See Marcus Cunliffe, *George Washington: Man and Monument* (New York: Mentor Books, 1982); Barry Schwartz, *George Washington: The Making of an American Symbol* (New York: Free Press, 1987); and Kirk Savage, "The Self-Made Monument: George Washington and the Fight to Erect a National Memorial," in Senie and Webster, *Critical Issues in Public Art,* 5–32. See also George B. Forgie, *Patricide in the House Divided: A Psychological Interpretation of Lincoln and His Age* (New York: Norton, 1979), especially chap. 1 and 184–90; and Peterson, *Lincoln in American Memory,* 27–29.

14. Robert H. Wiebe, *The Search for Order, 1877–1920* (New York: Hill and Wang, 1967), 27; David Donald, *Lincoln Reconsidered: Essays on the Civil War Era* (New York: Vintage Books, 1961), 8; and Peterson, *Lincoln in American Memory,* chap. 2.

15. See Eric Foner, *Reconstruction: America's Unfinished Revolution, 1863–1877* (New York: Harper and Row, 1988), 61–62 and passim.

16. The phrase appears in Donald, *Lincoln Reconsidered,* 6.

17. See Savage, *Standing Soldiers. Kneeling Slaves,* 103–13. On the other proposals, see ibid., chap. 4.

18. Cullom (1829–1914) had become acquainted with Lincoln through his father and followed Lincoln, whom he revered, into the Republican fold before the war. After the war Cullom served two terms as governor of Illinois and then represented the state in the U.S. Senate for thirty years. On him see *Dictionary of American Biography,* s.v. "Cullom, Shelby M." 4: 588–89; and "Lifelong Friend Draws Picture of Lincoln as He Saw Him," *New York Times,* March 22, 1908, pt. 5, 4:2.

19. See John Higham, *Strangers in the Land: Patterns of American Nativism 1860–1925,* 2d ed. (New York: Atheneum, 1965), chap. 2; and Foner's moving epilogue in *Reconstruction,* 602–12.

20. Savage, *Standing Soldiers, Kneeling Slaves,* 112.

21. On Ball's Freedmen's Memorial, see ibid., chap. 4 (ill., p. 91); on Ream's statue, see Charlotte Streifer Rubinstein, *American Women Sculptor: A History of Women Working in Three Dimensions* (Boston: G. K. Hall, 1990), 68–72. I am also grateful to Kirk Savage for letting me read in typescript his article "Vinnie Ream's *Lincoln* (1871): The Sexual Politics of a Sculptor's Studio."

22. On the first, see Marvin Trachtenberg, *The Statue of Liberty,* rev. ed. (New York: Penguin, 1986); and Boime, *Hollow Icons,* 113–39; on the second, see Henry Van Brunt, "The Washington Monument," *American Art Review* 1, 1st div. (1880): 57–65; and Savage, "Self-Made Monument," 19–22.

23. Congressional silence about memorializing Lincoln was broken only once, by a scheme for multiple obelisks: *Congressional Record,* 49th Cong., 1st sess. Senate, January 11, 1886, vol. 17, 570–71.

24. Kammen, *Mystic Chords of Memory,* 128–29.

25. Scott and Lee, *Buildings of the District of*

Columbia, 156–58 and 142–45, respectively. On the postwar city as a whole, see the sources cited in note 6.

26. Scott and Lee, *Buildings of the District of Columbia*, 72–76; and David C. Streatfield, "The Olmsteds and the Landscape of the Mall," in Longstreth, *The Mall in Washington*, 117–21.

27. See Alan Trachtenberg, *The Incorporation of America: Culture and Society in the Gilded Age* (New York: Hill and Wang, 1982), chap. 5; John Tomsich, *A Genteel Endeavor: American Culture and Politics in the Gilded Age* (Stanford, Calif.: Stanford University Press, 1971); and Peterson, *Lincoln in American Memory*, chap. 4.

28. New Englander and historian Francis Parkman, as quoted in Trachtenberg, *Incorporation of America*, 153. See Matthew Arnold, *Culture and Anarchy: An Essay in Political and Social Criticism*, published in London in 1867 and in New York in 1875.

29. See, for example, Woodrow Wilson, *A History of the American People* (New York: Harper and Brothers, 1902), 1:207; and Brand Whitlock, *Abraham Lincoln* (1909; Boston: Small, Maynard & Co., 1919), xi, 160, and passim.

30. Ida Minerva Tarbell, *The Life of Abraham Lincoln* (New York: Lincoln History Society, 1900), 2:261–62. On her contribution, see Peterson, *Lincoln in American Memory*, 148–54. A still more perfect Lincoln emerged from John G. Nicolay and John Hay, *Abraham Lincoln: A History*, 10 vols. (New York: Century Co., 1890).

31. On the statue, see John H. Dryfhout, *The Work of Augustus Saint-Gaudens* (Hanover, N.H.: University Press of New England, 1982), 158–62 (cat. no. 124); Peterson, *Lincoln in American Memory*, 63–66; and Savage, *Standing Soldiers, Kneeling Slaves*, 122–25.

32. Francis Trevelyan Miller, *The Photographic History of the Civil War in Ten Volumes* (New York: Review of Reviews, 1911), 1:15. See also Kammen, *Mystic Chords of Memory*, chap. 4.

33. See Cecilia O'Leary, " 'American All':

Reforging a National Brotherhood, 1876–1917," *History Today* 44, no. 10 (October 1994): 20–27.

34. See Scot M. Guenter, *The American Flag, 1777–1924: Cultural Shifts from Creation to Codification* (Rutherford, N.J.: Fairleigh Dickinson University Press, 1990), chaps. 5, 6; and Higham, *Strangers in the Land*, 103.

35. See Rhoads, *The Colonial Revival;* and Axelrod, *Colonial Revival in America*.

36. See Gaines M. Foster, *Ghosts of the Confederacy: Defeat, the Lost Cause, and the Emergence of the New South 1865–1913* (New York: Oxford University Press, 1987), chap. 6.

37. Arthur S. Link, "Woodrow Wilson: The American as Southerner," in *The Higher Realism of Woodrow Wilson, and Other Essays* (Nashville, Tenn.: Vanderbilt University Press, 1971), 21–37; and Richard Hofstadter, *The American Political Tradition and the Men Who Made It* (New York: Knopf, 1973), chap. 10, "Woodrow Wilson: The Conservative as Liberal."

38. Wilson, *History of the American People*, 5:49.

39. See Foster, *Ghosts of the Confederacy*, esp. 98–103, 158–59; and, on the Lee Monument, Savage, *Standing Soldiers, Kneeling Slaves*, chap. 5.

40. On this subject, see Michael Davis, *The Image of Lincoln in the South* (Knoxville: University of Tennessee Press, 1971), chap. 4.

41. On the election, see Wiebe, *Search for Order*, 100–107; on its effect on the party, see Franklin L. Burdette, *The Republican Party: A Short History*, 2d ed. (New York: D. Van Nostrand, 1972), chap. 7; on the flavor of Populism and the air of crisis, see Richard Hofstadter, *The Age of Reform: From Bryan to F.D.R.* (New York: Knopf, 1959), chap. 2.

42. Quoted in Wilfred E. Binkley, *President and Congress*, 3d rev. ed. (New York: Vintage Books, 1962), 234.

43. "Fifty Years of the Republican Party," speech given at Jackson, Michigan, July 6, 1904, in John Hay and Elihu Root, *The Republican Party: "A Party Fit to Govern"* (New York: privately printed, 1904), 12.

44. Between 1895 and 1899, Senator Shelby Cullom (Rep.-Ill.) introduced bills for the erection of a national monument at Gettysburg, which passed in the Senate but not in the House. Several other bills to build a memorial in Washington were introduced in the House, but these also failed, despite pressure from the Illinois legislature.

45. Donald, *Lincoln Reconsidered*, 3–18.

46. Quoted in Peterson, *Lincoln in American Memory*, 164. See also Hay, "Fifty Years of the Republican Party," 9.

47. On the McMillan Commission and McMillan Plan, see Charles Moore, ed., *The Improvement of the Park System of the District of Columbia*, 57th Cong., 1st sess., Senate Document 965 (Washington, D.C.: Government Printing Office, 1902); and the digest and illustrations in Reps, *Monumental Washington*, chaps. 4–6. See also Charles Moore, *Daniel H. Burnham, Architect, Planner of Cities* (Boston: Houghton Mifflin, 1921), vol. 1, chap. 11; idem, *The Life and Times of Charles Follen McKim* (Boston: Houghton Mifflin, 1929), chap. 15; and idem, *Washington, Past and Present* (New York: Century Co., 1929), 257–68; Jon A. Peterson, "The Hidden Origins of the McMillan Plan for Washington, D.C., 1900–1902," in *Historical Perspectives on Urban Design: Washington, D.C., 1890–1910*, ed. Antoinette J. Lee, Center for Washington Area Studies, Occasional Paper no. 1 (Washington, D.C.: George Washington University Press, 1983), 4–7; idem, "The Nation's First Comprehensive City Plan," *Journal of the American Planning Association* 51 (spring 1985): 134–50; and, for cognate areas, the sources cited in notes 49 and 51.

48. William V. Cox, comp., *Celebration of the One Hundredth Anniversary of the Establishment of the Seat of Government in the District of Columbia* (Washington, D.C.: Joint Committee on Printing, Government Printing Office, 1901), 21. See also Reps, *Monumental Washington*, chap. 3.

49. Lincoln Steffens's *The Shame of the Cities* (1904), based on a series in *McClure's*, drew the attention of a vast readership to the plight of the urban poor and the responsibility of plutocrats and political bosses for it. On turn-of-the-century urban reform, see Paul Boyer, *Urban Masses and Moral Order in America: 1820–1929* (Cambridge, Mass.: Harvard University Press, 1978), esp. pt. 3; William H. Wilson, *The City Beautiful Movement* (Baltimore: Johns Hopkins University Press, 1989), pt. 1; and John Milton Cooper Jr., *Pivotal Decades: The United States, 1900–1920* (New York: Norton, 1990), 82–89 and passim.

50. See Moore, *Daniel H. Burnham*, chaps. 4, 5; David F. Burg, *Chicago's White City of 1893* (Lexington: University Press of Kentucky, 1976); and Reid Badger, *The Great American Fair: The World's Columbian Exposition and American Culture* (Chicago: N. Hall, 1979), esp. chaps. 7, 8.

51. See Glenn Brown, *1860–1930, Memories: A Winning Crusade to Revive George Washington's Vision of a Capital City* (Washington, D.C.: W. F. Roberts, 1931); William B. Bushong, "Glenn Brown, the American Institute of Architects, and the Development of the Civic Core of Washington, D.C." (Ph.D. diss., George Washington University, 1988); and idem, "A City Beautiful Crusade," in William Bushong, Judith H. Robinson, and Julie Mueller, *A Centennial History of the Washington Chapter, the American Institute of Architects 1887–1987* (Washington, D.C.: Washington Architectural Foundation Press, 1987), 21–43. On his feelings for Georgian and Federal architecture, see Brown, *History of the United States Capitol*, 2 vols., 56th Cong., 1st sess., S. Doc. 60 (Washington, D.C.: Government Printing Office, 1900–1903; reprint, New York: Da Capo Press, 1970), esp. Charles Moore's introduction.

52. The conference papers were published as *Papers Relating to the Improvement of the City of Washington, District of Columbia*, 56th Cong., 2d sess., S. Doc. 94 (Washington, D.C.: Government Printing Office, 1901). See the digest in Reps, *Monumental Washington*, 83–93.

53. Richard Collin, *Theodore Roosevelt, Culture, Diplomacy, and Expansion* (Baton Rouge: Louisiana State University Press, 1985), 32. On

McMillan, see also *National Cyclopaedia of American Biography*, s.v. "McMillan, James."; and David J. Rothman, *Politics and Power: The United States Senate, 1869–1901* (Cambridge, Mass.: Harvard University Press, 1966), 45–53 and passim.

54. On Cannon, see *Dictionary of American Biography*, s.v. "Cannon, Joseph G."; L. White Busbey, comp., *Uncle Joe Cannon: The Story of a Pioneer American* (New York: H. Holt and Company, 1927), esp. xxii–xxx; and Richard B. Cheney and Lynne V. Cheney, *Kings of the Hill: Power and Personality in the House of Representatives* (New York: Continuum, 1983), chap. 6. On his feelings for the McMillan Plan, see Reps, *Monumental Washington*, 144.

55. For a summary of the commissioners' backgrounds, see Moore, *Washington, Past and Present*, 270–71. For more detail, see the biographical sources cited in note 47, plus Augustus Saint-Gaudens, *The Reminiscences of Augustus Saint-Gaudens*, ed. Homer Saint-Gaudens (1913; reprint, New York: Garland, 1976), esp. 1:42, 51.

56. See Rhoads, *Colonial Revival*; and Axelrod, *Colonial Revival in America*.

57. Lois Goldreich Marcus, "The Shaw Memorial: A History Painting in Bronze," *Winterthur Porfolio* 14, no. 1 (spring 1979): 5.

58. Dryfhout, *Work of Augustus Saint-Gaudens*, 110–15 (Farragut); 253–58 (Sherman); and 222–29 (Shaw).

59. Only Olmsted had not been a member of the fair's design board; his father, the more famous F. L. Olmsted Sr., had. The elder Olmsted could not serve on the McMillan Commission because, though still alive, he had been incapacitated by insanity since 1895.

60. See Dennis R. Montagna, "The Ulysses S. Grant Memorial in Washington, D.C.: A War Memorial for the New Century," in Senie and Webster, *Critical Issues in Public Art*, 115–27.

61. See Moore, *Improvement of the Park System*, 58; and Jill Bretherick, "Honor of Sacrifice: The Evolution of the Arlington National Cemetery," *Modulus* 17 (1984): 106–13.

62. Phillip C. Jessup, *Elihu Root* (New York: Dodd, Mead, 1938), 2:280–81; and Reps, *Monumental Washington*, 140–41, 150.

63. Moore, *Life and Times of Charles Follen McKim*, 202. In fact, Pericles made his oration over the dead of the First Peloponnesian War.

64. This suggestion is based on Roosevelt's feelings for Lincoln and his personal activity in realizing the Mall plan: Jessup, *Elihu Root*, 2:280–81.

65. On Newlands's role see Bushong, "Glenn Brown," 142–43, 171; and, for biographical data, *Dictionary of American Biography*, s.v. "Newlands, Francis Griffith."

66. See Donald J. Olsen, *The City as a Work of Art: London, Paris, Vienna* (New Haven, Conn.: Yale University Press, 1988).

67. Woodrow Wilson, *Congressional Government: A Study in American Politics* (1885; reprint, Baltimore: Johns Hopkins University Press, 1981), 54. See also Trachtenberg, *Incorporation of America*, 165–66.

68. See Edward Bellamy, *Looking Backward 2000–1887*, ed. John L. Thomas (1888; reprint, Cambridge, Mass.: Belknap Press of Harvard University Press, 1967). Bellamy's followers called their reform movement "Nationalism."

69. Henry James, *The American Scene*, ed. Leon Edel (1907; reprint, Bloomington: Indiana University Press, 1968), 356.

70. In "Ulysses S. Grant Memorial," Montagna argues that the designers and patrons of that monument used Civil War imagery "to embody turn-of-the-century ideas advocating military preparedness and the nobility of self-sacrifice for the nation's well-being" (117). Here, the argument is that references to the war had a larger and more partisan political context.

71. Hay, "Fifty Years of the Republican Party," 4, 8–9.

72. See Guenter, *The American Flag*, 134.

73. On Lincoln's understanding of the Union, see Wills, *Lincoln at Gettysburg*, chap. 3.

74. Binkley, *President and Congress*, chaps. 7–9.

75. Quoted in ibid., 185.

76. Wilson, *Congressional Government*, 48.

77. Ibid., 215. On Wilson's theory, see Walter Lippmann's introduction to the book, 7–17.

78. Quoted in Binkley, *President and Congress*, 203.

79. Wilson, *Congressional Government*, preface of 1900, 22.

80. The plan contains other evidence of this. It called for the aggrandizement of Lafayette Square and the zone around the White House occupied by executive departments: Reps, *Monumental Washington*, 131–32. In addition, the text hinted at inadequacies in the White House, which the Roosevelts and McKim's firm of McKim, Mead & White happily corrected in a major restoration campaign begun in 1902: Collin, *Theodore Roosevelt*, 35–46; Leland M. Roth, *McKim, Mead & White, Architects* (New York: Harper and Row, 1983), 267–71; and William Seale, *The President's House: A History* (Washington, D.C.: White House Historical Association/National Geographic Society, 1986), vol. 2, chap. 29.

81. See Binkley, *President and Congress*, 235–36. See also Edmund Morris, *The Rise of Theodore Roosevelt* (New York: Coward, McCann and Geoghegan, 1979); Lewis L. Gould, *The Presidency of Theodore Roosevelt* (Lawrence: University Press of Kansas, 1991); Collin, *Theodore Roosevelt*; and Cooper, *Pivotal Decades*, chaps. 2–4.

82. Quoted in Binkley, *President and Congress*, 250.

83. Quoted in ibid., 252.

84. Cooper, *Pivotal Decades*, xv, 122.

CHAPTER 2

1. Moore, *Life and Times of Charles Follen McKim*, 203. On Cullom's bill, see *Congressional Record*, 57th Cong., 1st sess., vol. 35, 127 and passim.

2. Kirk Savage, "Race, Memory, Identity: The National Monuments of the Union and the Con-federacy (Ph.D. diss., University of California at Berkeley, 1990), 29.

3. Reps, *Monumental Washington*, 142–43.

4. On the commission of 1902, see Concklin, *Lincoln Memorial*, 16–17. On Vest, see *Biographical Directory of the American Congress, 1774–1961* (Washington, D.C.: Government Printing Office, 1961), 1754. On Wetmore, see *National Cyclopaedia of American Biography*, s.v., "Wetmore, George Peabody"; and Rothman, *Politics and Power*, 46. On McCleary, see note 32.

5. McKim's builder, Norcross Brothers, had submitted a figure of $1,975,480 for a memorial in the Doric order, and $350,000 more if the more ornate Corinthian were used: National Archives, RG 66, project files, letter Norcross to Senate Park Commission, March 28, 1902. In his letter covering the estimate, McKim said, based on figures from Saint-Gaudens, that the statue of Lincoln would cost an additional quarter-million dollars.

6. *Congressional Record*, 35, 6884.

7. Ibid.

8. Quoted in Jessup, *Elihu Root*, 1:279–80. On Cannon's vulgarity, see also Henry F. Pringle, *The Life and Times of William Howard Taft* (Hamden, Conn.: Archon Books, 1964), 1:402.

9. Minutes of this meeting have not survived, but a digest appears in Concklin, *Lincoln Memorial*, 17, followed by a summary of later legislation and minutes of the Lincoln Memorial Commission created in 1911. Hereafter, minutes are not cited individually.

10. See Glenn Brown, "The Lincoln Memorial in Washington D.C.," part 1, "The Site," *American Architect* 118, no. 2339 (October 20, 1920): 489–99, 503–6 [hereafter Brown, "LM—Site"]; and Bushong, "Glenn Brown," chap. 5. On the attention to Potomac Park in 1906–7, see correspondence in the Daniel H. Burnham papers, Burnham and Ryerson Libraries of the Art Institute of Chicago, and Charles Moore and Olmsted Associates papers in the Library of Congress, Manuscript Division.

11. On the birthplace memorial, see Peterson,

Lincoln in American Memory, 177–82; and Steven McLeod Bedford, *John Russell Pope, Architect of Empire* (New York: Rizzoli, 1998), 118–22.

12. Donald, *Lincoln Reconsidered*, 162–63. See also Peterson, *Lincoln in American Memory*, chap. 4; and William Abbatt, comp., *The Lincoln Centenary in Literature: Selections from the Principal Magazines of February and March 1909, Together with a Few from 1907–1908*, 2 vols. (New York: Henry E. Huntington for Library of Congress, 1909).

13. Quoted in Peterson, *Lincoln in American Memory*, 141.

14. Quoted in Betts, *Lincoln and the Poets*, 65–68. Selections from the poem, slightly altered, also appear in Peterson, *Lincoln in American Memory*, 189–90.

15. An instance is Carl Sandburg's colossal, poetic "biography" of Lincoln, which appeared in two parts: *The Prairie Years*, 2 vols. (1925–26) and *The War Years*, 4 vols. (1936–37). On Sandburg's Lincoln, see Peterson, *Lincoln in American Memory*, 271–78 and passim.

16. See the sources cited in n. 11 above.

17. Cooper, *Pivotal Decades*, 143.

18. Herbert Croly, *The Promise of American Life* (New York: Macmillan, 1909; reprint, New Brunswick, N.J.: Transaction, 1993), esp. chap. 7.

19. Herbert Croly, "Consummate": "The Paradox of Lincoln," *New Republic* 21 (February 18, 1920), 352. "Shows us": *Promise of American Life*, 89. Though separated by more than a decade and a world war, Croly's views of Lincoln showed great consistency.

20. Cooper, *Pivotal Decades*, 182–83. Democrats first joined Republicans in marking Lincoln's Birthday in 1901. On Lincoln for the left wing, see Peterson, *Lincoln in American Memory*, 157–58.

21. Whitlock, *Abraham Lincoln*, 73; also, 118–21.

22. Unidentified poem quoted in Peterson, *Lincoln in American Memory*, 162.

23. Ida Minerva Tarbell, "Father Abraham: Another 'He Knew Lincoln' story," *American Magazine* 67, no. 4 (February 1909). Tarbell was the muckraking journalist who exposed the excesses of Standard Oil.

24. Wilson, *City Beautiful Movement*, 285–90.

25. James T. McCleary, "What Shall the Lincoln Memorial Be?" *American Review of Reviews* 38 (September 1908): 334–41. For a resumé, see Reps, *Monumental Washington*, 155–56. See also "The Lincoln Memorial," *New York Times*, July 3, 1908, 6:2.

26. Endorsements are found in Burnham papers, Library of the Art Institute of Chicago, DHB to McCleary, October 5, 1908; and AIA Archives, RG 801, series 7, box 5, folder "LM, letters," Gilbert to Newlands, January 28, 1909.

27. Brown, *1860–1930, Memories*, 286.

28. On the early history of the automobile and the Good Roads movement, see James J. Flink, *America Adopts the Automobile, 1895–1910* (Cambridge, Mass.: MIT Press, 1970); idem, *The Car Culture* (Cambridge, Mass.: MIT Press, 1975), esp. chaps. 1, 2; and David Halberstam, *The Reckoning* (New York: William Morrow, 1986), esp. chap. 4. On roads, see also Spiro Kostof, *America by Design* (New York: Oxford University Press, 1987), 188–203.

29. See "A Highway from Ocean to Ocean," *Horseless Age* 23 (April 23, 1902): 512; and Bellamy Partridge, *Fill 'er Up! The Story of Fifty Years of Motoring* (New York: McGraw-Hill, 1952), esp. 79–85.

30. On Ford's innovations, see Terry Smith, *Making the Modern: Industry, Art, and Design in America* (Chicago: University of Chicago Press, 1993), chap. 1. On Good Roads conventions, see Flink, *America Adopts the Automobile*, 208; and Partridge, *Fill 'er Up!* chap. 14, esp. 185. See also Partridge's chronology of the car, p. 221.

31. Wayne E. Fuller, *RFD: The Changing Face of Rural America* (Bloomington: Indiana University Press, 1964), 181.

32. See *Post-Office Department: Annual Reports for the Fiscal Year Ended June 30, 1907* (Washington, D.C.: Government Printing Office,

1907), 137; on automobile service, see p. 151. On McCleary, see also *Biographical Directory of the American Congress,* 1284; *Who Was Who in America,* vol. 1,*1897–1942* (Chicago: Marquis, 1942), 800; Champ Clark, *My Quarter-Century of American Politics,* 2 vols. (1920; reprint, New York: Kraus Reprint, 1968), 2:427–29; and Carl H. Chrislock, *The Progressive Era in Minnesota 1899–1918* (St. Paul: Minnesota Historical Society, 1971), 42–43, 81.

33. See Wayne E. Fuller, *The American Mail: Enlarger of the Common Life* (Chicago: University of Chicago Press, 1972), 105–7 and passim; Carl H. Scheele, *A Short History of the Mail Service* (Washington, D.C.: Smithsonian Institution Press, 1970), 114–18; and Fuller, *RFD,* esp. chap. 8.

34. McCleary, "What Shall the Lincoln Memorial Be?" 338.

35. See *Congressional Record,* 60th Cong., 2d sess., vol. 43, 1202, 1290 (Senate, January 21 and 22, 1909); "The Lincoln Boulevard," *New York Times,* December 13, 1908; and "Views of the Lincoln Memorial," *New York Times,* January 13, 1909. Previously in favor of the road, the *Times* had changed its position.

36. Bill H.R. 21985: *Congressional Record,* 60th Cong., 1st sess., vol. 42, 6520. See also 60th Cong., 1st sess., H. Rep. 1773 (report of McCleary's committee on the bill).

37. Brown, "LM—Site," 491.

38. See Brown, *1860–1930, Memories,* 56–60; and Bushong, "Glenn Brown," 138–39.

39. On the station and its environs, see Scott and Lee, *Buildings of the District of Columbia,* 140–42. On the difficulties the plaza presented, see LC, Manuscripts, Olmsted Associates Papers, B136, file 2836, letter F. L. Olmsted Jr. to Col. John Biddle, January 8, 1906.

40. For correspondence about the project, see Burnham papers, Library of the Art Institute of Chicago; and the Architect of the U.S. Capitol, curator's office, file "Lincoln Memorial: D.H. Burnham & Co." A number of Anderson's drawings appear in Bates Lowry, *Building a National Image:*

Architectural Drawings for the American Democracy, 1789–1912 (Washington, D.C.: National Building Museum, 1985), plates 96–99.

41. See Lawrence B. Evans, *Samuel W. McCall, Governor of Massachusetts* (Boston: Houghton Mifflin, 1916), esp. 34–35.

42. See Brown, *1860–1930, Memories,* 283–94; Reps, *Monumental Washington,* 156; Bushong, "Glenn Brown," chap. 6; Bushong, Robinson, and Mueller, *Centennial History,* 31–32; and Thomas, "Lincoln Memorial and Its Architect," 387–404.

43. See the sources cited in Brown, *1860–1930, Memories;* and AIA archives, RG 801, series 7, box 5.

44. See Brown, *1860–1930, Memories,* 37–38 (including text of Executive Order 1010); Moore, *Daniel H. Burnham,* 2:116–19; Reps, *Monumental Washington,* 153; Susan A. Kohler, *The Commission of Fine Arts: A Brief History, 1910–1976,* (Washington, D.C.: Commission of Fine Arts, 1985), 2–3; Bushong, "Glenn Brown," 181–84; and Bushong, Robinson, and Mueller, *Centennial History,* 31.

45. *Congressional Record,* 60th Cong., 2d sess., vol. 43, 2116. McCall's commission is never known to have met.

46. See Pringle, *Life and Times of William Howard Taft;* and Cooper, *Pivotal Decades,* esp. 117–25.

47. See LC, Manuscripts, Root and Wetmore papers, passim; and, especially, Moore papers, container 8, Letter of Root to Moore, April 22, 1935. See also Kohler, *Commission of Fine Arts,* 3–4; and Bushong, "Glenn Brown," 189–93. On the revolt against Cannon, see Clark, *My Quarter-Century,* 2:270–83; and Busbey, *Uncle Joe Cannon,* 247–69.

48. See Kohler, *Commission of Fine Arts,* 165; and, on discussions of membership, LC, Manuscripts, Wetmore papers, container 1, folder "Candidates for the Art Commission."

49. LC, Manuscripts, Wetmore papers, container 1, CFA correspondence, printed circular letter.

50. See Glenn Brown, *The Development of Washington with Special Reference to the Lincoln*

Memorial, address of December 13, 1910 (Washington, D.C.: Washington Chamber of Commerce, 1910).

51. *Congressional Record,* 61st Cong., 3d sess., vol. 46, 236.

52. Quoted in Pringle, *Life and Times of William Howard Taft,* 1:410.

53. Judith Icke Anderson, *William Howard Taft: An Intimate History* (New York: Norton, 1981), 189.

54. Ibid., 152.

55. AIA archives, RG 801, series 7, box 5, letter to editor of *New York Times,* dated March 28, 1911. See also "Plans for the Lincoln Memorial," *Architectural Record* 29 (May 1911): 436–47.

56. Summaries of the Lincoln Memorial Commission's minutes are found in Concklin, *Lincoln Memorial,* 20–28. For full versions, see National Archives, RG 42, no. 363. Minutes are not cited individually hereafter.

57. See H. Paul Caemmerer, *The Commission of Fine Arts, 1910–1963: A Brief History* (Washington, D.C.: Government Printing Office, 1964), 3–7; and Kohler, *Commission of Fine Arts,* 7–15. CFA minutes are held, on paper and indexed, in the commission's offices, and on microfilm in National Archives, RG 66. See also National Archives, RG 66, no. 17 (project files).

58. See Bogart, *Public Sculpture,* esp. 284–303. Applications concerning the Lincoln Memorial are found in National Archives, RG 42, no. 362, vol. 1, and RG 66, no. 17, project files; in CFA minutes; and in LC, Manuscripts, Taft papers, series 6, no. 301.

59. Savage, "Race, Memory, Identity," 99, quoting *Washington Post,* September 9, 1911.

60. See *Congressional Record,* 61st Cong., 3d sess., vol. 46, 2086 (McCall's speech); and "The Lincoln Memorial" (editorial), *Washington Evening Star,* April 13, 1911.

61. Cited in note 60.

62. See Sue A. Kohler and Jeffrey R. Carson, *Sixteenth Street Architecture* (Washington, D.C.: Commission of Fine Arts, 1978), 1:323–35; James M. Goode, *Capital Losses: A Cultural History of Washington's Destroyed Buildings* (Washington, D.C.: Smithsonian Institution Press, 1979), 106–8; Meridian House International, *Washington Renaissance: Architecture and Landscape of Meridian Hill,* ed. Steven Bedford (Washington, D.C.: Meridian House International, 1989); and Scott and Lee, *Buildings of the District of Columbia,* 297–316.

63. See Reps, *Monumental Washington,* fig. 49, p. 86; and Moore, *Improvement of the Park System,* 63–65. Since then, the White house had been restored and enlarged.

64. See Mary Henderson, "Suggests Memorial Arch," letter to editor, *Washington Post,* August 7, 1911.

65. See E.S.M., "Discusses the Site of Lincoln Memorial," *Washington Times,* July 31, 1911.

66. Moore, *Improvement of the Park System,* 101.

67. See Moore, *Daniel H. Burnham,* 2:135.

68. See Fred L. Fishback, "Fort Stevens and the Lincoln Memorial," *National Magazine,* January 1912, 589–92; idem, "Opposed to Location for Lincoln Memorial" (letter to editor), *Washington Star,* August 4, 1911; and "Old Fort Stevens Sold," *Washington Evening Star,* March 22, 1911.

69. National Archives, RG 66, no. 17, letter of Millet to Burnham, June 19, 1911. The report, on which the following paragraphs are based, is found in three places: Commission of Fine Arts, *Annual Report,* 1911–12; Lincoln Memorial Commission, *Lincoln Memorial Commission Report,* December 5, 1912, 62d Cong., 3d sess., S. Doc. 965 (Washington, D.C.: Government Printing Office, 1913) [hereafter *LMC Report,* 1912], appendix A, pp. 19–24; and Concklin, *Lincoln Memorial,* 31–39.

70. See Moore, *Daniel H. Burnham,* 1:95–113; Brown, *1860–1930, Memories,* 206–10; Bushong, "Glenn Brown," 87–90; and Antoinette J. Lee, *Architects to the Nation: The Rise and Decline of the Supervising Architect's Office* (New York: Oxford University Press, 2000), esp. chap. 6.

71. Moore, *Daniel H. Burnham,* 2:135.

72. Ibid., 135–36.

73. Then, even more than now, such things were not said directly, least of all in writing. See, however, Roth, *McKim, Mead & White*, 116, 335, and passim; New-York Historical Society, McKim, Mead & White Papers, 1950 collection, old mixed file no. 276, (auto?)biography of Kendall; and Columbia University, Avery Library, W. R. Ware Collection, reminiscences of Henry Bacon by William Partridge [hereafter "Partridge—Avery, Bacon"], 2d installment, March 8, 1948.

74. Moore, *Daniel H. Burnham*, 1:134.

75. LC, Manuscripts, Moore papers, box 9, correspondence 1909–36, unidentified address, pp. 2–3.

76. For a thorough biography, see Thomas, "Lincoln Memorial and Its Architect," pt. 1. Bacon's office papers, on which the following account is largely based, are in Wesleyan University, Olin Memorial Library, Archives and Special Collections.

77. National Archives, RG 42, no. 362. Millet's statement served most of the press as Bacon's official biography.

78. On Frank Bacon, see Thomas, "Lincoln Memorial and Its Architect," 9–30; and idem, "Francis H. Bacon: Master Draftsman as Archaeologist," *The Classicist* 2 (1995–96): 28–33.

79. See Francis H. Bacon, ed., *Investigations at Assos: Drawings and Photographs of the Buildings and Objects Discovered during the Excavations of 1882–1883 by Joseph T. Clarke, Francis H. Bacon, Robert Koldewey*, 2 vols. (Cambridge, Mass.: Archeological Institute of America, 1902, 1921).

80. Partridge—Avery, Bacon. See also Marcelle Robinson, "Pioneer, Scholar, and Victim: An Appreciation of Frank Calvert (1828–1908)," *Anatolia* 14 (1994): 153–68.

81. See books by Leland M. Roth and Richard Guy Wilson, both titled *McKim, Mead & White, Architects* and both published in 1983, the former by Harper and Row, the latter by Rizzoli; and Susannah Lessard, *The Architect of Desire: Beauty and Danger in the Stanford White Family* (London: Phoenix, 1997).

82. See Francis S. Swales, "Henry Bacon as a Draftsman," *Pencil Points* 5 (May 1924): 43; and Egerton Swartwout, "An Architectural Decade," unpublished typescript in Walker Cain's office (copy in possession of Leland Roth).

83. See Arthur Drexler, ed., *The Architecture of the Ecole des Beaux-Arts* (New York: Museum of Modern Art, 1977); Robin Middleton, ed., *The Beaux-Arts and Nineteenth-Century French Architecture* (Cambridge, Mass.: MIT Press, 1982); and Richard Oliver, *The Making of an Architect, 1881–1981: Columbia University in the City of New York* (New York: Rizzoli, 1981), esp. 13–85.

84. Royal Cortissoz, "The Architect," *Architectural Record* 55 (March 1924): 276.

85. Besides Thomas, "Lincoln Memorial and Its Architect," chap. 3 and appendix A, see Richman, *Daniel Chester French*; and idem, "Daniel Chester French and Henry Bacon: Public Sculpture in Collaboration, 1897–1908," *American Journal of Art* 12, no. 3 (summer 1980): 46–64.

86. See *Dictionary of American Biography*, s.v. "Hanna, Marcus A."; and Herbert Croly, *M. A. Hanna, His Life and Work* (New York: Macmillan, 1912; reprint, Temecula, Calif.: Reprint Services, 1988), esp. 456.

87. He had designed monuments to other Republican leaders, too, including President Benjamin Harrison, in Indianapolis; Carl Schurz, in New York City; and Garrett A. Hobart, McKinley's first vice president, in Paterson, N.J: Thomas, "Lincoln Memorial and Its Architect," appendix A.

88. Although Cannon's motion, once defeated, was expunged from the record at his own request, a trace of it is found in National Archives, RG 42, no. 362, 1;64, 78.

89. See Architect of the Capitol, curator's office, file "proposed Lincoln Memorial—J. R. Pope." The abortive consultative committee Cannon had proposed would have consisted of Pope, Bacon, and Woods.

90. "Clark Wants Highway Monument to Lincoln," *New York Globe*, August 9, 1911.

91. See Bedford, *John Russell Pope*; also Her-

bert Croly, "Recent Works of John Russell Pope," *Architectural Record* 29 (June 1911): 441–509; and Steven Bedford, "John Russell Pope and Meridian Hill," in Meridian House International, *Washington Renaissance*, 13–27.

92. See National Archives, RG 66, project files, letters of Pope to Charles Moore, November 18 and 23, 1931, recalling events of 1911.

93. *Congressional Record*, 62d Cong., 1st sess., vol. 47, 3323–24.

94. The request appears in National Archives, RG 42, no. 362, 2:128, letter of Borland to Taft, July 2 [*sic*: means August], 1911.

95. See "Want Site Changed," *Washington Star*, August 4, 1911; "Lincoln Memorial Highway Is Urged on President Taft," *Washington Times*, August 4, 1911; "May Change Memorial Plan," *Washington Post*, August 5, 1911; and "Congress to Decide," *Washington Star*, August 9, 1911 (source of "nation-wide agitation").

96. Senate bill 3197, copy in National Archives, RG 42, no. 362, 1:76.

97. See the sources cited in note 28; and Cooper, *Pivotal Decades*, 133–35.

98. See Lee Shipley, "Building a National Turnpike," *Collier's*, January 6, 1912, auto section; and National Archives, RG 42, no. 362, 2:141: letter of Mary Henderson to Taft, February 3rd, [1912].

99. Partridge, *Fill 'er Up!* 221. On Ford, see Smith, *Making the Modern*, chap. 2.

100. The index to National Archives, RG 42, no. 362, vol. 1, lists letters from the Packard and United States motorcar companies, but the letters themselves are missing.

101. *Biographical Directory of the American Congress*, 1284.

102. *The Lincoln Memorial Road Association of America*, pamphlet, copy in National Archives, RG 42, no. 362, 2:128.

103. Jessup, *Elihu Root*, 1:280.

104. Drake Hokanson, *The Lincoln Highway: A Main Street across America* (Iowa City: University of Iowa Press, 1988), 9.

105. W.E.B. [*sic*], "Urging Lincoln Road," *Boston Evening Transcript*, December 30, 1911.

106. Brown, "LM—Site," 494.

CHAPTER 3

1. For these and other models, see general sources, such as Spiro Kostof, *A History of Architecture: Settings and Rituals*, 3d ed. (New York: Oxford University Press, 1995); Nikolaus Pevsner, *A History of Building Types*, Bollingen Series xxxv.19 (Princeton, N.J.: Princeton University Press, 1976), chap. 1; and James Stevens Curl, *A Celebration of Death: An Introduction to Some of the Buildings, Monuments, and Settings of Funerary Architecture in the Western European Tradition* (London: Constable and Co., 1980), chaps. 11, 12. On Civil War commemoration, specifically, see Savage, *Standing Soldiers, Kneeling Slaves*, passim.

2. Opinion expressed in answer to a query of January 1912 from the Lincoln Memorial Commission on the advisability of building an obelisk to Lincoln.

3. See Hugh Honour, *Neoclassicism* (Harmondsworth: Penguin, 1968); J. Mordaunt Crook, *The Greek Revival: Neo-classical Attitudes in British Architecture 1760–1870* (London: J. Murray, 1972), pt. 1; and Roger G. Kennedy, *Greek Revival America* (New York: Stewart, Tabori and Chang, 1989).

4. Leila Mechlin, "The Proposed Lincoln Memorial," *The Century* 83 (January 1912): 374. Secretary of the American Federation of Arts, Mechlin was an associate of Glenn Brown's and a friend of the Bacon brothers. The accuracy of her testimony to Bacon's intentions can be relied on.

5. Royal Cortissoz, "A Memorial to Lincoln Worthy Alike of the Nation and the Man," *New York Tribune*, January 7, 1912.

6. Mechlin, "Proposed Lincoln Memorial," 374.

7. Cortissoz, "Memorial to Lincoln."

8. Brooklyn Museum, *The American Renais-*

sance, 1876–1917, exhibition catalog (Brooklyn, N.Y.: Brooklyn Institute of Arts and Sciences, 1979), chap. 1.

9. See John M. Bryan, ed., *Robert Mills, Architect* (Washington, D.C.: American Institute of Architects Press, 1989), 159–60.

10. Wesleyan University, Bacon papers, misc. correspondence, letter of Royal Cortissoz to HB, August 28 [1911], referring to an idea expressed in a letter from HB.

11. On the idea—but not the phrase—see Anthony Vidler, *Claude-Nicolas Ledoux: Architecture and Social Reform at the End of the Ancien Régime* (Cambridge, Mass.: MIT Press, 1990), especially 145–49.

12. Letter cited in note 10.

13. On his work, see Jules Vallée Guérin, *Jules Guérin, Master Delineator: An Exhibition* (Houston: Rice University, 1983).

14. See *LMC Report*, 1912, appendix. Typescript copies are found in National Archives, RG 42, and in Wesleyan University, Bacon papers, box 6. Illustrations from Bacon's design were also published in *The Century* 83 (January 1912), and *Architecture* 25 (February 1912).

15. Moore, *Daniel H. Burnham*, 2:151.

16. See J. J. Coulton, *Ancient Greek Architects at Work: Problems of Structure and Design* (Ithaca, N.Y.: Cornell University Press, 1977), 108–12.

17. See William H. Goodyear, "Horizontal Curves in Columbia University," *Architectural Record* 9 (July–September 1899): 82–93; and idem, *Greek Refinements: Studies in Temperamental Architecture* (New Haven, Conn.: Yale University Press, 1912).

18. Though not mentioned in Bacon's report of December 1911, this refinement was clearly intended, for he incorporated extensive horizontal curvature in the executed design.

19. See essays by Neil Levine, Robin Middleton, and David Van Zanten in Middleton, *The Beaux-Arts and Nineteenth-Century Architecture*.

20. Mechlin, "Proposed Lincoln Memorial," 374.

21. Ibid.

22. See William H. Pierson Jr., *American Buildings and Their Architects: The Colonial and Neoclassical Styles* (Garden City, N.Y.: Anchor Books, 1976), chap. 8.

23. On these, see Frank Sear, *Roman Architecture* (Ithaca, N.Y.: Cornell University Press, 1983), esp. chap. 2.

24. See Ernest Nash, *The Pictorial Dictionary of Ancient Rome*, 2d ed., revised (New York: Praeger, 1968), 1:292–94.

25. See David Watkin and Tilman Mellinghoff, *German Architecture and the Classical Ideal* (Cambridge, Mass.: MIT Press, 1987).

26. Wesleyan University Archives, Bacon collection, drawings for Lincoln Memorial.

27. See *LMC Report*, 1912, appendix C. National Archives, RG 42, contains an original, illustrated copy of Pope's report. Several original renderings survive in National Archives, cartographic collection, RG 42, and are reproduced in Dunlap Society, *The Architecture of Washington, DC*, microfiche collection, ed. Bates Lowry (Washington, D.C.: Dunlap Society, 1976–79), I, ix, 1-E; and in Lowry, *Building a National Image*, plates 100–106. Prints of others survive in the photo collection of the Commission of Fine Arts. See also the sources on Pope cited in note 28 and in chapter 2, notes 11, 91.

28. Steven Bedford, "The Architectural Career of John Russell Pope" (Ph.D. diss., Columbia University, 1994), 255. In "John Russell Pope and Meridian Hill" (in *Washington Renaissance* [Washington, D.C.: Meridian House International, 1989], 13–27), Bedford had identified as Pope's model the so-called Temple of Neptune at Paestum, now known to be of Hera.

29. The report suggests: "TO ABRAHAM LINCOLN PIONEER ORATOR JURIST STATESMAN PARDONER RECONCILER EMANCIPATOR LOVER AND PROTECTOR OF ALL LIFE WHO THROUGH THE BITTERNESS OF WAR PRESERVED THE UNION AND WHO THROUGH A MAR-

TYR'S DEATH HEALED THE WOUNDS OF THE SWORD AND CEMENTED IN LOVE A REUNITED PEOPLE." A longer quotation from a speech by Lincoln would appear inside, on the frieze above the colonnade.

30. Architect of the Capitol, curator's office, file on Lincoln Memorial, letter of Woods to Pope, November 6, 1911.

31. The summary of press commentary here is based largely on scrapbooks of clippings in the Wesleyan University Archives, Bacon collection. Important reviews of the designs are listed in the bibliography.

32. Mechlin "Proposed Lincoln Memorial," 374, 376. See also Mechlin's shorter review, "The Lincoln Memorial," in *Art and Progress* 3 (February 1912): 484–85.

33. "The Proposed Lincoln National Memorial," *Harper's Weekly*, January 20, 1912, 21.

34. Architect of the Capitol, curator's office, file on Lincoln Memorial, letter of Pope to Woods, n.d.

35. [Title missing], *Washington Star*, December 30, 1911; copy in Wesleyan University Archives, Bacon collection, clipping scrapbook.

36. See AIA Archives, RG 801, series 7.

37. See note 2.

38. Copies of a brochure showing the design, issued at her expense, are found in National Archives, RG 42, no. 362. See also "Congress Urged to Place Lincoln Memorial on Meridian Hill," *Washington Herald*, January 21, 1912. In fact, the design eventually adopted for Meridian Hill Park incorporated similar water features.

39. See LC, Manuscripts, Taft papers, series 6, letters of MacVeagh to Taft, March 8, 1912, and Taft to MacVeagh, March, 12, 1912.

40. "Name Lincoln Memorial Site," *Washington Post*, February 4, 1912, 1.

41. Brown, "LM—Site," 499, quoting a letter of the Lincoln Memorial Road Association.

42. Ibid., 498.

43. On living memorials, see Bogart, *Public Sculpture*, 284–292.

44. On modernity and modernism, its literary and artistic parallel, see *The Dictionary of Art*, ed. Jane Turner (London: Macmillan, 1996), 21:775–79; and Daniel Joseph Singal, "Towards a Definition of Modernism," *American Quarterly* 39, no. 1 (spring 1987): 7–26.

45. Henry F. May, *The End of American Innocence: A Study of the First Years of Our Own Time, 1912–1917* (New York: Knopf, 1959).

46. See Smith, *Making the Modern*. His argument, though applied mainly to the 1920s and 1930s, is useful for the prewar period, too.

47. Walter Lippmann, *Drift and Mastery: An Attempt to Diagnose the Current Unrest* (1914; new edition, Englewood Cliffs, N.J.: Prentice-Hall, 1961), 16.

48. Quoted in Smith, *Making the Modern*, 4.

49. See U.S. Congress, *Hearings before the Committee on the Library, House of Representatives, on H.R. 13045* (Washington, D.C.: Government Printing Office, 1912). On Slayden's support for the plan, see Ellen Maury Slayden, *Washington Wife: Journal of Ellen Maury Slayden from 1897–1919* (New York: Harper and Row, 1963), 193, 364.

50. Slayden, *Washington Wife*, 193.

51. *LMC Report*, appendix E. A copy of Pope's revised design and the report on it is in National Archives, RG 42, no. 362. For illustrations, see Dunlap Society, *Architecture of Washington, DC*, vol. 1, chap. 9, fiche 2: A4–B3; and idem, *Building a National Image*, plates 102 and 104–6.

52. Lowry, *Building a National Image*, plate 104; and *Antiques* 128 (October 1985): 731.

53. On Bacon's revised designs see the same sources as for Pope's, listed in note 51.

54. Dunlap Society, *Architecture of Washington, DC*, vol. 1, chap. 9, shows a perspective (2-B9), "probably representing Bacon's scheme A." This is incorrect: it shows his design of December 1911. An elevation (ibid., 2-C7), reproduced from *American Architect* 27 (October 1920), is said to represent a preliminary or intermediate design, but this is also wrong. Rather, it shows Bacon's "final" design of June 1912. No known drawing corresponds to the plan in Figure 3.25 and Bacon's description of his scheme A.

55. *LMC Report*, appendix F. Copies of the original, again drafted by Moore and revised by Millet, are in National Archives, RG 42, no. 362; and RG 66, no. 17, project files.

56. "Leader": National Archives, RG 66, project files, letter of Pope to Charles Moore, November 23, 1931. "Too modest": Architect of the U.S. Capitol, curator's office, project file, letter of Pope to Woods, April 1, 1912.

57. See National Archives, RG 42, no. 362, letter of Pope to Lincoln Memorial Commission, April 1, 1912. Enclosed are supporting letters from two contractors, the George A. Fuller Co., which went on to build the superstructure, and Norcross Brothers, formerly H. H. Richardson's builders.

58. LC, Manuscripts, Taft papers, series 6, no. 301.

59. In 1931, wanting to get to the bottom of the bad taste the competition had left, Charles Moore approached Pope for his version of events: see National Archives, RG 66, project file, letters of Pope to Charles Moore, November 18 and 23, 1931.

60. See sources on Pope cited in note 28 and in chapter 2, note 11; and Christopher A. Thomas, *The Architecture of the West Building of the National Gallery of Art* (Washington, D.C.: National Gallery of Art, 1992).

61. Bacon's final scheme is the best-documented stage of the evolution of his design in his papers and drawings at Wesleyan University and in National Archives, Cartographic division, RG 42. See also *LMC Report*, December 1912, appendix G; and Dunlap Society, *Architecture of Washington, DC*, vol. 1, chap. 9, fiche 2, C1–D1.

62. National Archives, RG 42, no. 362, transcript of hearing before the Senate Library Committee, December 7, 1912, Bacon agreeing with Wetmore.

63. See Wesleyan University Archives, Bacon collection, Lincoln Memorial correspondence, letter of Cullom to Bacon, June 4, 1912.

64. "Lincoln as a Greek God," *New York Independent*, February 8, 1912.

65. F. W. Fitzpatrick, "An Architect's Protest," *The Outlook* (New York), March 31, 1912.

66. See Brooklyn Museum, *American Renaissance*, esp. pt. 1.

67. See May, *End of American Innocence*, pt. 3, chap. 2; and, on literature, Dorothy Anne Dondore, *The Prairie and the Making of Middle America: Four Centuries of Description* (1926; reprint, New York: Antiquarian Press, 1961), esp. chap. 8.

68. Cited in May, *End of American Innocence*, 249.

69. Resolution paraphrased in "Fight Lincoln Plan," *Chicago Sunday Record*, January 19, 1913.

70. "Discuss Design of Lincoln Statue," *Chicago Inter-Ocean*, January 19, 1913.

71. See Rex Alan Smith, *The Carving of Mount Rushmore* (New York: Abbeville Press, 1985); and Boime, *Unveiling of the National Icons*, chap. 3.

72. "The Nation's Memorial to Abraham Lincoln" (letter to the editor), *New York Sun*, January 15, 1912.

73. Borglum, letter to Wetmore of February 22, 1912; copies in National Archives, RG 42, no. 362; and LC, Manuscripts, Taft and Wetmore Papers.

74. "Mr. Gutzon Borglum Says Never Use a Fork," unidentified clipping in Wesleyan University Archives, Bacon collection, clipping scrapbook. See also "Borglum Scolds Again," *American Art News*, March 9, 1912.

75. Wesleyan University Archives, Bacon collection, Lincoln Memorial correspondence, letter of Bacon to Cullom, June 1, 1912. See also National Archives, RG 42, no. 362, letter of Borglum to Henry Vale, April 4, 1912.

76. 62d Cong., 3d sess., S. Rept. 1071 (of the Senate Library Committee, drafted by Root).

77. "Love for Senator to Win," *Philadelphia Record*, January 16, 1913.

78. 62d Cong., 3d sess., H. Rept. 1294.

79. "The Lincoln Memorial and After" (editorial), *Brooklyn Standard*, February 9, 1913.

1. See lengthy reports in National Archives, RG 66, project files, letter of Cass Gilbert to Col. S. Cosby, June 6, 1913; and ibid., RG 42, no. 366, letter of Frederick Law Olmsted, Jr., to Bacon, May 25, 1913.

2. On him, see "The Foundations of the Lincoln Memorial," *Pencil Points* 5 (June 1924): 74–75.

3. See Thomas, "Marble of the Lincoln Memorial," 42–63; and David Roberts, "Magical Marble, That Gleaming Rock for the Ages," *Smithsonian* 22, no. 10 (January 1992): 98–107.

4. "Whiteness": National Archives, RG 42, no. 362, architect's report, September 25, 1913. "I remember": ibid., transcript of LMC hearing, September 26, 1913, p. 50.

5. This claim became standard, but Bacon himself said only that the memorial was larger than any Greek Doric temple. "Some of the temples in Sicily are larger than the Lincoln Memorial, but coarse tufa stone was used in their construction": Wesleyan University Archives, Bacon collection, box 6, description of memorial.

6. See National Archives, RG 42, no. 366, anonymous memorandum for General Crowder, October 10, 1913. The bidder was Arthur Cowsill, of Washington, D.C.

7. "Splendid company": National Archives, RG 42, no. 366, letter Bacon to J. F. Bethune, September 29, 1913. "Simply glorious": Wesleyan University Archives, Bacon collection, Lincoln Memorial correspondence, letter Bacon to Shelby Cullom, September 27, 1913.

8. See George A. Fuller Co., *Fireproof Building Construction: Prominent Buildings Erected by the George A. Fuller Company* (New York: 1904, 1910); and idem, *George A. Fuller Company, General Contractors, 1882–1937* (New York: George A. Fuller Company, 1937).

9. See, e.g., Bogart, *Public Sculpture*, 168–70.

10. National Archives, RG 42, no. 366, "Memorandum on the Approaches . . . ," 2.

11. Page Smith, *America Enters the World: A People's History of the Progressive Era and World War I* (New York: Penguin, 1985), 79.

12. Arthur S. Link, *Wilson: The New Freedom* (Princeton, N.J.: Princeton University Press, 1956), 119.

13. See National Archives, RG 42, no. 362, letter of Root (who had framed the bill) to Cullom, November 6, 1913. On the corps' activities in Washington, see Albert E. Cowdrey, *A City for the Nation: The Army Engineers and the Building of Washington, D.C., 1790–1967* (Washington, D.C.: Historical Division, Office of Administrative Services, Office of the Chief Engineer, Government Printing Office, 1979).

14. National Archives, RG 42, no. 366, anonymous memorandum for General Crowder, October 10, 1913.

15. Wesleyan University, Bacon papers, box 6, incomplete copy of a legal opinion by Cullom, probably addressed to Attorney General J. C. McReynolds. He told Bacon, "I feel terribly disgusted at the conduct of the Secretary of War. . . . He had the reputation of being a gentleman and a man of affairs but he is neither"; ibid., letter of Cullom to Bacon, January 3, 1914. Cullom died on January 28.

16. National Archives, RG 42, no. 362, letter of Daniel C. French (as chair of CFA) to Garrison, January 23, 1914, enclosed in letter of Garrison to Taft, January 26, 1914.

17. "Memorial Ground Broken," *Washington Herald*, February 13, 1914.

18. A copy of Blackburn's remarks accompanies LMC minutes for February 7, 1914, in National Archives, RG 42, no. 362.

19. See Office of Public Buildings and Grounds (hereafter OPB&G), monthly reports of operations on the Lincoln Memorial, 1913–20 (intermittent toward the end), in National Archives, RG 42, no. 366 (to May 1914) and no. 365 (thereafter). These are not cited here individually.

20. Col. W. W. Harts, "Cylinder-Pier Founda-

tions for Lincoln Memorial, Washington, D.C.,"
Engineering News 71 (May 7, 1914): 1019. See
also A. Sylvester Edmonds, "Engineering Feats in
Building Lincoln Memorial," *Manufacturers
Record* 67, no. 1 (January 7, 1915): 47–48; "Foun-
dations of the Lincoln Memorial"; and Maj. D. L.
Weart, "The Foundations of the Lincoln Memor-
ial," in Concklin, *Lincoln Memorial,* 55–61.

21. Edmonds, "Engineering Feats," 48.

22. "Beautiful Lincoln Memorial Dedicated
with Simple Ceremonies," *New York Sun,* February 26, 1915.

23. Wesleyan University Archives, Bacon collection, Lincoln Memorial correspondence, letter of
Bacon to Cullom, July 28, 1913.

24. On these, see Henry Bacon, "The Architecture of the Lincoln Memorial," in Concklin, *Lincoln Memorial,* 42.

25. National Archives, RG 42, no. 366, letter of
July 8, 1914, by which time much of the marble
had been quarried and cut to size. Harts's reply of
the next day (ibid.) confirms that Bacon was referring to the memorial's walls only.

26. See Fred J. Maroon, Suzy Maroon, and
Daniel J. Boorstin, *The United States Capitol* (New
York: Stewart, Tabori, and Chang, 1993), 83, 87, 92.

27. Henry Bacon, "Exterior Decorations," in
Concklin, *Lincoln Memorial,* 49.

28. On the decision to raise the attic, see
National Archives, RG 42, no. 366, letters of Bacon
(per Lincoln) to Harts, September 23, 1914; and
Harts to Bacon, October 24, 1914. New drawings
were made for the attic in spring 1915.

29. National Archives, RG 42, no. 366, letter of
Bacon to Olmsted, October 6, 1915.

30. See "Lincoln Address for Memorial,"
Washington Herald, March 24, 1913. Isaac
Markens, considered the authority on the address,
sent Bacon a copy of his article on its wording
and an endorsement by Robert Lincoln of his
position.

31. Wesleyan University Archives, Bacon collection, "Building the Lincoln Memorial," typescript by J. F. Manning, enclosed in letter of

Manning to Bacon, October 19, 1916. Manning
was president of the Colorado-Yule Marble Company. Here, the account of quarrying and fabrication is based on Manning's article; Roberts,
"Magical Marble"; and the transcript of an interview in October 1985 between the late Paul Goeldner, U.S. National Park Service, and the late Henry
Bacon McKoy, the architect's nephew, who represented the Fuller Company at the quarry in
1914–15. See also my article "Marble of the Lincoln Memorial."

32. The same chamber supplied the block for
the Tomb of the Unknown Soldier in Arlington
National Cemetery.

33. J. P. Kirsch, "The Marble Columns of the
Lincoln Memorial," *Scientific American* 112
(March 20, 1915): 267.

34. Papers of Henry Bacon McKoy, copy of letter of Shafroth to Manning, February 12, 1915. A
copy of the letter was deposited in the memorial's
cornerstone: see Concklin, *Lincoln Memorial,*
65–66.

35. "The Heart-Gift" by Arthur Chapman, in
clipping enclosed in letter of Manning to Bacon,
February 18, 1915, Wesleyan University Archives,
Bacon collection, box 4.

36. "Supreme altar": filmmaker Paul Strand,
quoted in Richard Guy Wilson, Dianne H. Pilgrim,
and Dickran Tashjian, *The Machine Age in America 1918–1941* (New York: Brooklyn Museum and
Harry N. Abrams, 1986), 23. "New Messiah" title
of an article by Ford (1928), cited in ibid., 351 note
25. On perceptions of America's prophetic role, see
Reyner Banham, *A Concrete Atlantis: U.S. Industrial Building and European Modern Architecture
1900–1925* (Cambridge, Mass.: MIT Press, 1986);
and Jean-Louis Cohen, *Scenes of the World to
Come: European Architecture and the American
Challenge, 1893–1960,* preface by Hubert Damisch
(Paris: Flammarion; Montreal: Canadian Centre for
Architecture, 1995).

37. Le Corbusier, *Towards a New Architecture,*
trans. Frederick Etchells (1927; reprint, New York:
Holt, Rinehart and Winston, 1982), 42.

38. On the ceremony, see Concklin, *Lincoln Memorial*, 65–67.

39. Ibid., 43.

40. "Comment on Passing Events Heard in Washington Hotels," *Washington Post*, June 30, 1916.

41. Quoted by Bacon in Wesleyan University Archives, Bacon collection, typescript, "The Lincoln Memorial."

42. *Congressional Record*, 64th Cong., 1st sess. House, February 15, 1916, 2593.

43. Richman, *Daniel Chester French*, 123.

44. See J. J. Pollitt, *Art in the Hellenistic Age* (Cambridge: Cambridge University Press, 1986), 65–70.

45. See Fryd, *Art and Empire*, chap. 3.

46. The seated figure of *Lincoln the Statesman* was not dedicated until 1926 but had been cast in 1908 and was well known by 1911: see Dryfhout, *Work of Augustus Saint-Gaudens*, 278; and Ira J. Bach, *A Guide to Chicago's Public Sculpture* (Chicago: University of Chicago Press, 1983), 28.

47. Wesleyan University Archives, Bacon collection, box 4, copy of letter from Bacon to Prof. Franklin W. Hooper, May 23, 1913.

48. Ibid., memo to file, April 24, 1914.

49. Ibid., letter of May 23, 1913 (see note 47).

50. Ibid., letters of Bacon to Hooper, February 15, 1913; and French to Hooper, March 1, 1913.

51. "Unconditional surrender": ibid., box 4, Lincoln Memorial correspondence, telegram French to Bacon, January 8, 1915.

52. Ibid., letter of French to Bacon, May 29, 1915. Published sources on the statue and its modeling include: [French], "The Statue," in Concklin, *Lincoln Memorial*, 44–45; Richman, *Daniel Chester French*, 171–86; idem, "The Lincoln Memorial: The Impact of the Columbian Exposition on Washington, D.C." (abstract), *Journal of the Society of Architectural Historians* 35 (December 1976): 275–76; and idem, "Sculptor Daniel Chester French and Architect Henry Bacon Labored Long and Hard to Give the Nation Its

Favorite Statue, 'Abraham Lincoln,' in Lincoln Memorial," *Smithsonian*, 7, no. 11 (February 1977): 54–61.

53. Copy of contract in National Archives, RG 66, project files; see also related correspondence in National Archives, RG 42, no. 366.

54. National Archives, RG 42, letter of Bacon to Harts, September 17, 1917, cited in Richman, *Daniel Chester French*, 179–80.

55. Memo cited in note 48.

56. See Glenn B. Opitz, ed., *Dictionary of American Sculptors: 18th Century to Present* (Poughkeepsie, N.Y.: Apollo, 1984), 313–14; and Josef Vincent Lombardo, *Attilio Piccirilli: Life of an American Sculptor* (New York: Pitman, 1944), esp. 54–63. See also W. M. Berger, "Making a Great Statue: How French's Lincoln Was Put into Marble," *Scribner's Magazine* 66 (October 1919): 424–31; and the sources cited in note 52.

57. See National Archives, RG 42, no. 366, letter of Bacon to Fuller Co., November 24, 1916.

58. National Archives, RG 42, no. 366, letter of Bacon, per L. J. Lincoln, to Col. Ridley, August 14, 1918.

59. Richman, *Daniel Chester French*, 182, citing letter to Newton MacKintosh, February 13, 1920.

60. Ibid., quoting letter of French to Ridley, May 24, 1920.

61. Quoted in Eleanor Carroll, "Colossal Statue of Lincoln in Place," *New York Evening Post*, March 10, 1920.

62. See Wills, *Lincoln at Gettysburg*.

63. See Jesse Lynch Williams, "The Guérin Decorations for the Lincoln Memorial: How They Were Done," *Scribner's Magazine* 66 (October 1919): 416–23; Jules Guérin, "The Mural Decorations, Described by the Painter," *Art and Archaeology* 13 (June 1922): 258–59; [idem], "The Interior Decorations," in Concklin, *Lincoln Memorial*, 45–46; and F. S. Swales, "Jules Guérin," *Pencil Points*, 5 (May 1924): 63–66. Other sources are cited in Guérin, *Jules Guérin, Master Delineator*, 14–15.

64. See "An Appearing Act at Lincoln Memor-

ial," *Boston Globe,* July 23, 1996, D1. Here, the painting restorer Christiana Cunningham-Andrews observes, "It would be ideal to put some doors on the Lincoln Memorial, but for some reason I don't think that would fly." I am also grateful to Audrey Tepper, restoration architect for the National Park Service, for information on the deterioration of the murals.

65. See Cooper, *Pivotal Decades,* 207–10, 309.

66. Ibid., 331.

67. See Constance M. Green, *The Secret City: A History of Race Relations in the Nation's Capital* (Princeton, N.J.: Princeton University Press, 1967); "The Other Washington," *Wilson Quarterly* 13 (New Year's, 1989), 76–117; and Helen B. Stern and Philip M. Stern, *"O, Say Can You See?": A Bifocal Tour of Washington* (Washington, D.C.: Colortone Press, 1965).

68. Wills, *Lincoln at Gettysburg,* esp. prologue and chap. 4.

69. Savage, *Race, Memory, Identity,* 162.

70. National Archives, RG 42, no. 366, letter of Bacon to Harts, December 16, 1916.

71. The offers are found in National Archives, RG 42, no. 362 and no. 366. Some correspondents also thought the memorial commission could *supply* information and Lincolniana.

72. 64th Cong., 1st sess., H.R. 4712, December 14, 1915.

73. National Archives, RG 66, project files, letters of W. G. Leland (secretary of American Historical Association) to Charles Moore, June 26 and July 15, 1915; and of Gaillard Hunt (of Library of Congress) to Moore, July 29, 1915.

74. National Archives, RG 42, no. 366, letter of Ridley to Rep. W. S. Vane (Pa.), November 17, 1917.

75. "Congressman 'Rediscovers' Lincoln Memorial Cavern," *Washington Star,* July 18, 1961.

76. "Plan for Museum within Memorial Has Backer in Lujan," *Washington Post,* February 17, 1992.

77. Lincoln, *Speeches and Writings,* 199. See also Henry B. Rankin, *Personal Recollections of Abraham Lincoln* (New York: Putnam's, 1916).

78. Wesleyan University Archives, Bacon collection, Lincoln Memorial correspondence, letter of Rankin to Bacon, May 2, 1916, in reply to one, now lost, from Bacon, of April 27, 1916.

79. Ibid., letter of Bacon to Rankin, July 2, 1919. For the Bixby letter, see Lincoln, *Speeches and Writings,* 644.

80. CFA minutes, August 20, 1919.

81. Wesleyan University, Bacon papers, Lincoln Memorial correspondence, letter of French to Bacon, August 28, 1919.

82. See Wesleyan University Archives, Bacon collection, Lincoln Memorial correspondence, letter of Bacon to Taft, April 29, 1922, enclosing an explanatory letter from Cortissoz to Bacon, April 28, 1922.

83. See Henry Louis Mencken, *Prejudices: Fifth Series* (New York: Knopf, 1926), 199–202.

84. National Archives, RG 66, project files, letter of Howe to Moore, January 17, 1935.

85. See National Archives, RG 66, project files, letter of Gilbert to Harts, June 15, 1915.

86. National Archives, RG 66, project files, circular letter from Olmsted to CFA members, May 26, 1915.

87. CFA minutes, February 9, 1920, quoting recent letter of Bacon to Colonel Ridley recalling his intentions of 1915.

88. See National Archives, RG 66, project files, passim; and Kohler, *Commission of Fine Arts,* 13–15.

89. "I hear": Wesleyan University Archives, Bacon collection, Lincoln Memorial correspondence, letter of French to Bacon, August 12, 1919. "Of all the works": ibid., Bacon to French, August 15, 1919. On his terms of employment, see National Archives, RG 42, no. 366, letter of Harts to J. C. Courts, February 15, 1916.

90. Wesleyan University Archives, Bacon collection, audit of Bacon's income taxes, 1921.

91. National Parks Service, Goeldner-McKoy interview, transcript.

92. Ibid.

93. LC, Manuscripts, Charles Moore papers,

container 5, letter of Gilbert to Moore, February 19, 1918.

94. "Obtrusively ugly": National Archives, RG 42, no. 362, memorandum (by Glenn Brown?) to Congress behind unsigned letter to Taft, March 29, 1919. See also "Plea Made for Early Removal of Army and Navy Buildings from Potomac Park Grounds," *Washington Evening Star*, June 12, 1919.

95. See Kohler, *Commission of Fine Arts*, 15, 36; and Richard Guy Wilson, "High Noon on the Mall," in Longstreth, *The Mall in Washington*, 146–47.

96. Margaret French Cresson, *Journey into Fame: The Life of Daniel Chester French* (Cambridge, Mass.: Harvard University Press, 1947), 277–78. See also idem, "Lighting Lincoln's Statue," *American Heritage* 7, no. 2 (February 1956): 56–57.

97. Elbert Peets, "The Interior of the Lincoln Memorial," *American Mercury*, June 1925; reprinted in Paul D. Spreiregen, ed., *On the Art of Designing Cities: Selected Essays of Elbert Peets* (Cambridge, Mass.: MIT Press, 1968), 102.

98. See Richman, *Daniel Chester French*, 183–84.

99. See Charles Linn, "Study Finds Lincoln Looks Best Basking in Incandescent Glow," *Architectural Record* 186 (February 1998): 205–6.

100. See Concklin, *Lincoln Memorial*, 58–61; and National Archives, RG 42, no. 366, [Colonel C. S. Ridley], "Memorandum (for Taft) on the Approaches and Terrace Wall of the Lincoln Memorial," January 1921.

101. See National Archives, RG 42, no. 366, memorandum by superintending engineer F. F. Gillen, March 13, 1919.

102. National Archives, RG 66, project files, letter of Taft to Moore, April 7, 1920.

103. See *The Lincoln Memorial: Letter from the Secretary of the Treasury . . .* , 66th Cong., 3d sess., S. Doc. 372, February 2, 1921.

104. See Scott and Lee, *Buildings of the District of Columbia*, 104; and U.S. Department of the Interior, National Park Service, *Rock Creek and Potomac Parkway, Washington, D.C.* (n.d.).

105. See Concklin, *Lincoln Memorial*, 51–52; and Kohler, *Commission of Fine Arts*, 15.

106. "Mall the Predestined Site for Lincoln Memorial," *Washington Post*, May 14, 1922; and "Lincoln Memorial Typifies Culture of the Emancipator," *Washington Post*, May 21, 1922. Charles Moore may have ghostwritten both articles.

107. Grace Phelps, "America's Tribute to the Rail Splitter," *New York Tribune*, May 28, 1922. See also *Literary Digest* 73 (June 17, 1922): 28. Could "Grace Phelps" have been a pseudonym for Cortissoz, the *Tribune*'s art critic?

108. "Simplicity to Mark Dedication Tomorrow of Noble Memorial to Abraham Lincoln," *Christian Science Monitor*, May 29, 1922, 5.

109. *Proceedings of the 55th Annual Convention of the AIA* (Washington, D.C.: American Institute of Architects, 1922); also quoted in *Architecture* 46 (July 1922): 216.

110. On the ceremony see *Journal of the American Institute of Architects* 11 (June 1923): passim; and *Journal of the American Institute of Architects* 11 (July 1923): 270 (poem); and Richard Guy Wilson, *The AIA Gold Medal* (New York: McGraw-Hill, 1984), 12–14, 150–51. Royal Cortissoz's after-dinner speech appears in *Architectural Record* 55 (March 1924): 276.

111. Brown, *1860–1930, Memories*, 295.

112. "The Lincoln Memorial," *Architectural Record* 53 (June 1923): 480.

113. Louis Sullivan, *The Autobiography of an Idea*, foreword by Claude Bragdon (1926; reprint, New York: Dover, 1956), 325–36. On the context of the passage, see Thomas E. Tallmadge, *The Story of Architecture in America* (New York: Norton, 1936), 223.

114. Frank Lloyd Wright, "Some Aspects of the Past and Present of Architecture," in Baker Brownell and Frank Lloyd Wright, *Architecture and Modern Life* (New York: Harper and Brothers, 1938), 56. For related comments, see also Wright, *The Future of Architecture* (1953; reprint, New

York: New American Library, 1963), 134; and idem, *A Testament* (New York: Horizon Press, 1957), 178.

115. Mumford, *Sticks and Stones,* 141–42.

CHAPTER 5

1. District of Columbia Public Library, Martin Luther King Jr. Memorial Library, Washingtoniana Division, vertical files on Lincoln Memorial, offer a reasonably full survey of events that have taken place there.

2. David Kertzer, quoted in *Encyclopedia of Social and Cultural Anthropology,* ed. Alan Barnard and Jonathan Spencer (New York: Routledge, 1996), 490.

3. Nora, "Between Memory and History." Nora is a French cultural historian.

4. See, e.g., Clifford Geertz, "Centers, Kings, and Charisma: Reflections on the Symbolics of Power," in Geertz, *Local Knowledge: Further Essays in Interpretive Anthropology* (New York: Basic Books, 1983), 121–46; and Victor W. Turner, *The Ritual Process: Structure and Anti-structure* (Chicago: Aldine, 1969).

5. As in the view of Memorial Day rituals advanced by W. Lloyd Warner, in *The Living and the Dead: A Study of the Symbolic Life of Americans* (New Haven, Conn.: Yale University Press, 1959), chap. 8.

6. In *The Ritual Process,* Turner, in particular, emphasizes this function of ritual.

7. Bodnar, *Remaking America,* chap. 1.

8. See Robert N. Bellah, "Civil Religion in America," *Daedalus* 96, no. 1 (winter 1967): 1–21; and Michael W. Hughey, *Civil Religion and Moral Order: Theoretical and Historical Dimensions* (Westport, Conn.: Greenwood Press, 1983), 66–69.

9. See National Archives, RG 66, project files on Lincoln Memorial.

10. In *The Ritual Process,* Turner emphasizes liminality as crucial to the success of ritual. On the theme of threshold, see also *Parabola* 25, no. 1 (February 2000).

11. Wesleyan University, Bacon papers, LM correspondence, letter of Harlan to HB, June 19, 1922.

12. LC, Manuscripts, French family papers, general correspondence, project files, enclosure in letter of Mrs. Arthur H. Cilly to DCF, June 20, 1924 [copy in Wesleyan University Archives, Bacon collection]; italics in original.

13. On the remarkable decade, see Geoffrey Perrett, *America in the Twenties: A History* (New York: Simon and Schuster, 1982); and Paul Goodman and Frank Otto Gatell, *America in the Twenties: The Beginnings of Contemporary America* (New York: Holt, Rinehart and Winston, 1972). See also Richard Wightman Fox and T. J. Jackson Lears, eds., *The Culture of Consumption: Critical Essays in American History, 1880–1980* (New York: Pantheon, 1983), passim; Warren I. Susman, *Culture as History: The Transformation of American Society in the Twentieth Century* (New York: Pantheon, 1984), chap. 7; and Wilson, Pilgrim, and Tashjian, *The Machine Age in America,* esp. foreword and chap. 1.

14. "The Interior of the Lincoln Memorial," *American Mercury,* June 1925; reprinted in Spreiregen, *On the Art of Designing Cities,* 101–4.

15. See Wills, *Lincoln at Gettysburg.*

16. Frank C. Capra, director, *Mr. Smith Goes to Washington,* Columbia Pictures, 1939. See Charles J. Maland, *American Visions: The Films of Chaplin, Ford, Capra, and Welles, 1936–1941* (New York: Arno Press, 1977), 254–68; and Charles Affron, *Cinema and Sentiment* (Chicago: University of Chicago Press, 1982), 118–31.

17. Quoted in Maland, *American Visions,* 263.

18. In *Lincoln in American Memory,* Peterson applies "Zenith," the title of chapter 7, to the three decades leading to the sesquicentennial of Lincoln's birth in 1959.

19. See Smith, *Carving of Mount Rushmore;* Boime, *Unveiling of the National Icons.*

20. See Sandburg, *The Prairie Years* and *The*

War Years; Peterson, *Lincoln in American Memory,* 271–78 and passim.

21. *The Public Papers and Addresses of Franklin D. Roosevelt,* comp. Samuel Irving Rosenman (New York: Random House, 1938), 5:557–58.

22. National Archives, RG 66, supplies early attendance figures at the Lincoln Memorial. Since 1960, figures for all the memorials in the capital come from Department of the Interior, National Capital Parks–Central. I am grateful to Arnold Goldstein and Jeff Gaumer for these.

23. "Most Beloved Memorial," *Boston Herald,* May 26, 1947.

24. See Boime, *Unveiling of the National Icons,* 300, where no source is cited.

25. "Nixon Praises 'Firm' Lincoln," *Raleigh (N.C.) News and Observer,* February 13, 1974.

26. *JFK,* written, produced, and directed by Oliver Stone, Warner Brothers, 1991. The sequence, it may be noted, contains an anachronism: the appearance, in the background, of Constitution Gardens, which did not replace the wartime temporary buildings, northeast of the memorial, until after 1970.

27. On the parallels, see Boime, *Unveiling of the National Icons,* 304.

28. William Manchester, *The Death of a President: November 20–November 25, 1963* (New York: Harper and Row, 1967), 602–3.

29. *The Washington Post Guide to Washington,* ed. Laura Longely Babb (1942; reprint, New York: McGraw-Hill, 1976), 92.

30. Norman Mailer, *The Armies of the Night: History as a Novel, the Novel as History* (New York: New American Library, 1968), esp. 89–94.

31. AIA archives, RG 806, series 1, box 1, folder 8, unidentified newspaper story.

32. A full report of the dedication, including texts of the addresses, appears in Concklin, *Lincoln Memorial,* 73–91. All major newspapers reported the ceremony in their issues of May 30 and May 31, 1922; e.g., "Harding Lauds Lincoln as Nation's Savior . . . ," *Washington Post,* May 31, 1922, 1. The size of the crowd is estimated in "Greatest Throng in City's History Takes Part in Honoring Heroes," *Washington Post,* May 31, 1922, 3; Harding's text appears on pp. 1 and 6.

33. "Harding on Lincoln," *Washington Post,* May 31, 1922, 2. For the regulations governing overflight, see "Ban on Airplanes," *Washington Evening Star,* May 30, 1922, 3.

34. Sean Dennis Cashman, *America in the Twenties and Thirties: The Olympian Age of Franklin Delano Roosevelt* (New York: New York University Press, 1989), 306.

35. E.g., *Washington Post,* May 31, 1922, 3.

36. Warner, *The Living and the Dead,* chap. 8. See especially pp. 270–73, on the symbolic function of Lincoln.

37. It was long said that Moton was not seated on the platform. See, e.g., Thomas, "Lincoln Memorial and Its Architect," 637–38. Scott Sandage, in "A Marble House Divided," 141, however, identified Moton in the photo in Figure 5.4. On Moton, see *Who Was Who in America,* 374.

38. Cashman, *America in the Twenties and Thirties,* 263; and W. E. Burghardt Du Bois, *The Souls of Black Folk: Essays and Sketches* (1903; reprint, Greenwich, Conn.: Fawcett, 1961), esp. 42–54.

39. Boime, *Unveiling of the National Icons,* 295–96, based on reports in several black newspapers.

40. Copy in archives of the Commission of Fine Arts, file on Lincoln Memorial.

41. Saunders Redding, introduction to Du Bois, *Souls of Black Folk,* viii.

42. See Perrett, *America in the Twenties,* chap. 4; and Cashman, *America in the Twenties and Thirties,* chap. 8. The number of lynchings appears in Goodman and Gatell, *America in the Twenties,* 127.

43. *Defender,* June 10, 1922, as quoted in Boime, *Unveiling of the National Icons,* 296.

44. Susman's characterization of the thirties as the "new era of nationalism" (see *Culture as History,* 157–58) can be extended, if in more attenuated fashion, to the postwar period. I am grateful

to Sandage, for drawing my attention to the concept, in "A Marble House Divided," 137–38.

45. Sandage, "A Marble House Divided," 165.

46. See ibid., 143–49 (including bibliography); and Marian Anderson, *My Lord, What a Morning* (New York: Viking, 1956), chap. 17.

47. Sandage, "A Marble House Divided," 145.

48. Ibid., 152.

49. On the event, see Thomas Gentile, *March on Washington*, (Washington, D.C.: New Day Publications, 1983); and Taylor Branch, *Parting the Waters: America in the King Years, 1954–63* (New York: Simon and Schuster, 1988), chap. 22. Other important accounts, along with thorough bibliography, appear in Sandage, "A Marble House Divided," 155–59; and Boime, *Unveiling of the National Icons*, 297–302.

50. *Unveiling of the National Icons*, 297.

51. Vincent Scully, "American Architecture: The Real and the Ideal," in *American Architecture: Innovation and Tradition*, ed. David G. De Long, Helen Searing, and Robert A. M. Stern (New York: Rizzoli, 1986), 22.

52. See Ghirardo, *Architecture after Modernism*; Jencks, *Post-modernism*.

53. Sandage, "A Marble House Divided," 166.

54. Kammen, *Mystic Chords of Memory*, 662.

55. Richard Harrington, "At the Memorial, Songs in the Key of Hope," *Washington Post*, January 18, 1993, C1.

56. See "Gays Demand Rights in 6-Hour March: A Call for Equality, Tolerance," *Washington Post*, April 26, 1993, A1. The article is the source of the other quotations in the paragraph.

57. Suggested by Savage, in *Standing Soldiers, Kneeling Slaves*, 212.

58. "Plan for Museum within Memorial Has Backer in Lujan," A27.

59. See *Congressional Record*, 103d Cong., 1st sess., April 21, 1993, Senate 4774–4775.

60. See Jan C. Scruggs and Joel L. Swerdlow, *To Heal a Nation: The Vietnam Veterans Memorial* (New York: Harper and Row, 1985); Charles L. Griswold, "The Vietnam Veterans Memorial and the Washington Mall: Philosophical Thoughts on Political Iconography," *Critical Inquiry* 12 (summer 1986): 688–719; Boime, *Unveiling of the National Icons*, epilogue; Bodnar, *Remaking America*, prologue; and Jeffrey Karl Ochsner, "A Space of Loss: The Vietnam Veterans Memorial," *Journal of Architectural Education*, 50, no. 3 (February 1997), 156–71.

61. Scruggs and Swerdlow, *To Heal a Nation*, 16, 18.

62. After the Vietnam Memorial was dedicated, attendance at the Lincoln Memorial dropped to pre-1960 levels, where it has largely remained. See note 22.

63. Allan Greenberg, "Discourses in Stone: Meaning in War Memorial Architecture," unpublished essay (1995) in collection of Allan Greenberg, architect. For the comment's context, see *Allan Greenberg: Selected Works*, Architectural Monographs no. 39 (London: Academy Editions, 1995).

64. "Introduction," in Gillis, ed., *Commemorations*, 20.

65. "At the Lincoln Memorial" (1962), in Archibald MacLeish, *New and Collected Poems, 1917–1976* (Boston: Houghton Mifflin, 1976), 435.

BIBLIOGRAPHY

PRIMARY SOURCES

American Institute of Architects, Washington, D.C. (A). Archives. Record groups (RGs) 801 (office files, especially series 7.2, miscellany); 803 (membership files); and 806 (awards). (B) Prints and Drawings Collection, Octagon Museum, The American Architectural Foundation. Drawings by Henry Bacon.

Architect of the U.S. Capitol. Curator's office. Files on Lincoln Memorial.

Architectural League of New York. Archives. Letter of Francis H. Bacon to Horace Moran, October 25, 1936.

Art Institute of Chicago. Burnham and Ryerson Architectural Libraries. Daniel H. Burnham Papers.

Bacon-McKoy family papers, Greenville, South Carolina, and Wilmington, North Carolina.

Boney Architects, Wilmington, North Carolina. Collection of Leslie N. Boney Jr., FAIA.

Columbia University. Avery Library of Art and Architecture. Drawings and Archives. Papers of Francis Henry Bacon, William Partridge, McKim, Mead & White, Stanford White, and William Rotch Ware.

Commission of Fine Arts, Washington, D.C. Records at Commission offices. Annual reports and photographs of Lincoln Memorial.

Congressional Globe. 1867–73.

Congressional Record. 1873–1993.

District of Columbia Public Library. Martin Luther King Jr. Memorial Library. Washingtoniana Division. Vertical files on Lincoln Memorial.

Greenberg, Allan, Architect. Office collection. "Discourses in Stone: Meaning in War Memorial Architecture." Unpublished typescript, 1995.

Library of Congress, Manuscript Division. Papers of William Howard Taft, Charles Moore, George P. Wetmore, Elihu Root, Cass Gilbert, Olmsted Associates, and French Family.

National Academy of Design, New York City. Archives. Biographical file on Henry Bacon.

National Archives and Records Administration (NARA). RGs 42 (Office of Public Buildings and Grounds, esp. no. 362–74: records of the Lincoln Memorial Commission); 66 (Commission of Fine Arts, esp. nos. 1, 17 [project files], and 21); 79 (National Park Service); and 328 (National Capital Planning Commission, esp. box 105: reminiscences by W. T. Partridge).

National Gallery of Art, Washington, D.C. Photographic Division. Collection of Dunlap Society.

National Park Service, National Capital Region, Washington, D.C. Transcript of an interview of Henry Bacon McKoy by Paul Goeldner, October 1985.

National Trust for Historic Preservation. Chesterwood (Daniel Chester French estate), Glendale, Mass. Archives.

————. Saint-Gaudens National Historic Site, Cornish, New Hampshire. Archives.

New-York Historical Society. Drawings Collection. McKim, Mead & White papers.

Richman, Michael, Takoma Park, Maryland. Research collection on D. C. French.

Roth, Leland M., University of Oregon, Eugene. Research collection. Egerton Swartwout, "An Architectural Decade." Unpublished typescript, formerly in office of Walker Cain, Architect (successor to McKim, Mead & White).

University of Pittsburgh. Research Collection. Savage, Kirk. "Vinnie Ream's *Lincoln* (1871): The Sexual Politics of a Sculptor's Studio." Unpublished typescript.

Wesleyan University, Middletown, Connecticut. Archives and Special Collections. Henry Bacon collection.

SECONDARY SOURCES

I. Books

Abbatt, William, comp. *The Lincoln Centenary in Literature: Selections from the Principal Magazines of February and March 1909, Together with a Few from 1907–1908.* 2 vols. New York: Henry E. Huntington for Library of Congress, 1909.

Affron, Charles. *Cinema and Sentiment.* Chicago: University of Chicago Press, 1982.

Anderson, Benedict. *Imagined Communities: Reflections on the Origin and Spread of Nationalism.* Rev. ed. London: Verso, 1991.

Anderson, Judith Icke. *William Howard Taft: An Intimate History.* New York: Norton, 1981.

Anderson, Marian. *My Lord, What a Morning.* New York: Viking, 1956.

Arnold, Matthew. *Culture and Anarchy: An Essay in Political and Social Criticism.* New York: Macmillan, 1875.

Ashcroft, Bill, Gareth Griffiths, and Helen Tiffen, eds. *The Post-colonial Studies Reader.* London: Routledge, 1995.

Axelrod, Alan, ed. *The Colonial Revival in America.* New York: Norton, with the Henry Francis du Pont Winterthur Museum, 1985.

Bach, Ira J. *A Guide to Chicago's Public Sculpture.* Chicago: University of Chicago Press, 1983.

Bacon, Francis H., ed. *Investigations at Assos: Drawings and Photographs of the Buildings and Objects Discovered during the Excavations of 1881–1882–1883 by Joseph T. Clarke, Francis H. Bacon, Robert Koldewey.* 2 vols. Cambridge, Mass.: Archeological Institute of America, 1902–21.

Badger, Reid. *The Great American Fair: The World's Columbian Exposition and American Culture.* Chicago: N. Hall, 1979.

Banham, Reyner. *A Concrete Atlantis: U.S. Industrial Building and European Modern Architecture 1900–1925.* Cambridge, Mass.: MIT Press, 1986.

Bedford, Steven McLeod. "The Architectural Career of John Russell Pope." Ph.D. diss., Columbia University, 1994.

———. *John Russell Pope, Architect of Empire.* New York: Rizzoli, 1998.

———., ed. *Washington Renaissance.* Washington, D.C.: Meridan House International, 1989.

Bellamy, Edward. *Looking Backward 2000–1887.* Ed. John L. Thomas. 1888. Reprint, Cambridge, Mass.: Belknap Press of Harvard University Press, 1967.

Betts, William W., ed. *Lincoln and the Poets.* Pittsburgh: University of Pittsburgh Press, 1965.

Binkley, Wilfred E. *President and Congress.* 3d rev. ed. New York: Vintage Books, 1962.

Biographical Directory of the American Congress, 1774–1961. Washington, D.C.: Government Printing Office, 1961.

Bodnar, John. *Remaking America: Public Memory, Commemoration, and Patriotism in the Twentieth Century.* Princeton, N.J.: Princeton University Press, 1992.

Bogart, Michele H. *Public Sculpture and the Civic Ideal in New York City, 1890–1930.* Chicago: University of Chicago Press, 1989.

Boime, Albert. *Hollow Icons: The Politics of Sculpture in Nineteenth-Century France.* Kent, Ohio: Kent State University Press, 1987.

———. *The Unveiling of the National Icons: A Plea for Patriotic Iconoclasm in a Nationalist Era.* Cambridge: Cambridge University Press, 1998.

Boritt, Gabor S., ed. *The Historian's Lincoln: Pseudohistory, Psychohistory, and History.* Urbana: University of Illinois Press, 1988.

Boyer, Paul. *Urban Masses and Moral Order in America: 1820–1929.* Cambridge, Mass.: Harvard University Press, 1978.

Branch, Taylor. *Parting the Waters: America in the King Years, 1954–63.* New York: Simon and Schuster, 1988.

Brooklyn Museum. *The American Renaissance, 1876–1917*. Exhibition catalog. Brooklyn, N.Y.: Brooklyn Institute of Arts and Sciences, 1979.

Brown, Glenn. *The Development of Washington with Special Reference to the Lincoln Memorial*. Washington, D.C.: Washington Chamber of Commerce, 1910.

———. *1860–1930, Memories: A Winning Crusade to Revive George Washington's Vision of a Capital City*. Washington, D.C.: W. F. Roberts, 1931.

———. *History of the United States Capitol*. 2 vols. 56th Cong., 1st sess., S. Doc. 60. Washington, D.C.: Government Printing Office, 1900–3. Reprint, New York: Da Capo Press, 1970.

———, ed. *Papers Relating to the Improvement of the City of Washington, District of Columbia*. 56th Cong., 2d sess., S. Doc. 94. Washington, D.C.: Government Printing Office, 1901.

Bryan, John M., ed. *Robert Mills, Architect*. Washington, D.C.: American Institute of Architects Press, 1989.

Burdette, Franklin L. *The Republican Party: A Short History*. 2d ed. New York: D. Van Nostrand, 1972.

Burg, David F. *Chicago's White City of 1893*. Lexington: University Press of Kentucky, 1976.

Busbey, L. White, comp. *Uncle Joe Cannon: The Story of a Pioneer American*. New York: H. Holt, 1927.

Bushong, William Brian. "Glenn Brown, the American Institute of Architects, and the Development of the Civic Core of Washington, D.C." Ph.D. diss., George Washington University, 1988.

Bushong, William, Judith H. Robinson, and Julie Mueller. *A Centennial History of the Washington Chapter, the American Institute of Architects*. Washington, D.C.: Washington Architectural Foundation Press, 1987.

Caemmerer, H. Paul. *The Commission of Fine Arts, 1910–1963: A Brief History*. Washington, D.C.: Government Printing Office, 1964.

Cashman, Sean Dennis. *America in the Twenties and Thirties: The Olympian Age of Franklin Delano Roosevelt*. New York: New York University Press, 1989.

Cheney, Richard B., and Lynne V. Cheney. *Kings of the Hill: Power and Personality in the House of Representatives*. New York: Continuum, 1983.

Chrislock, Carl H. *The Progressive Era in Minnesota 1899–1918*. St. Paul: Minnesota Historical Society, 1971.

Clark, Champ. *My Quarter-Century of American Politics*. 2 vols. 1920. Reprint, New York: Kraus Reprint, 1968.

Cohen, Jean-Louis. *Scenes of the World to Come: European Architecture and the American Challenge, 1893–1960*. Preface by Hubert Damisch. Paris: Flammarion; Montreal: Canadian Centre for Architecture, 1995.

Collin, Richard H. *Theodore Roosevelt, Culture, Diplomacy, and Expansion*. Baton Rouge: Louisiana State University Press, 1985.

Concklin, Edward F., ed. *The Lincoln Memorial, Washington*. Washington, D.C.: Government Printing Office, 1927.

Cooper, John Milton, Jr. *Pivotal Decades: The United States, 1900–1920*. New York: Norton, 1990.

Coulton, J. J. *Ancient Greek Architects at Work: Problems of Structure and Design*. Ithaca, N.Y.: Cornell University Press, 1977.

Cowdrey, Albert E. *A City for the Nation: The Army Engineers and the Building of Washington, D.C., 1790–1967*. Washington, D.C.: Historical Division, Office of Administrative Services, Office of the Chief Engineers, Government Printing Office, 1979.

Cox, William Van Zandt, comp. *Celebration of the One Hundredth Anniversary of the Establishment of the Seat of Government in the District of Columbia*. Washington, D.C.: Joint Committee on Printing, Government Printing Office, 1901.

Craig, Lois, and the staff of the Federal Architecture Project. *The Federal Presence: Architecture, Politics, and Symbols in U.S. Government Building*. Cambridge, Mass.: MIT Press, 1978.

Cresson, Margaret French. *Journey into Fame: The Life of Daniel Chester French*. Cambridge, Mass.: Harvard University Press, 1947.

Croly, Herbert. *M. A. Hanna, His Life and Work*. New York: Macmillan, 1912. Reprint, Temecula, Calif.: Reprint Services Corp., 1988.

————. *The Promise of American Life*. New York: Macmillan, 1909. Reprint, New Brunswick, N.J. : Transaction Publishers, 1993.

Crook, J. Mordaunt. *The Greek Revival: Neo-classical Attitudes in British Architecture 1760–1870*. London: J. Murray, 1972.

Culler, Jonathan. *Structuralist Poetics: Structuralism, Linguistics, and the Study of Literature*. Ithaca, N.Y.: Cornell University Press, 1975.

Cunliffe, Marcus. *George Washington: Man and Monument*. New York: Mentor Books, 1982.

Curl, James Stevens. *A Celebration of Death: An Introduction to Some of the Buildings, Monuments, and Settings of Funerary Architecture in the Western European Tradition*. London: Constable and Co., 1980.

————. *A Dictionary of Architecture*. Oxford: Oxford University Press, 1999.

Davis, Michael. *The Image of Lincoln in the South*. Knoxville: University of Tennessee Press, 1971.

De Long, David G., Helen Searing, and Robert A. M. Stern, eds. *American Architecture: Innovation and Tradition*. New York: Temple Hoyne Buell Center for the Study of American Architecture/Rizzoli, 1986.

Dictionary of American Biography. New York: Charles Scribner's Sons, various dates.

The Dictionary of Art. 34 vols. Ed. Jane Turner. London: Macmillan, 1996.

Donald, David. *Lincoln Reconsidered: Essays on the Civil War Era*. New York: Vintage Books, 1961.

Dondore, Dorothy Anne. *The Prairie and the Making of Middle America: Four Centuries of Description*. 1926. Reprint, New York: Antiquarian Press, 1961.

Drexler, Arthur, ed. *The Architecture of the Ecole Des Beaux-Arts*. New York: Museum of Modern Art, 1977.

Dryfhout, John H. *The Work of Augustus Saint-Gaudens*. Hanover, N.H.: University Press of New England, 1982.

Du Bois, W. E. Burghardt. *The Souls of Black Folk: Essays and Sketches*. 1903. Reprint, Greenwich, Conn.: Fawcett, 1961.

Dunlap Society. *The Architecture of Washington, DC*. Ed. Bates Lowry. 88 sheets of microfiche in 2 vols. Washington, D.C.: Dunlap Society, 1976–79.

Eagleton, Terry. *Ideology: An Introduction*. London: Verso, 1991.

————. *Literary Theory: An Introduction*. 2d ed. Oxford: Blackwell, 1996.

Encyclopedia of Social and Cultural Anthropology. Ed. Alan Barnard and Jonathan Spencer. New York: Routledge, 1996.

Evans, Lawrence B. *Samuel W. McCall, Governor of Massachusetts*. Boston: Houghton Mifflin, 1916.

Flink, James F. *America Adopts the Automobile, 1895–1910*. Cambridge, Mass.: MIT Press, 1970.

————. *The Car Culture*. Cambridge, Mass.: MIT Press, 1975.

Foner, Eric. *Reconstruction: America's Unfinished Revolution, 1863–1977*. New York: Harper and Row, 1988.

Forgie, George B. *Patricide in the House Divided: A Psychological Interpretation of Lincoln and His Age*. New York: Norton, 1979.

Foster, Gaines M. *Ghosts of the Confederacy: Defeat, the Lost Cause, and the Emergence of the New South 1865–1913*. New York: Oxford University Press, 1987.

Fox, Richard Wightman, and T. J. Jackson Lears, eds. *The Culture of Consumption: Critical Essays in American History, 1880–1980*. New York: Pantheon, 1983.

Friedberg, Robert. *Paper Money of the United States: A Complete Illustrated Guide with Valuations*. 8th ed. With additions and revisions by Jack Friedberg. New York: Coin and Currency Institute, 1975.

Fryd, Vivien Green. *Art and Empire: The Politics of*

Ethnicity in the United States Capitol, 1815–1860. New Haven, Conn.: Yale University Press, 1992.

Fuller, Wayne E. *The American Mail: Enlarger of the Common Life*. Chicago: University of Chicago Press, 1972.

———. *RFD: The Changing Face of Rural America*. Bloomington: Indiana University Press, 1964.

Geertz, Clifford. *The Interpretation of Cultures: Selected Essays by Clifford Geertz*. New York: Basic Books, 1973.

Gentile, Thomas. *March on Washington, August 28, 1963*. Washington, D.C.: New Day Publications, 1983.

George A. Fuller, Company. *Fireproof Building Construction: Prominent Buildings Erected by the George A. Fuller Company*. 1904. 2d ed., New York: George A. Fuller Company, 1910.

———. *George A. Fuller Company, General Contractors, 1882–1937*. New York: George A. Fuller Company, 1937.

Ghirardo, Diane. *Architecture after Modernism*. New York: Thames and Hudson, 1996.

Gillis, John R., ed. *Commemorations: The Politics of National Identity*. Princeton, N.J.: Princeton University Press, 1994.

Goode, James M. *Capital Losses: A Cultural History of Washington's Destroyed Buildings*. Washington, D.C.: Smithsonian Institution Press, 1979.

———. *The Outdoor Sculpture of Washington, D.C.: A Comprehensive Historical Guide*. Washington, D.C.: Smithsonian Institution Press, 1974.

Coodman, Paul, and Frank Otto Gatell. *America in the Twenties: The Beginnings of Contemporary America*. New York: Holt, Rinehart and Winston, 1972.

Goodyear, William H. *Greek Refinements: Studies in Temperamental Architecture*. New Haven, Conn.: Yale University Press, 1912.

Gordon, Suzanne. *In This Temple: A Guide Book to the Lincoln Memorial*. Washington, D.C.: Museum Press, 1973.

Gould, Lewis L. *The Presidency of Theodore Roosevelt*. Lawrence: University Press of Kansas, 1991.

Green, Constance M. *The Secret City: A History of Race Relations in the Nation's Capital*. Princeton, N.J.: Princeton University Press, 1967.

———. *Washington: A History of the Capital, 1800–1950*. Princeton, N.J.: Princeton University Press, 1962.

[Greenberg, Allan.] *Allan Greenberg: Selected Works*. Architectural Monographs 39. London: Academy Editions, 1995.

Greenthal, Kathryn. *Augustus Saint-Gaudens, Master Sculptor*. New York: Metropolitan Museum of Art, 1985.

Guenter, Scot M. *The American Flag, 1777–1924: Cultural Shifts from Creation to Codification*. Rutherford, N.J.: Fairleigh Dickinson University Press, 1990.

[Guérin, Jules Vallée.] *Jules Guérin: Master Delineator*. Houston: Rice University, 1983.

Gutheim, Frederick. *Worthy of the Nation: The History of Planning for the National Capital*. Washington, D.C.: Smithsonian Institution Press, 1977.

Halberstam, David. *The Reckoning*. New York: William Morrow, 1986.

Hay, John, and Elihu Root. *The Republican Party: "A Party Fit to Govern."* New York: Privately printed, 1904.

Higham, John. *Strangers in the Land: Patterns of American Nativism 1860–1925*. 2d ed. New York: Atheneum, 1965.

Hobsbawm, Eric J., and Terence Ranger, eds. *The Invention of Tradition*. Cambridge: Cambridge University Press, 1983.

Hofstadter, Richard. *The Age of Reform: From Bryan to F.D.R.* New York: Knopf, 1959.

———. *The American Political Tradition and the Men Who Made It*. 25th anniversary edition. Ed. Christopher Lasch. New York: Knopf, 1973.

Hokanson, Drake. *The Lincoln Highway: A Main Street across America*. Iowa City: University of Iowa Press, 1988.

Honour, Hugh. *Neoclassicism*. Harmondsworth: Penguin, 1968.

Hughey, Michael W. *Civil Religion and Moral Order: Theoretical and Historical Dimensions*. Westport, Conn.: Greenwood Press, 1983.

James, Henry. *The American Scene*. Ed. Leon Edel. 1907. Reprint, Bloomington: Indiana University Press, 1968.

Jencks, Charles. *Post-modernism: The New Classicism in Art and Architecture*. London: Academy Editions, 1987.

Jessup, Phillip C. *Elihu Root*. 2 vols. New York: Dodd, Mead, 1938.

Kammen, Michael. *Mystic Chords of Memory: The Transformation of Tradition in American Culture*. New York: Vintage Books, 1991.

Kaplan, Robert D. *Balkan Ghosts: A Journey through History*. New York: St. Martin's Press, 1993.

Katz, Peter. *The New Urbanism: Toward an Architecture of Community*. New York: McGraw-Hill, 1994.

Kennedy, Roger G. *Greek Revival America*. New York: Stewart, Tabori and Chang, 1989.

Kohler, Sue A., and Jeffrey R. Carson. *Sixteenth Street Architecture*. Vol. 1. Washington, D.C.: Commission of Fine Arts, 1978.

Kohler, Susan A. *The Commission of Fine Arts: A Brief History, 1910–1976*. With additions, 1977–84. Washington, D.C.: Commission of Fine Arts, 1985.

Kostof, Spiro. *A History of Architecture: Settings and Rituals*. 3d ed. New York: Oxford University Press, 1995.

———. *America by Design*. Based on the PBS series by Guggenheim Productions. New York: Oxford University Press, 1987.

Le Corbusier. *Towards a New Architecture*. Trans. Frederick Etchells. 1927. Reprint, New York: Holt, Rinehart and Winston, 1982.

Lee, Antoinette J. *Architects to the Nation: The Rise and Decline of the Supervising Architect's Office*. Foreword by William Seale. New York: Oxford University Press, 2000.

———, ed. *Historical Perspectives on Urban Design: Washington, D.C., 1890–1910*. Center for Washington Area Studies, Occasional Paper no. 1. Washington, D.C.: George Washington University Press, 1983.

Leech, Margaret. *Reveille in Washington, 1860–1865*. New York: Harper and Brothers, 1941.

Lessard, Susannah. *The Architect of Desire: Beauty and Danger in the Stanford White Family*. London: Phoenix, 1997.

Lewis, Lloyd. *Myths after Lincoln*. New York: Harcourt, Brace, 1929.

Lincoln, Abraham. *Speeches and Writings, 1859–1865: Speeches, Letters, and Miscellaneous Writings, Presidential Messages and Proclamations*. Ed. Don E. Fehrenbacher. Library of America, vol. 46. New York: Literary Classics of the U.S., 1989.

Lincoln Memorial Commission. *Lincoln Memorial Commission Report: Message from the President of the United States Transmitting a Report . . . in Accordance with the Act. Approved February 9, 1911*. Dated December 5, 1912. 62d Cong., 3d sess., S. Doc. 965. Washington, D.C.: Government Printing Office, 1913.

Link, Arthur S. *The Higher Realism of Woodrow Wilson, and Other Essays*. Foreword by Dewey W. Grantham. Nashville, Tenn.: Vanderbilt University Press, 1971.

———. *Wilson: The New Freedom*. Princeton, N.J.: Princeton University Press, 1956.

Lippmann, Walter. *Drift and Mastery: An Attempt to Diagnose the Current Unrest*. 1914. Rev. ed. Ed. William E. Leuchtenburg. Englewood Cliffs, N.J.: Prentice-Hall, 1961.

Lombardo, Josef Vincent. *Attilio Piccirilli: Life of an American Sculptor*. New York: Pitman, 1944.

Longstreth, Richard, ed. *The Mall in Washington, 1791–1991*. CASVA Studies in the History of Art, no. 30. Washington, D.C.: National Gallery of Art, 1991.

Lowenthal, David. *The Past Is a Foreign Country*. Cambridge: Cambridge University Press, 1985.

Lowry, Bates. *Building a National Image: Architectural Drawings for the American Democracy, 1789–1912.* Catalog of inaugural exhibition. Washington, D.C.: National Building Museum, 1985.

MacLeish, Archibald. *New and Collected Poems, 1917–1976.* Boston: Houghton Mifflin, 1976.

Mailer, Norman. *The Armies of the Night: History as a Novel, the Novel as History.* New York: New American Library, 1968.

Maland, Charles J. *American Visions: The Films of Chaplin, Ford, Capra, and Welles, 1936–1941.* New York: Arno Press, 1977.

Manchester, William. *The Death of a President: November 20–November 25, 1963.* New York: Harper and Row, 1967.

Maroon, Fred J., Suzy Maroon, and Daniel J. Boorstin. *The United States Capitol.* New York: Stewart, Tabori, and Chang, 1993.

May, Henry F. *The End of American Innocence: A Study of the First Years of Our Own Time, 1912–1917.* New York: Knopf, 1959.

McPherson, James M. *Abraham Lincoln and the Second American Revolution.* New York: Oxford University Press, 1990.

Mencken, Henry Louis. *Prejudices: Fifth Series.* New York: Knopf, 1926.

Meridian House International. *Washington Renaissance: Architecture and Landscape of Meridian Hill.* Ed. Steven Bedford. Exhibition catalog. Washington, D.C.: Meridian House International, 1989.

Middleton, Robin, ed. *The Beaux-Arts and Nineteenth-Century French Architecture.* Cambridge, Mass.: MIT Press, 1982.

Miller, Francis Trevelyan. *The Photographic History of the Civil War in Ten Volumes.* New York: Review of Reviews, 1911.

Mitchell, W. J. T., ed. *Art and the Public Sphere.* Chicago: University of Chicago Press, 1992.

Moore, Charles. *Daniel H. Burnham, Architect, Planner of Cities.* 2 vols. Boston: Houghton Mifflin, 1921.

———. *The Life and Times of Charles Follen McKim.* Boston: Houghton Mifflin, 1929.

———. *Washington, Past and Present.* New York: Century Co., 1929.

———, ed. *The Improvement of the Park System of the District of Columbia.* 57th Cong., 1st sess., S. Doc. 965. Washington, D.C.: Government Printing Office, 1902.

Morris, Edmund. *The Rise of Theodore Roosevelt.* New York: Coward, McCann and Geoghegan, 1979.

Mumford, Lewis. *Sticks and Stones: A Study of American Architecture and Civilization.* 1924. 2d rev. ed. New York: Dover, 1955.

Nash, Ernest. *The Pictorial Dictionary of Ancient Rome.* 2d ed., revised. 2 vols. New York: Praeger, 1968.

National Cyclopaedia of American Biography. 63 vols. New York: J. T. White, 1898–1984.

Neely, Mark E., Jr. *The Last Best Hope of Earth: Abraham Lincoln and the Promise of America.* Cambridge, Mass.: Harvard University Press, with the Huntington Library and the Illinois State Historical Society, 1993.

Nicolay, John G., and John Hay. *Abraham Lincoln: A History.* 10 vols. New York: Century Co., 1890.

Oliver, Richard. *The Making of an Architect, 1881–1981: Columbia University in the City of New York.* New York: Rizzoli, 1981.

Olsen, Donald J. *The City as a Work of Art: London, Paris, Vienna.* New Haven, Conn.: Yale University Press, 1988.

Opitz, Glenn B., ed. *Dictionary of American Sculptors: 18th Century to Present.* Poughkeepsie, N.Y.: Apollo, 1984.

Partridge, Bellamy. *Fill 'er Up! The Story of Fifty Years of Motoring.* New York: McGraw-Hill, 1952.

Perrett, Geoffrey. *America in the Twenties: A History.* New York: Simon and Schuster, 1982.

Peterson, Merrill D. *Lincoln in American Memory.* New York: Oxford University Press, 1994.

Pevsner, Nikolaus. *A History of Building Types.* The A. W. Mellon Lectures in the Fine Arts, 1970, National Gallery of Art, Washington.

Bollingen Series XXXV.19. Princeton, N.J.: Princeton University Press, 1976.

Pierson, William H., Jr. *American Buildings and Their Architects: The Colonial and Neoclassical Styles*. Garden City, N.Y.: Anchor Books, 1976.

Pollitt, J. J. *Art in the Hellenistic Age*. Cambridge: Cambridge University Press, 1986.

Post-Office Department: Annual Reports for the Fiscal Year Ended June 30, 1907. Washington, D.C.: Government Printing Office, 1907.

Pringle, Henry F. *The Life and Times of William Howard Taft*. 2 vols. Hamden, Conn.: Archon Books, 1964.

Proceedings of the 55th Annual Convention of the AIA. Washington, D.C.: American Institute of Architects, 1922.

The Public Papers and Addresses of Franklin D. Roosevelt. Samuel Irving Rosenman. Vol. 5. New York: Random House, 1938.

Rankin, Henry B. *Personal Recollections of Abraham Lincoln*. New York: Putnam's, 1916.

Reps, John H. *Monumental Washington: The Planning and Development of the Capital Center*. Princeton, N.J.: Princeton University Press, 1967.

Rhoads, William B. *The Colonial Revival*. New York: Garland, 1977.

Richman, Michael. *Daniel Chester French, An American Sculptor*. Landmark Reprint Series. Washington, D.C.: National Trust for Historic Preservation, 1976.

Roth, Leland M. *McKim, Mead & White, Architects*. New York: Harper and Row, 1983.

Rothman, David J. *Politics and Power: The United States Senate 1869–1901*. Cambridge, Mass.: Harvard University Press, 1966.

Rubinstein, Charlotte Streifer. *American Women Sculptors: A History of Women Working in Three Dimensions*. Boston: G. K. Hall, 1990.

Saint-Gaudens, Augustus. *The Reminiscences of Augustus Saint-Gaudens*. 2 vols. Ed. Homer Saint-Gaudens. 1913. Reprint, New York: Garland, 1976.

Samuels, Ernest, ed. *The Education of Henry Adams*. Boston: Houghton Mifflin, 1974.

Sandburg, Carl. *Abraham Lincoln: The Prairie Years* [2 vols., 1925–26]; *The War Years* [4 vols., 1936–37]. Condensed into one volume. New York: Harcourt, Brace, 1954.

Sarasohn, David. *The Party of Reform: Democrats in the Progressive Era*. Jackson: University Press of Mississippi, 1989.

Savage, Kirk. "Race, Memory, Identity: The National Monuments of the Union and the Confederacy." Ph.D. diss., University of California at Berkeley, 1990.

———. *Standing Soldiers, Kneeling Slaves: Race, War, and Monument in Nineteenth-Century America*. Princeton, N.J.: Princeton University Press, 1997.

Scheele, Carl H. *A Short History of the Mail Service*. Washington, D.C.: Smithsonian Institution Press, 1970.

Schwartz, Barry. *George Washington: The Making of an American Symbol*. New York: Free Press, 1987.

Scott, Pamela, and Antoinette J. Lee. *Buildings of the District of Columbia*. New York: Oxford University Press, 1993.

Scruggs, Jan C., and Joel L. Swerdlow. *To Heal a Nation: The Vietnam Veterans Memorial*. New York: Harper and Row, 1985.

Seale, William. *The President's House: A History*. Washington, D.C.: White House Historical Association/National Geographic Society, 1986.

Sear, Frank. *Roman Architecture*. Ithaca, N.Y.: Cornell University Press, 1983.

Senie, Harriet F., and Sally Webster, eds. *Critical Issues in Public Art: Content, Context, and Controversy*. New York: HarperCollins, 1992.

Slayden, Ellen Maury. *Washington Wife: Journal of Ellen Maury Slayden from 1897–1919*. New York: Harper and Row, 1963.

Smith, Page. *America Enters the World: A People's History of the Progressive Era and World War I*. New York: Penguin, 1985.

Smith, Rex Alan. *The Carving of Mount Rushmore*. New York: Abbeville Press, 1985.

Smith, Terry. *Making the Modern: Industry, Art, and Design in America*. Chicago: University of Chicago Press, 1993.

Sprague, Claire, ed. *Van Wyck Brooks, The Early Years: A Selection from His Works*. Boston: Northeastern University Press, 1993.

Spreiregen, Paul D., ed. *On the Art of Designing Cities: Selected Essays of Elbert Peets*. Cambridge, Mass.: MIT Press, 1968.

Steffens, Lincoln. *The Shame of the Cities*. 1904. Reprint, Mattick, N.Y.: Amereon, 1966.

Stern, Helen B., and Philip M. Stern. *"O, Say Can You See?": A Bi-focal Tour of Washington*. Washington, D.C.: Colortone Press, 1965.

Sullivan, Louis. *The Autobiography of an Idea*. Foreword by Claude Bragdon. 1926. Reprint, New York: Dover, 1956.

Susman, Warren I. *Culture as History: The Transformation of American Society in the Twentieth Century*. New York: Pantheon, 1984.

Tallmadge, Thomas E. *The Story of Architecture in America*. New York: Norton, 1936.

Tarbell, Ida Minerva. *The Life of Abraham Lincoln: Drawn from Original Sources and Containing Many Speeches, Letters and Telegrams Hitherto Unpublished*. 2 vols. New York: Lincoln History Society, 1900.

Thomas, Christopher A. *The Architecture of the West Building of the National Gallery of Art*. Published in conjunction with exhibition *John Russell Pope and the Building of the National Gallery of Art*, March–July 1991. Washington, D.C.: National Gallery of Art, 1992.

———. "The Lincoln Memorial and Its Architect, Henry Bacon (1866–1924)." 4 vols. Ph.D. diss., Yale University, 1990.

Tomsich, John. *A Genteel Endeavor: American Culture and Politics in the Gilded Age*. Stanford, Calif.: Stanford University Press, 1971.

Trachtenberg, Alan. *The Incorporation of America: Culture and Society in the Gilded Age*. New York: Hill and Wang, 1982.

Trachtenberg, Marvin. *The Statue of Liberty*. Rev. ed. New York: Penguin, 1986.

Turner, Victor W. *The Ritual Process: Structure and Anti-structure*. Chicago: Aldine, 1969.

U.S. Congress. *Hearings before the Committee on the Library, House of Representatives, on H.R. 13045*. March 5 and 6, 1912. Washington, D.C.: Government Printing Office, 1912.

U.S. Department of the Interior, National Park Service. *Highways in Harmony: Rock Creek and Potomac Parkway, Washington, D.C.,* 1994.

U.S. Senate, Committee on the District of Columbia. *The Mall Parkway: A Hearing before the Committee on the District of Columbia of the United States Senate, Saturday, March 12, 1904 . . . .* Washington, D.C.: Government Printing Office, 1904.

Vidler, Anthony. *Claude-Nicolas Ledoux: Architecture and Social Reform at the End of the Ancien Régime*. Cambridge, Mass.: MIT Press, 1990.

Warner, W. Lloyd. *The Living and the Dead: A Study of the Symbolic Life of Americans*. New Haven, Conn.: Yale University Press, 1959.

The Washington Post Guide to Washington. Ed. Laura Longely Babb. 1942. Reprint, New York: McGraw-Hill, 1976.

Watkin, David, and Tilman Mellinghoff. *German Architecture and the Classical Ideal*. Cambridge, Mass.: MIT Press, 1987.

Whitlock, Brand. *Abraham Lincoln*. 1909. Reprint, Boston: Small, Maynard & Co., 1919.

Who Was Who in America. Vol. 1, *1897–1942*. Chicago: Marquis, 1942.

Wiebe, Robert H. *The Search for Order, 1877–1920*. New York: Hill and Wang, 1967.

Wills, Garry. *Lincoln at Gettysburg: The Words That Remade America*. New York: Simon and Schuster, 1992.

Wilson, Richard Guy. *The AIA Gold Medal*. New York: McGraw-Hill, 1984.

———. *McKim, Mead & White, Architects*. New York: Rizzoli, 1983.

Wilson, Richard Guy, Dianne H. Pilgrim, and Dickran Tashjian. *The Machine Age in America 1918–1941*. New York: Brooklyn Museum and Harry N. Abrams, 1986.

Wilson, William H. *The City Beautiful Movement*. Baltimore: Johns Hopkins University Press, 1989.

Wilson, Woodrow. *Congressional Government: A Study in American Politics*. 1885. Reprint, Baltimore: Johns Hopkins University Press, 1981.

———. *A History of the American People*. 5 vols. New York: Harper and Brothers, 1902.

Wright, Frank Lloyd. *The Future of Architecture*. 1953. Reprint, New York: New American Library, 1963.

———. *A Testament*. New York: Horizon Press, 1957.

II.   Articles

"An Appearing Act at Lincoln Memorial." *Boston Globe*, July 23, 1996.

"Ban on Airplanes." *Washington Evening Star*, May 30, 1922, 3.

"Beautiful Lincoln Memorial Dedicated with Simple Ceremonies." *New York Sun*, February 26, 1915.

Bellah, Robert N. "Civil Religion in America." *Daedalus* 96, no. 1 (winter 1967): 1–21.

Berger, W. M. "Making a Great Statue: How French's Lincoln Was Put into Marble." *Scribner's Magazine* 66 (October 1919): 424–31.

Bhabha, Homi K. "Postmodernism/Postcolonialism." In *Critical Terms for Art History*, edited by Robert S. Nelson and Richard Shiff, 307–22. Chicago: University of Chicago Press, 1996.

"Borglum Scolds Again." *American Art News*, March 9, 1912.

Bretherick, Jill. "Honor of Sacrifice: The Evolution of the Arlington National Cemetery." *Modulus* 17 (1984): 106–13.

Brooks, Van Wyck. "On Creating a Usable Past." In *Van Wyck Brooks, the Early Years: A Selection*

from His Works, edited by Claire Sprague, 219–26. Boston: Northeastern University Press, 1993.

Brown, Glenn. "The Lincoln Memorial, Washington, D.C." Part 1, "The Site." Part 2, "The Design." *American Architect* 118, no. 2339 (October 20, 1920): 489–99, 503–6.

Carroll, Eleanor. "Colossal Statue of Lincoln in Place." *New York Evening Post*, March 10, 1920.

"Clark Wants Highway Monument to Lincoln." *New York Globe*, August 9, 1911.

"Comment on Passing Events Heard in Washington Hotels." *Washington Post*, June 30, 1916.

"Congress to Decide." *Washington Star*, August 9, 1911.

"Congress Urged to Place Lincoln Memorial on Meridian Hill." *Washington Herald*, January 21, 1912.

"Congressman 'Rediscovers' Lincoln Memorial Cavern." *Washington Star*, July 18, 1961.

Corn, Wanda M. "Coming of Age: Historical Scholarship in American Art." *Art Bulletin* 70 (June 1988): 188–207.

Cortissoz, Royal. "The Architect." *Architectural Record* 55 (March 1924): 276.

———. "A Memorial to Lincoln Worthy Alike of the Nation and the Man." *New York Tribune*, January 7, 1912.

Cresson, Margaret French. "Lighting Lincoln's Statue." *American Heritage* 7, no. 2 (February 1956): 56–57.

Croly, Herbert D. "The Paradox of Lincoln." *New Republic* 21 (February 18, 1920): 350–53.

———. "Recent Works of John Russell Pope." *Architectural Record* 29 (June 1911): 441–509.

"Discuss Design of Lincoln Statue." *Chicago Inter-Ocean*, January 19, 1913.

Edmonds, A. Sylvester. "Engineering Feats in Building Lincoln Memorial." *Manufacturers Record* 67, no. 1 (January 7, 1915): 47–48.

"E.S.M. Discusses the Site of Lincoln Memorial." *Washington Times*, July 31, 1911.

"Fight Lincoln Plan." *Chicago Sunday Record*, January 19, 1913.

"Fight Now Impending over Lincoln Memorial." *Washington Star*, December 18, 1912.

Fishback, Fred L. "Fort Stevens and the Lincoln Memorial." *National Magazine*, January 1912, 589–92.

———. "Opposed to Location for Lincoln Memorial." Letter to editor. *Washington Star*, August 4, 1911.

Fitzpatrick, F. W. "An Architect's Protest." *The Outlook* (New York), March 31, 1912.

"The Foundations of the Lincoln Memorial." *Pencil Points* 5 (June 1924): 74–75.

"Gays Demand Rights in 6–Hour March: A Call for Equality, Tolerance." *Washington Post*, April 26, 1993, A1.

Geertz, Clifford. "Centers, Kings, and Charisma: Reflections on the Symbolics of Power." In Clifford Geertz, *Local Knowledge: Further Essays in Interpretive Anthropology*, 121–46. New York: Basic Books, 1983.

Goodyear, William H. "Horizontal Curves in Columbia University." *Architectural Record* 9 (July–September 1899): 82–93.

"Greatest Throng in City's History Takes Part in Honoring Heroes." *Washington Post*, May 31 1922, 3.

Greenberg, Allan. "Lutyen's Cenotaph." *Journal of the Society of Architectural Historians* 48, no. 1 (March 1989): 5–23.

Griswold, Charles L. "The Vietnam Veterans Memorial and the Washington Mall: Philosophical Thoughts on Political Iconography." *Critical Inquiry* 12 (summer 1986): 688–719.

Guérin, Jules. "The Mural Decorations, Described by the Painter." *Art and Archaeology* 13 (June 1922): 258–59.

"Harding Lauds Lincoln as Nation's Savior. . . . " *Washington Post*, May 31, 1922, 1.

"Harding on Lincoln." *Washington Post*, May 31 1922, 2.

Harrington, Richard. "At the Memorial, Songs in the Key of Hope." *Washington Post*, January 18, 1993, C1.

Harts, Col. W. W. "Cylinder-Pier Foundations for Lincoln Memorial, Washington, D.C." *Engineering News* 71 (May 7, 1914): 1019.

Hawthorne, Nathaniel. "Chiefly about War Matters, by a Peaceable Man." In Hawthorne, *Tales, Sketches, and Other Papers*, 299–345. 1883. Reprint, Freeport, N.Y.: Books for Libraries Press, 1972.

Hay, John. "Fifty Years of the Republican Party." In John Hay and Elihu Root, *The Republican Party: "A Party Fit to Govern."* New York: Privately printed, 1904.

Henderson, Mary. "Suggests Memorial Arch." Letter to the editor. *Washington Post*, August 7, 1911.

"A Highway from Ocean to Ocean." *Horseless Age* 23 (April 23, 1902): 512.

Kirsch, J. P. "The Marble Columns of the Lincoln Memorial." *Scientific American* 112 (March 20, 1915): 267.

Ledderose, Lothar. "Die Gedenkhalle für Mao Zedong: Ein Beispiel von Gedächtnisarchitektur." In *Kultur und Gedächtnis*, edited by Jan Assmann and Tonio Hölscher, 311–39. Suhrkamp Taschenbuch Wissenschaft 724. Frankfurt am Main: Suhrkamp, 1988.

"Lifelong Friend Draws Picture of Lincoln as He Saw Him." *New York Times*, March 22, 1908, pt. 5, 4:2.

"Lincoln Address for Memorial." *Washington Herald*, March 24, 1913.

"Lincoln as a Greek God." *New York Independent*, February 8, 1912.

"The Lincoln Boulevard." *New York Times*, December 13, 1908, pt. 3, 12:2.

"The Lincoln Memorial." Editorial. *New York Times*, July 3, 1908, 6:2.

"The Lincoln Memorial." Editorial. *Washington Evening Star*, April 13, 1911.

"The Lincoln Memorial." *Architectural Record* 53 (June 1923): 480.

"The Lincoln Memorial and After." Editorial. *Brooklyn Standard*, February 9, 1913.

"Lincoln Memorial Highway Is Urged on President Taft." *Washington Times*, August 4, 1911.

"Lincoln Memorial Typifies Culture of the Emancipator." *Washington Post*, May 21, 1922.

[Lincoln Memorial, photos of Henry Bacon's design.] *Architecture* 25 (February 1912).

Linn, Charles. "Study Finds Lincoln Looks Best Basking in Incandescent Glow." *Architectural Record* 186, no. 2 (February 1998): 205–6.

"Love for Senator to Win." *Philadelphia Record*, January 16, 1913.

"Mall the Predestined Site for Lincoln Memorial." *Washington Post*, May 14, 1922.

Marcus, Lois Goldreich. "The Shaw Memorial: A History Painting in Bronze." *Winterthur Portfolio* 14, no. 1 (spring 1979): 1–23.

"May Change Memorial Plan." *Washington Post*, August 5, 1911.

McCleary, James T. "What Shall the Lincoln Memorial Be?" *American Review of Reviews* 38 (September 1908): 334–41.

Mechlin, Leila. "The Lincoln Memorial." *Art and Progress* 3 (February 1912): 484–85.

———. "The Proposed Lincoln Memorial." Includes photos of Henry Bacon's design. *The Century* 83 (January 1912): 367–76.

"Memorial Ground Broken." *Washington Herald*, February 13, 1914.

"Most Beloved Memorial." *Boston Herald*, May 26, 1947.

"Name Lincoln Memorial Site." *Washington Post*, February 4, 1912.

National Magazine 35 (January 1912): frontispiece.

"The Nation's Memorial to Abraham Lincoln." Letter to the editor. *New York Sun*, January 15, 1912.

"Nixon Praises 'Firm' Lincoln." *Raleigh News and Observer*, February 13, 1974.

Nora, Pierre. "Between Memory and History: *Les Lieux de Mémoire*." *Representations* 26 (spring 1989): 7–25.

Ochsner, Jeffrey Karl. "A Space of Loss: The Vietnam Veterans Memorial." *Journal of Architectural Education* 50, no. 3 (February 1997): 156–71.

"Old Fort Stevens Sold." *Washington Evening Star*, March 22, 1911.

O'Leary, Cecilia. "'American All': Reforging a National Brotherhood, 1876–1917." *History Today* 44, no. 10 (October 1994): 20–27.

"The Other Washington." *Wilson Quarterly* 13 (New Year's, 1989): 76–117.

Parabola 25, no. 1 (February 2000). Issue on theme of threshold.

Peets, Elbert. "The Interior of the Lincoln Memorial." *American Mercury*, June 1925; reprinted in *On the Art of Designing Cities: Selected Essays of Elbert Peets*, edited by Paul Spreiregen. Cambridge, Mass.: MIT Press, 1968.

Peterson, Jon A. "The Nation's First Comprehensive City Plan." *Journal of the American Planning Association* 51 (spring 1985): 134–50.

Phelps, Grace. "America's Tribute to the Rail Splitter." *New York Tribune*, May 28, 1922; *Literary Digest* 73 (June 17, 1922): 28.

"Plan for Museum within Memorial Has Backer in Lujan." *Washington Post*, February 17, 1992, A27.

"Plans for the Lincoln Memorial." *Architectural Record* 29 (May 1911): 436–37.

"Plea Made for Early Removal of Army and Navy Buildings from Potomac Park Grounds." *Washington Evening Star*, June 12, 1919.

"The Proposed Lincoln National Memorial." *Harper's Weekly*, January 20, 1912, 21.

Richman, Michael. "Daniel Chester French and Henry Bacon: Public Sculpture in Collaboration, 1897–1908." *American Journal of Art* 12, no. 3 (summer 1980): 46–64.

———. "The Lincoln Memorial: The Impact of the Columbian Exposition on Washington, D.C." Abstract of conference paper presented at twenty-ninth annual meeting. *Journal of the Society of Architectural Historians* 35 (December 1976): 275–76.

———. "Sculptor Daniel Chester French and Architect Henry Bacon Labored Long and Hard to Give the Nation Its Favorite Statue, 'Abraham Lincoln,' in Lincoln Memorial." *Smithsonian* 7, no. 11 (February 1977): 54–61.

Roberts, David. "Magical Marble, That Gleaming Rock for the Ages." *Smithsonian* 22, no. 10 (January 1992): 98–107.

Robinson, Marcelle. "Pioneer, Scholar, and Victim: An Appreciation of Frank Calvert (1828–1908)." *Anatolia* 44 (1994): 153–68.

Sandage, Scott A. "A Marble House Divided: The Lincoln Memorial, the Civil Rights Movement, and the Politics of Memory, 1939–1963." *Journal of American History* 80 (June 1993): 135–67.

Shipley, Lee. "Building a National Turnpike." *Collier's*, January 6, 1912, auto section, 27–29.

"Simplicity to Mark Dedication Tomorrow of Noble Memorial to Abraham Lincoln." *Christian Science Monitor*, May 29, 1922, 5.

Singal, Daniel Joseph. "Towards a Definition of Modernism." *American Quarterly* 39, no. 1 (spring 1987): 7–26.

Swales, Francis S. "Henry Bacon as a Draftsman." *Pencil Points* 5 (May 1924): 42–62.

———. "Jules Guérin." *Pencil Points* 5 (May 1924): 63–66.

Tarbell, Ida Minerva. "Father Abraham: Another 'He Knew Lincoln' Story." *American Magazine* 67, no. 4 (February 1909): n.p.

Thomas, Christopher. "Francis H. Bacon: Master Draftsman as Archaeologist." *The Classicist* 2 (1995–96): 28–33.

———. "Lincoln as Theodore Roosevelt: The Politics of the Lincoln Memorial, 1901–1911." Paper presented at a symposium of the Latrobe Chapter of the Society of Architectural Historians and the National Building Museum, Washington, D.C., March 1997.

———. "The Marble of the Lincoln Memorial: 'Whitest, Prettiest, and . . . Best.'" *Washington History* 5, no. 2 (fall/winter 1993–94): 42–63.

"Urging Lincoln Road." *Boston Evening Transcript*, December 30, 1911.

Van Brunt, Henry. "The Washington Monument." *American Art Review* 1 1st division (1880): 7–12, 57–65.

"Views of the Lincoln Memorial." *New York Times*, January 13, 1909, pt. 6, 5:5–6.

"Want Site Changed." *Washington Star*, August 4, 1911.

W.E.B. [*sic*]. "Urging Lincoln Road." *Boston Evening Transcript*, December 30, 1911.

Williams, Jesse Lynch. "The Guérin Decorations for the Lincoln Memorial: How They Were Done." *Scribner's Magazine* 66 (October 1919): 416–23.

Wright, Frank Lloyd. "Some Aspects of the Past and Present of Architecture." In Baker Brownell and Frank Lloyd Wright, *Architecture and Modern Life*. New York: Harper and Brothers, 1937.

INDEX

Italic page numbers refer to figures.

Sullivan, Louis, 95, 142
Susman, Warren I., 191n44

Taft, William Howard: actions as president, 35–39; choosing a designer, 50, 89; congressional hostility to the Memorial, 138; constructing the Memorial, 104; dedication ceremony, 153, *154*, 155–57; dedicatory inscription, 131; election of 1912, 82; Lincoln Memorial Commission of 1902, 25–27; siting the Memorial, 43, 51–53, 80–81
Tarbell, Ida M., 9–10, 29, *30*
Temple of the Scottish Rite, *51*
Thornton, James, 15
Tiananmen Square, Mao Zedong mausoleum, 169n4
"To Laugh Or Not to Laugh," *97*

UCV. *See* United Confederate Veterans
Underpinning & Foundation Company, 101, 105
Union Square Bank, *47*
Union Station, 33–34
United Confederate Veterans (UCV), 12
urban reform, 14
uses of the Memorial, xvii, xix, xxviii, 144–45, 166–68; official and vernacular ritual, 158–67; private visitation, 145–52; public rituals, 152–58

Venturi, Robert, xxvi
Vest, George Graham, 26
Vietnam Veterans Memorial, xvii, xxvi, 165–66, *166*

Waco, Texas, Art League, 80
Warner, W. Lloyd, 156
Washington, D.C.: African-Americans in, 128; buildings and monuments in (*see* names of specific sites); centennial of, 14; Civil War, during the, 3; Gilded Age, in the, 8–9; history and development of, 2–3; Mall, the (*see* Mall, the); McMillan Commission plans for (*see* McMillan Commission/Plan); perception of Lincoln in, 10, 12–13; race relations in, 156, 159–60
Washington, George, 3, 5, 119–20, *120*
Washington Monument: building of, 3, 8; design of, 61, *62*; McMillan Commission proposal for, 17, 104–5
Webster, Mary P., 147
Weinman, Adolph, 73, 80, 84
Wetmore, George Peabody, 26–27, 37–38, 97
White, Henry, 89
White, Stanford, *10*, 17, 45
White House, naming and restoring of, 22
Whitlock, Brand, 29
Wiest, D. T., *5*
Wilson, Woodrow: centralization of government, 20; election of 1912, 53, 82, 94, 99; electoral use of Lincoln, 29; Lincoln Memorial and, 103–4, 135; New South movement and, 11–12; the presidency, strength of, 22–23; Roosevelt, opinion of, 23; segregation and, 128
Woods, Elliott, 33–34, 50–51, 77, 79
World's Columbian Exposition, 14–15, 17, 45, 56, 156
Wright, Frank Lloyd, 24, 95, 142–43